# CONTEMPORARY
# DECORATIVE
# ARTS
from 1940 to the present

*'Rainbow's End' by Patrick Hughes. Published as a postcard in the late seventies by the London firm Artist's Cards.*

# CONTEMPORARY
# DECORATIVE
# ARTS

### from 1940 to the present

## Philippe Garner

# FACTS ON FILE, INC.

119 West 57th Street,
New York, N.Y. 10019

A QUARTO BOOK

Published in the USA by
Facts on File, Inc.
119 West 57th Street, New
York, NY 10019 Library of
Congress Number: 80-68782

ISBN 0-87196-472-4

9 8 7 6 5 4 3 2 1


This book was designed and
produced by Quarto
Publishing Limited
32 Kingly Court
London, W1

Art director: Robert Morley
Designer: Moira Clinch
Editor: Victoria Funk
Filmset in Great Britain by
Abettatype, London and
Brown, Knight and Truscott
Ltd, Tunbridge. Colour
origination by Sakai
Lithocolour Company Ltd.,
Hong Kong.
Printed in Hong Kong by
Leefung Asco Limited.

**Acknowledgements**
Geoffrey Allen
Brian Aris
David Bailey
David Brown
Graham Bush
Cartier
Barbara Cartlidge
Wendell Castle
Prunella Clough
Michael Coffey
John Coleman
John Culme
James Danziger
Daum
Dior
Celia Farmer

Vere French
Lucilla Garner
Hazel Gates
Howard Grey
Grima
Interspace
John Jesse
Allen Jones
Simon Kentish
Calvin Klein
Dan Klein
Josef Kostick for Norma Kamali
Jeanette Kynch
John Makepeace
Annette Meach
Steve Newall
Helmut Newton

Rabanne
Janet E. Robinson
Rudolph Schoëwandt (Braun)
Andrew Stewart
Jon Weallans
Robert Webster
Adrian Woodhouse
Lorenz Zatecky


**Special thanks to:**
Robert Adkinson
Roger Daniels
Nick Clark
Clive Haybal
Heather Jackson
Marion Eason

# CONTENTS

INTRODUCTION 6

EVOLUTION OF STYLE 14

FURNITURE AND THE INTERIOR 50

SILVER AND METALWORK 84

CERAMICS 98

JEWELLERY DESIGN 108

GLASS DESIGN 122

TEXTILE DESIGN 136

FASHION DESIGN 144

INDUSTRIAL DESIGN 176

GRAPHIC DESIGN 192

FILM AND PHOTOGRAPHY 208

INDEX AND BIBLIOGRAPHY 222

# INTRODUCTION

*Film star and cult figure Marilyn Monroe as portrayed by Pop painter Andy Warhol, an artist who has become as much a cult figure as the subject of this silk screen portrait.*

AN APPRECIATION OF THE HISTORY of design and decoration, a concern for the styles of the past, would seem futile unless its end goal were a higher set of standards in the assessment of modern design. Nor is it justifiable to place full responsibility on artist, designer or manufacturer for the quality of modern design. The decorative arts are a direct reflection of aspirations in the quality of life which a society sets for itself and goods and styles are as worthy as their market. It is the demanding consumer who will encourage designer or manufacturer to aim higher. It would seem logical, therefore, for any study of the history and evolution of styles to conclude, not with yesterday's achievements, nor even today's, but with our hopes for the future.

The compiling of this survey has been a journey of discovery, providing a clarification of ideas, images and impressions absorbed in a fragmented way over a period of years. It has demonstrated that the exploration of recent history can be as uncertain as any archaeological foray into distant history. So much is ephemeral; artists and designers are often their own worst enemies, never satisfied with their past achievements, concerned only with the present and the future; a healthy attitude but the despair of the archivist. From a multitude of facts and documents, however, patterns start to form themselves. Putting the pieces together, a more distinct picture or rather sequence of pictures has emerged of the Contemporary era.

A survey of the decorative arts would seem sadly empty, however, if some mention were not made of just a few of the numerous personalities who have injected style, glamour and character into the recent decades: those people who, without necessarily being artists themselves, have contributed to the creation of the image of their era. Theirs has been, and will always be, a valuable though often intangible role, their looks, ideas, poses or personalities expressing a moment in time or giving a lead to the talents of others. These are the great hosts, art patrons, art collectors and dealers, authors and critics, stars of stage or screen, musicians and pop stars, models and professional beauties and the characters who, through a combination in varying proportions of wit, looks, charm or wealth make up the style-setting *beau monde*.

In 1951 the *beau monde* enjoyed its first truly lavish grand international ball since before the war, the legendary costumed ball hosted in Venice by Carlos de Bestegui. It was a glittering occasion and one which will probably never again be equalled, a magical, élitist expression of post-war romanticism. The arrival of many of the guests in opulent historical costumes underlined all the more effectively the feeling that such a manifestation of the ideals of a courtly age was out of key with the spirit of the second half of the twentieth century. There have been other social gatherings since in the same grand manner, such as the Proust Ball thrown by the Rothschilds in 1971, but the Venice Ball was a landmark, a celebration of a way of life which has receded from view. Today's jet set lives out its dramas in less magical surroundings, with the impersonal glamour of discothèques providing the currently most fashionable stage. The ball gown of 1951 has been replaced by the disco leotard of the late seventies.

More in tune with the spirit of a young post-war generation was a figure who, albeit unwittingly, influenced styles. This was French philosopher Jean-Paul Sartre, who in his advocacy of the philosophy of Existentialism provided the starting point for the life-style and appearance of a whole generation. Juliette Greco became the Existentialists' muse; Audrey Hepburn came to popularity with a similar look, before Givenchy lifted her forever from

The Honourable Mrs Reginald Fellowes photographed by Cecil Beaton making her entrance at Carlos de Bestegui's spectacular Venice Ball of 1951. The courtly image makes a defiant protest against the inexorable progress of the twentieth century.

the Left to the Right Bank; the Existentialists found their American and British counterparts in the Beatniks. Bernard Buffet became the hero of the hour in French painting, his sad, skeletal subjects managing to strike precisely the right chord.

Meanwhile Peggy Guggenheim was wrestling with American Abstract Expressionism, encouraging its critical acceptance and billing Pollock as the leading man of the new school. On the screen, Brando and Dean created a new style of hero; Monroe, Eckberg and a generation of sultry Italian beauties promoted a new ideal of celluloid glamour, while the cool, haughty looks of such models as Dovima, Dorian Leigh, Barbara Goalen and Suzy Parker were paraded in newspapers and magazines and left a strong image of a stylish epoch. As for music, what use a Contemporary teak sideboard with built-in record player without the right kind of record, most likely some fashionable modern jazz from the Dave Brubeck Quartet, or the earthy sound of Sydney Bechet.

The sixties were to see the arrival of a

*Today's ideals of beauty and of style are more likely to be derived from the street than from aristocratic tradition. Many designers today draw their vitality from popular culture. Two top English models photographed in 1977 by Brian Aris conform to a lively, popular image of glamour.*

*Left: French philosopher Jean-Paul Sartre, guiding light of the Existentialist movement.
Right: Audrey Hepburn in Left Bank, Existentialist costume in a scene from the film 'Funny Face' of 1957.*

new cast of characters, new sounds, new social habits and a new idea of beauty. Andy Warhol emerged as a Pop painter of note but above all as a cult figure who has become a magnet to the talented, the rich and the beautiful, a position which he seemingly maintains with a dead-pan expression and a carrier-bag full of spare film. Pop Art made its impact on the market in the sixties through the crusading appreciation of such dealers as Leo Castelli and Ivan Karp in New York and Robert Fraser in London. Fraser ran the avant-garde Mayfair gallery and promoted both British and American artists. He was immortalized by Richard Hamilton in a print showing him handcuffed to Mick Jagger in the back of a police car after their arrest on a drugs charge.

Pop Art found its most ethusiastic early patrons in Mr and Mrs Robert Scull of New York and the sale at auction in 1973 of a part of their collection confirmed the transition of Pop from the avant-garde to the pantheon of art history. The New York art scene was enlivened by Henry Geldzahler, described evocatively in 1965 in *Harper's Bazaar* as '. . . a familiar figure at Happenings, gallery openings, Underground movies and dinner parties, he is persistently on the scene, dead-center in the concentric circles of New York, professionally as the Metropolitan

*Right: Portrait of new York contemporary art dealer Ivan Karp by Roy Lichtenstein in comic strip style.
Far right: Andy Warhol self-portrait. Silk screen on canvas, 1964.
Below: 'Swinging London 1967', etching and aquatint by Richard Hamilton.*

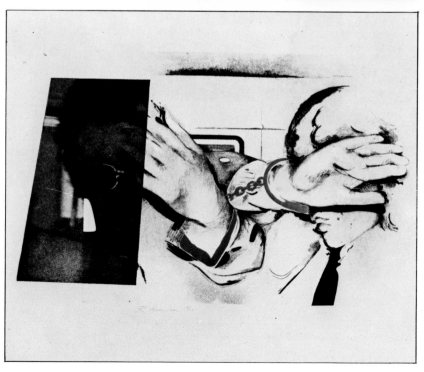

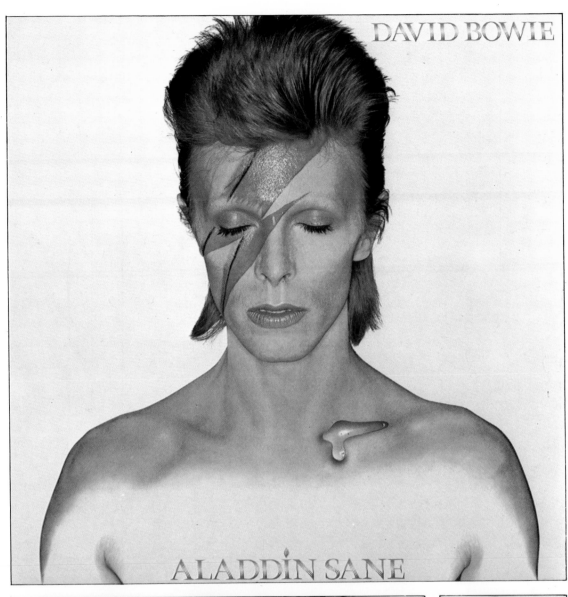

DAVID BOWIE

ALADDIN SANE

| Gene Vincent | Joe Brown | Billy Fury | Eddie Cochran | 153 |

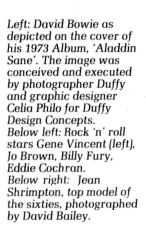

*Left: David Bowie as depicted on the cover of his 1973 Album, 'Aladdin Sane'. The image was conceived and executed by photographer Duffy and graphic designer Celia Philo for Duffy Design Concepts.*
*Below left: Rock 'n' roll stars Gene Vincent (left), Jo Brown, Billy Fury, Eddie Cochran.*
*Below right: Jean Shrimpton, top model of the sixties, photographed by David Bailey.*

*Paloma Picasso photographed by Helmut Newton in 1973. She is wearing a dress by Karl Lagerfeld and the heavy bracelets are of her own design.*

Museum's Associate Curator of American Paintings and Sculpture, and privately as a pop personality . . .'

In the sixties the young ruled the world of style and the British young set the pace. The Beatles and the Rolling Stones made the music, while Jill Kennington, Sue Murray and above all Jean Shrimpton set the look, long, straight-haired, pale-lipped, dark-eyed. The sixties saw the consecration of the pop star as cult hero, a trend started in the fifties and now the basis of a vast industry and the starting point of many a fad or fashion. The sixties found one of its most talented troubadours in the wistful Bob Dylan. Among the many music idols of more recent years one of the most intriguing and influential has been the epicene David Bowie, while, for better or worse, Punk or New Wave musicians have made a strong mark on fashion.

Among the taste-makers of the seventies are a host of characters who gravitate between New York and the capitals of Europe, in several cases within the entourages of leading designers in the world of fashion, notably Yves Saint-Laurent and Karl Lagerfeld. They include Saint-Laurent's aide, Lou-Lou de La Falaise, Italian fashion editor Anna Piaggi, Paloma Picasso, whose famous name has perhaps overshadowed her genuine talent as a jewellery designer, and restaurateur Michael Chow, who has been painted by Peter Blake and David Hockney and who has consistently set the pace with his taste in decoration.

If this sampling of names has been all too brief or seems too random, it is because the aim of this study is above all to observe the evolution in styles of decoration and design of the last forty years and the concern is therefore primarily with the tangible relics of the passage of time. This mention of names serves only as a reminder that styles exist as a reflection of people's tastes and that for certain people style becomes a way of life.

*'Frisco and Lorenzo Wong and Wildman Michael Chow'. English artist Peter Blake's 1966 collage painting of restaurateur Michael Chow.*

# EVOLUTION OF STYLE

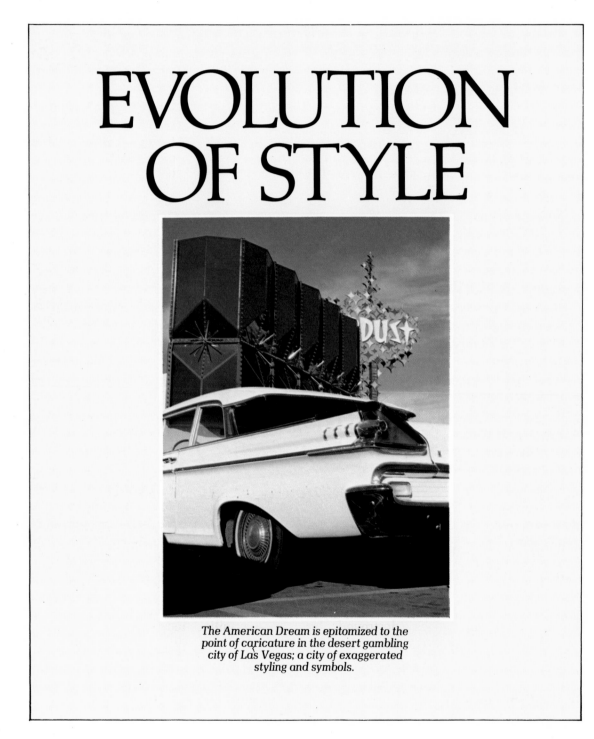

The American Dream is epitomized to the
point of caricature in the desert gambling
city of Las Vegas; a city of exaggerated
styling and symbols.

## 1940 – Present
### Style and Design

FOUR COMPLEX AND OFTEN CONFUSING DEC-
ADES have elapsed since the start of the
Second World War. Styles in design and
decoration, the social and artistic influences which have helped shape these
styles through this contemporary period
emerge in a rich confusion with so many
overlapping, at times seemingly contradictory threads, that the true nature of this
varied era would risk being misrep-
resented by any attempt to confine them
to very strict categories.

Social and political factors are often
closely interwoven with artistic development. The early forties were stagnant
years in the creative arts: the war effort
claiming so much energy, so many
resources. Indeed, even the late forties
remained austere years in a world
rebuilding and reassessing itself after the
destruction of the war. Christian Dior may
have launched his extravagant New Look
in 1947, but in Britain rationing remained
a way of life until the fifties. From the
ruins of the war years, however, there
emerged a new sense of hope, an optimism which was to survive through the
late fifties and sixties before coming to
grief in the essentially cynical seventies.

Industry set about rebuilding itself in
the immediate post-war period, exploring
new technologies and materials, among
them the new synthetics and alloys which
were often the direct product of wartime
experiment. After the pre-war era of technological dreams and nightmares, in
which the machine had become a love-
hate symbol in the arts, the technological
age had at last arrived. Germany and
Japan, their industries destroyed by
defeat, were forced to rebuild from the
drawing board and have risen from the
ashes as the most industrially advanced
countries, setting the pace during the sixties and seventies.

The fifties and sixties were decades of

new affluence and technology was welcomed into middle and working class
homes in terms of consumer hardware
which raised standards of living as never
before.

The lead in this new consumerism came
from the United States, where the brash
and confident styling and packaging of
consumer goods, the exaggerated scale of
supermarkets and cars, freeways and skys-
crapers made 'The Big Country' into the
very image of the promised land. Perhaps
the most striking feature of the American
import was its emphasis on a previously
ignored market, the young, who for the
first time had money to spend and a
determination to carve out a style for
themselves.

In 1957 the launch of the first Russian
Sputnik started the 'space race', which
became the perfect vehicle for the pres-
ervation, through the sixties, of the American Dream, culminating in the realization,
in 1969, of President Kennedy's promise
that the United States would put a man
on the moon before the close of the
decade. A science-fiction idea became a
reality, which in turn has provided a rich
fund of stylish imagery and has nourished
what is still essentially a fantasy

The decade of the conquest of space,
the 'swinging' sixties, saw a frenetic explosion of talent in the arts: young, raw
talents breaking down class and age barriers, creating a new aristocracy revolving
around the worlds of fashion, advertising,
film-making, commercial photography,
Pop music and Pop Art. Never had success
seemed within such easy reach, nor the
trappings of success so superficially
appealing. The essential shallowness of
this neophiliac decade found its reaction
in the strong undercurrent of disquiet
which characterized the hopeless, escapist
idealism of the 'love' movement, the 'hippie' or 'flower power' drug culture which
developed into a strong, if short-lived cult
in 1967. Whilst N.A.S.A. literally extended

NASA 75 -HC- 159

*Top left: The Russian 'Sputnik', launched in 1957 became the opening move in what was known as the 'Space Race'.*
*Top right: NASA photograph of an American astronaut exploring the surface of the moon.*
*Above: A space fantasy. The space station from Stanley Kubrick's film '2001: A Space Odyssey'.*

man's frontiers, Timothy Leary, prophet of the drug cult invited his followers to explore the frontiers of their minds, to 'turn on, tune in, drop out' into the psychedelic fantasy world of hallucinogenic drugs. The cult inspired a richly decorative style in dress and decoration, most especially in graphic art, in the work of British and West Coast American artists.

If the corpse of the sixties has already been thoroughly dissected and analyzed, the seventies await their post-mortem. The decade will be remembered for the pervasiveness of political anarchy, for the international tightrope act between inflation and major economic recession. In the worlds of fashion, art, design and decoration this was a hard, polished decade, a decade of cynical sophistication which contrasts sharply with the naive energy of the sixties.

The architectural symbol of the decade is Richard Rogers and Renzo Piano's Centre Pompidou in Paris, opened in 1977. There is no false 'modernist' chic in the structure, but rather a beautiful and brutally logical pursuit of a raw architectural 'truth', appropriate to the technological age; it is one of the most stylishly 'honest' buildings since the Crystal Palace, its true precursor. The structure and the very entrails of the building are bared in a design of dynamic, skeletal beauty: an art refinery which resembles an oil refinery, a new optic. In music, the raw energy of American 'underground' themes, nurtured in New York circles, found a wider expression in the aggressive British 'New Wave' and its accompanying visual vernacular and nihilistic anti-philosophy.

In the fine art world there has been a cynical back-lash against many of the abstract and conceptual trends of the post-war years, none more savage than Tom Wolfe's essay on the avant-garde machine, *The Painted Word* (1975), or David Hockney's tirade (London *Sunday Times*, March 1979) against policies of the Tate.

## Youth and America

The threatening atmosphere overshadowing the closing years of the seventies is in marked contrast to the mood of hope which characterized the post-war beginnings of this contemporary era, the bright optimism of the 'Britain Can Make It' exhibition of 1946. The post-war generation was living for the future, and for the young that future, so full of promise, was symbolized by America. It was, to quote from the *The Neophiliacs* by Christopher Booker, '. . . an enticing, far-off New World of shining buildings, gaudy advertisements, chromium-plated cars, flashing lights and pulsating, thrilling music.' When John McHale, a member of the

London Institute of Contemporary Arts Independent Group returned from a visit to the United States in 1955 '... with a trunk full of new magazines, such as *Playboy* and *Mad*', the group looked on America as '... the source of a new and unexpected inspiration, as a romantic land with an up-to-date culture ...'

The young, first in America and then in Europe, were enjoying the first taste of an independence born of a new affluence and rallying to the rhythms of their own new music idols, the purveyors of rock 'n' roll. Nothing could hold back the surge of

*The architectural symbol of the seventies, the 'Centre Pompidou', Paris. Designed by Richard Rogers and Renzo Piano and opened in 1977.*

this musical expression of the new mood. No watch committees, no Chief Constables, no red-neck Americans of the North Alabama White Citizens Council like the one who, in May 1956, proclaimed that rock 'n' roll 'is a means of pulling down the white man to the level of the negro ... part of a plot to undermine the youth of our generation ... sexualistic, unmoralistic and the best way to bring peoples of both races together.' The film industry was prompt to take advantage of the new, youthful markets with a spate of low-budget rock'n'roll films, such as *Rock Around the Clock* (1955), *Don't Knock the Rock* (1956), *Untamed Youth* (1957), *The Duke Wore Jeans* (1958), *Juke Box Rhythm* (1959), *Hot Rod Gang* (1959) and *Because They're Young* (1960). How revealing are even these titles, how evocative the key words, 'Youth', 'Jeans', 'Juke Box' and 'Hot Rod'.

The monolithic juke-boxes manufactured in the United States by Wurlitzer, Ami, Seeburg and the Rock-Ola Manufacturing Corporation have become symbols of the emergence of the young market and the pervasiveness of American popular culture. In their styling they incorporate every visual feature of this culture, elaborate chrome trims, moulded plastic and gaudy lights. The only all-British juke-box, the 'Chantal Meteor 200', designed in 1952 by David Fry, is an early and stylish homage to the American Dream.

The extraordinary and symptomatic youth sub-culture of car customizing which grew up in the United States, especially on the West Coast, has never been better described than in Tom Wolfe's essay published in *Esquire* magazine in 1963 under the title 'There Goes (Varoom! Varoom!) That Kandy-Kolored Tangerine-Flake Streamline Baby.' 'Here,' wrote Wolfe, 'was this incredible combination of form plus money in a place nobody ever thought about finding it, namely, among teenagers.' The car became a symbol, ...

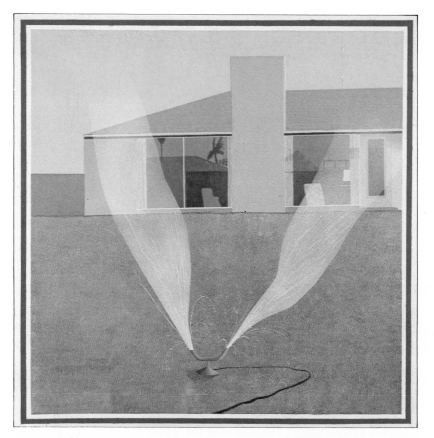

'The Sprinkler', by David Hockney, acrylic on canvas, 1967. British artist Hockney evolved an elegant and highly individual visual language to express his fascination with the life and landscape of California.

a pure piece of curvilinear abstract sculpture. If Brancusi is any good then this thing (an "XPAK 400" model) belongs on a pedestal too. There is not a straight line in it, and only one true circle, and those countless planes, and tremendous baroque fins ...' The streamline principle is divorced from functionalism and becomes pure style, '... baroque abstract or baroque modern or whatever you want to call it, which curves around and swoops and flows just for the thrill of it.' The colours, too, created a new, synthetic beauty. One example, the source of the essay's title, 'makes the car look like it has been encrusted with chips of some kind of semi-precious ossified tangerine, all coated with a half-inch of clear lacquer.'

The young expressed their new-found identity in the cult of distinctive fashion uniforms. From the States came casual styles: the college-campus style and the blouson jacket, blue-jean and T-shirt look inspired by the new celluloid heroes, Brando and Dean. In London, young dandyism found its expression in the neo-Edwardian 'Teddy-Boy' styles of the early fifties. Later in the fifties came slick and influential new styles from Italy, notably in male attire: a silhouette tapering down from a short boxy jacket, through narrow tapered trousers to the stylistic extreme of the winkle-picker pointed shoe.

By 1960 the centre of creative activity in fashion and style had begun to move from America to London. An article, 'London – the Most Exciting City', published in the London *Weekend Telegraph* (30 April

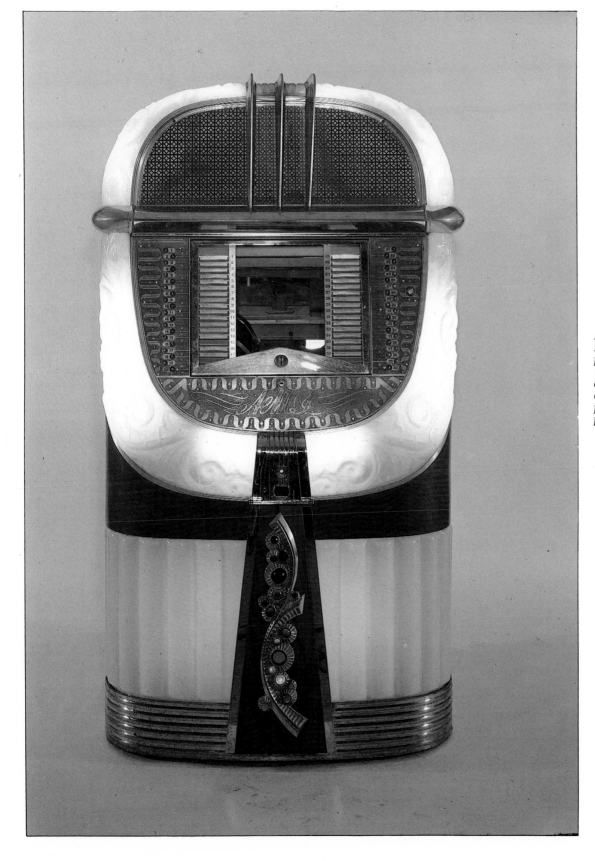

*Ami Model 'A' juke box, in production for a brief period between 1946 and 1948 and a striking example of the exaggerated styling of juke box casings in the post war years.*

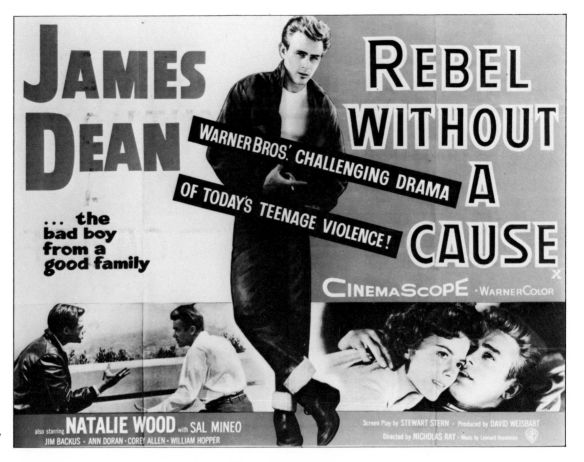

Advertising poster for the film which immortalized the sulky, rebellious looks of the young James Dean, 'Rebel Without a Cause', 1955.

1965) pinpointed '... the turbulence that boiled up in Britain around – if we must date it – 1958, although some say as late as 1960. In that period youth captured this ancient island and took command in a country where youth had always before been kept properly in its place. Suddenly the young own the town.' British youth found its own music idols in the Beatles and the Rolling Stones. The Stones have, to this day, preserved intact their image of raw rebellion, while managing to reconcile themselves to the material advantages of success. The Beatles have followed a more symbolic path, becoming leading figures, indeed the pied pipers of the 'love' movement of the late sixties, the search for salvation in mysticism.

The sixties in Britain saw the domination of every aspect of the arts by young and often working-class talent. These were the heroes of David Bailey's 'Box of Pin-Ups', of 1965, the cast of characters to whom he bid farewell in his *Goodbye Baby & Amen*, subtitled 'A Saraband for the Sixties.'

Through the seventies the fashion and music industries and so many other aspects of design and marketing have been dominated by the demands of the young market. The decade has produced a tougher, perhaps more bitter youth, inheritors of the tarnished relic of the post-war dream. Nineteen seventy-seven

saw the coming of Punk and, in the following summer, a commentator in the London *Sunday Times* (11 June 1978) sought to define the underlying significance of this bizarre neo-Dada movement and saw the 'deliberate self-denigration ... cynicism ... lack of purpose' as profoundly disturbing traits, asking, 'What statement is made by the use of rubbish – rusty blades, empty cans, bent pins ... for decorative jewellery?'

## Consumerism

If the contemporary era has witnessed the emergence and development of a new young market for style and design, it has witnessed, equally, the wide development of middle-class awareness of style in domestic and product design, a concern with taste of far wider social implications than ever before. This concern was stimulated during the fifties by the growing range of household magazines and by such media coverage as Lord Clarke's television broadcast of 1 December 1958, *What is good taste?*, in which he showed for discussion a room which epitomized what he called 'ghastly good taste', a too-perfect celebration of the discreet, elegant, late fifties 'Contemporary' style – 'very simple

*John Lennon and Paul McCartney. A double portrait of the celebrated song-writing team by sixties enfant terrible photographer, David Bailey. This is one of the thirty-six portraits included in his 'Box of Pin-Ups' of 1965. Bottom left: Punk characters from Derek Jarman's film. 'Jubilee' of 1978.*

*Above: Design for a living room by Olavi Hanninen shown in the 'Housing in Finland' section of the Milan Triennale exhibition of 1957. Finnish designers won wide acclaim in the Triennale shows of the fifties.*
*Right: The 'Trattoria' style is well demonstrated in this Mario and Franco restaurant interior. The vaulted rough-cast ceiling and tiled floor are characteristic features.*

shapes, very pale colour, furniture perched on rather thin legs.'

The Contemporary Style, drawing elements from American designs, but most especially from Scandinavia, was the realization of the middle-class post-war dream of good living. It has been observed that '... design-conscious consumers, mainly from the middle-classes, would accumulate a quite amazing store of knowledge on who designed what when and where to go and look for it. Numerous suburban homes were a shrine to the Design Centre ... A sign of the times was the mania in England for things from Scandinavia. Fifties Contemporary had a very special character, not exactly stark but not exactly cosy. Perhaps it was a little too self-conscious to relax in, perhaps the gaiety seemed slightly earnest ...'

In Harold Pinter's *The Caretaker* of 1960, the character Mick makes a revealing speech in discussing his plans for redecorating and, to quote Martin Esslin, '... transmutes the jargon of contemporary brand names into a dream-like world of wish-fulfillment.' 'You could have an off-white pile linen rug, a table in ... afromosia teak veneer, sideboard with matt black drawers, curved chairs with cushioned seats, armchairs in oatmeal tweed, beech-frame settee with woven sea-grass seat, white-topped, heat-resistant coffee table, white tile surround ...'

This newly affluent and self-conscious middle class was extending its consumer horizons in every respect, to include not just the home, but entertainment and travel. In England eating out became a regular luxury and a previously insular

middle class, fresh from the exciting novelty of continental holidays, was catered for by the French and especially the new Italian restaurants which mushroomed first in London and subsequently in the provinces during the sixties. With the emergence during that decade of such enterprising restaurateurs as Lorenzo Apicetta, 'Alvaro' and the Mario (Cassandro) and Franco (Lazatolla) team, the 'trattoria' style was elevated to the design peerage and became a significant ingredient of that middle-class phenomenon of the sixties and seventies, the 'Habitat style', brain-child of designer Terence Conran. Conran had tested himself in the Contemporary mode, but hit a commercial gold mine with an amalgam of mainstream Modernist and reassuringly cosy 'good taste' styles. The Habitat formula, exported to Europe and to the United States, has proved a successful commercial solution to the yearning of a design-conscious middle class.

The new design-awareness of the middle class was nowhere more marked, or more self-conscious, than in Britain. Consumerism was a new thrill to be judiciously enjoyed and the tastes of this new public were to be nourished after 1962 by the colour supplements to the Sunday newspapers – first with the *Sunday Times*, then with the *Observer*. With such features as the *Sunday Times*' 'Design for Living,' the supplements, as much in their advertising as in their editorial content, provided a pot-pourri of instant consumer culture and contributed to the visual education of a very wide market.

Since the late fifties and the advent of commercial television in Britain, the development and widening of the consumer market has in turn encouraged the increased sophistication of packaging and marketing skills, the development of the giant advertising agencies and their spin-off industries. The increasingly vast sums spent on advertising demanded a new

*Left: A selection of kitchen goods from the Habitat range. The Habitat formula for the wide marketing of 'good taste' has established itself internationally and was the brainchild of designer Terence Conran.*

professionalism in copywriting and design. In 1962 the Designers and Art Directors Association was formed in London to define and improve the standards of graphic communication.

## Design and Sponsorship

The contemporary period has undoubtedly witnessed the most significant general raising of standards, both in product design and buyer awareness, since the theorists of the nineteenth century first lamented the growing gulf between Art and Industry. Credit for a great deal of this improvement must go to the specialized government departments, independent commercial or non-commercial organizations which have sponsored and organized the promotion of good design, the exploration of craft and the rational exploitation of materials and technology.

In the most industrially advanced nations, notably in Britain, Germany, Japan and the United States, a spirit of adventure in the technological and design fields has produced a wide range of goods, from space rocket to electric razor, in which the pursuit of a new aesthetic is a major feature.

In the United States, museums and universities have become actively involved in the promotion of good design and craft. At the forefront, the Museum of Modern Art, New York, has inspired a spirit of experiment with such notable events as the 'Organic Design in Home Furnishing' competition and exhibition of 1940-41 and the 'Low-cost Furniture Competition' of 1948. M.O.M.A. has also consistently provided an educational showcase for the best of international contemporary design with such exhibitions as 'Italy: the New Domestic Landscape' of 1972. The Smithsonian Institution has similarly involved itself in visual education projects, such as the sponsorship in 1957 of a travelling exhibition throughout the United States of the work of the Lunning prize-winners since 1951, the very best of contemporary Scandinavian design.

In Britain the crucial event in the history of government sponsorship was the establishment in 1944 of the Council of Industrial Design. In his letter of acknowledgement to the newly-appointed chairman, Sir Thomas Barlow, Hugh Dalton set out the aims of the Council. The primary

*Above: The Design Centre label is a reassuring seal of approval.*
*Right: Sculptured wood bench seat by Wendell Castle, the American furniture designer-craftsman whose work has put him at the forefront of the seventies crafts revival.*

*Above left: The installation of the Museum of Modern Art's 1946 Charles Eames exhibition.*
*Above: 'AX Chair 6003' designed by Peter Hvidt and Orla Molgaard-Nielsen. Laminated beech frame, teak seat and back, 1950.*

aim was '... to promote by all practicable means the improvement of design in the products of British industry.' The practical functions would be '... to encourage and assist the establishment ... of Design Centres by industries ... to provide a national display of well-designed goods ... to co-operate with the Education Authorities and other bodies in matters affecting the training of designers ... (and) to be a centre of information and advice ... on all matters of industrial art and design.' In 1956 the Duke of Edinburgh opened the now internationally respected Design Centre in London's Haymarket. Here are displayed the winners of the Centre's coveted awards, instituted in 1957. The government-sponsored Crafts Advisory Committee, now restyled as the Crafts Council, was set up in 1971 to encourage individual artisans in every craft medium. Both the Council and the Victoria and Albert Museum, by holding regular exhibits of contemporary craft and design, have helped establish Britain's pre-eminence in the field of craft.

In the Scandinavian countries government support and the rationalism of both industry and artisans in establishing their own high design criteria have shaped the character of contemporary Scandinavian craft and assured the international export success of the Scandinavian style.

The Finns, showed a remarkably well co-ordinated surge of design energy after the sterile war years. Tapio Wirkkala is

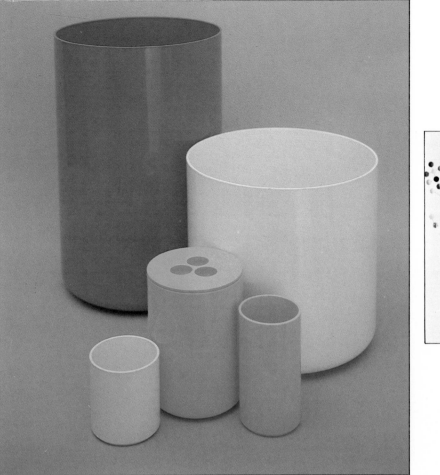

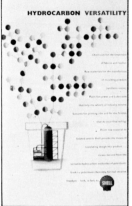

*Right: A selection from the 'Input' range of ABS plastic vessels designed in 1974 by Martin Roberts of Conran Associates and manufactured under the trademark 'Crayonne' by the Airfix Plastics Group.*
*Far right: 'Hydrocarbon Versatility'. 1949 advertisement for Shell emphasizing the company's involvement in the exploration of the chemistry of petroleum-derived synthetics.*

probably Finland's leading contemporary designer and has led his country to great success in international exhibitions and in the international market. From 1951 to 1954 he was artistic director at the Institute of Industrial Arts. Finland's influential promotional groups include Ornamo (the Association of Industrial Designers), the Finnish Society of Crafts and Design, the Friends of Finnish Handicrafts and the Finnish Council for Furniture Export Promotion.

Den Permanente, opened in 1931 in Copenhagen, provides a fine permanent exhibition of the best in contemporary Danish craft and domestic design and its co-operative policy offers equal opportunity to small studio or larger manufacturing concern. The Danes have their Society of Arts and Crafts and Industrial Design and the high standards of their furniture industry are maintained by the Danish Furniture Manufacturer's Quality Control Board which tests every design at Copenhagen's Technological Institute. The creation in 1951 of the Lunning Prize by Danish-born Frederik Lunning, on the occasion of his seventieth birthday, has rewarded the best of Scandinavian design, annually bestowing two generous travel/research grants. The first and highly deserving winners were Tapio Wirkkala from Finland and Hans Wegner from Denmark.

In Sweden the Svenska Slöjdföreningen is a non-commercial body which 'works steadfastly to raise quality and consumer taste conducive to gracious living for everyone.'

In France, despite the continuing work and 'Formes Utiles' exhibitions of the Union des Artistes Modernes, a strongly conservative streak has lost French designers their former pre-eminence, which had in 1925 made France the undisputed centre of fine craft and decorative

Left: Central well of the Charles de Gaulle airport, Paris, opened in 1972. One is reminded of the futuristic architecture of Fritz Lang's 'Metropolis'; a vision has become a reality.
Above: Catalogue of the 1955 'Formes Utiles' exhibition of the Union des Artistes Modernes.

*Left: The Guggenheim Museum, New York, designed by Frank Lloyd Wright and completed in 1959. This breathtaking spiral is a confident and masterful expression of Wright's mature style.*

design. The French government, however, has shown a willingness to make a few major statements in the technological design field with such projects as the Anglo-French 'Concorde' and such architectural hymns to the technological age as the prestigious Charles de Gaulle Airport of 1972 and the Centre Pompidou of 1977.

Internationally, a major contribution of industry in the contemporary era has been the development of synthetic materials, loosely described as plastics, but including a remarkable variety of compounds with an equally remarkable variety of intrinsic qualities. These plastics are the product of costly and complex research for which the corporate giants of industry, notably in Britain, the United States and Germany, have provided the facilities. Dr. Otto Bayer of the Bayer Corporation made important progress with polyurethanes during the war. In 1953 Professor Karl Ziegler of the Max Planck Institute for Coal Research at Mulheim announced further discoveries. In Britain Imperial Chemical Industries and in the United States such corporations as Standard Oil, du Pont, Philips Petroleum, and the General Electric Company have led the field in research. In 1942 the Dow Chemical Company formed a partnership with the Corning Glass Works to further the development of silicones. Industry has provided the materials of the modern age, the synthetics or plastics which, appearing at first cautiously during the late forties and fifties, then more confidently during the sixties and seventies, have come to dominate our environment.

## 1945 – Present
### Art and Style

In purely stylistic terms the contemporary era unfolds in a pattern of more or less identifiable phases, though the overlap, the sometimes contradictory parallel

*The TWA terminal at New York's Kennedy Airport, designed by Eero Saarinen and opened in 1961. The taut, elegant, free-flowing curves are a perfect example of Organic Modernism.*

developments and the unbroken thread of some influences would render inaccurate any very rigid analysis. The decorative arts owe a considerable debt to the fine arts and to pre-war stylistic and ethical precursors, notably in the continuing evolution of the International Modernist aesthetic.

The first pointers towards a distinctive new style in design and decoration came in the early forties from the United States where Charles Eames and Eero Saarinen were evolving the language of Organic Modernism, exploring free forms and the balance of slender lines and abstract masses which were to become so distinctive a feature of the post-war years. In the hands of essentially rational rather than decorative designers Organic Modernism became a style which somehow seemed to reconcile the conflicts between form and function explored since the Art Nouveau era. The clean-lined logic of International Modernism combined with the effortless grace of curvilinear Art Nouveau, with more than a nod at the American Stream-

lined Moderne of the thirties. In architecture the style was to find a late but perfect expression in Frank Lloyd Wright's Guggenheim Museum, completed in 1959, and in the taut, elegant, free-flowing curves of Saarinen's T.W.A. Terminal at Kennedy Airport of 1961.

The free form acquired a symbolic decorative value and was to be found in every medium. Its painterly origins were in the symbolic abstract forms of the Surrealist painters, the melting shapes in Dali's deserts, the ambiguous forms invented by Miró. Charles Eames' prototype *chaise* of 1948 is a pure exercise in the new style. Raised on the distinctive thin legs, which he had been the first to introduce, the amoeboid, free-form seat, asymmetrical, curving in every direction and with an off-centre cut-out, might have been the creation of a sculptor, perhaps of Barbara Hepworth or Jean Arp. The latter has been described as 'a one-man laboratory for the discovery of new form', and his two-and-three dimensional abstract forms were indeed quickly absorbed into the language of the decorative arts.

The Organic Modernist free form is to be found in the pure, simple, abstract, asymmetrical vases blown at Murano or at the Scandinavian glassworks of Orrefors, Kosta or Karhula-Littala; in the carved

*Top left: Chair designed by Carlo Mollino for Apelli & Varesio of Turin. c.1952.*
*Top right: 'Moving and Non-Moving Things'. Mural by Jo v. Kalckreuth, Munich, c. 1950.*
*Center: Prototype chaise by Charles Eames, 1948.*
*Right: Metal and glass dish by Fontana Arte.*

*Below: French painted wood and metal coat stand of the fifties. Bottom left: The typical thin scratchy lines and counter-balancing masses of the post war years on a British fabric. Bottom right: Mobiles in wood, wire, and plastic*

*by W.D. Wlodarczyk. Illustrated in 'International Window Display'.*

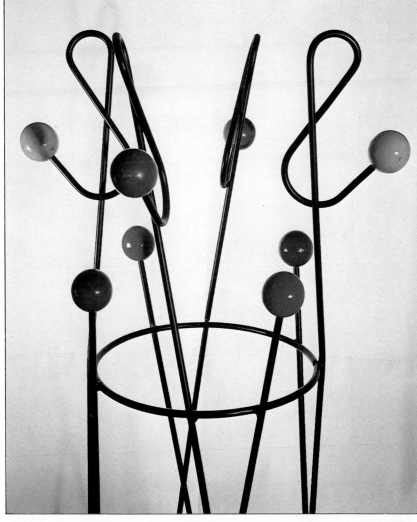

wood and glass tables conceived in the forties by sculptor Isamu Noguchi for Herman Miller; in the elegant silver of Georg Jensen; in textile and graphic design and, with more than a dash of the surreal, in such stylish eccentricities as the furniture of American Paul Laszlo or Italian designer Carlo Mollino. The Surrealist element was not always restricted to experiments in form. It appeared also in the more decorative aspects of design. From Bonwit Teller's New York window displays, through British advertising graphics to wall light fittings by the Italian firm of Fontana Arte, Surrealism was plundered for motifs and absorbed into the language of post-war romanticism.

The fashionable abstract free form was very often counterbalanced by thin lines. This relationship, successfully evolved within the applied arts in the Eames-Saarinen projects of the early forties, would seem to have had, as one of its primary sources of stylistic influence from within the fine arts, the mobiles of Calder.

The thin line and counterbalancing masses found a specific and highly popular area of exploitation in the 'molecular-structure' motifs which so perfectly expressed the optimistic post-war mood of scientific progress. Explored in depth by the Festival Pattern Group in a project which began in May 1949, molecular structures became the basis for patterns in every medium and indeed for certain elements of the very structure of the Fes-

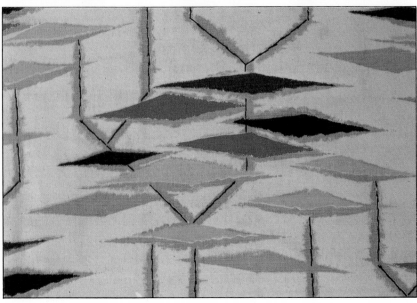

tival of Britain. In the States, for Herman Miller, George Nelson designed a molecular structure clock in 1949 and a stylish sofa made up of circular units on stick-like infrastructure and legs in 1956.

The thin, scratchy line, however, developed a quite independent life of its own and was used in graphic and three-dimensional contexts, often in romantic and whimsical frivolities, such as the cartoons and creations of the British Rowland Emmett, or the sweet lovers of French illustrator Peynet, in a magical and senti-

*Far left: Engraved glass windows for Coventry Cathedral by John Hutton.*
*Center: Composition in black, brown and yellow by Hans Hartung. 1951.*
*Above right: Printed satin. Enrico Prampolini for Socota, before 1957.*
*Bottom left: Whimsical 1949 drawing for 'Punch' by Rowland Emmett.*
*Bottom right: 'Antelope' chair designed by Ernest Race, steel and ply, 1950.*

mental post-war Paris. The painter Bernard Buffet, ably promoted by Pierre Bergé, a public relations wizard who was later to transfer his attentions to another rising star, Yves Saint-Laurent, found considerable success during the fifties with a seemingly scratchy style which combined the fashionable spontaneous graffiti texture of the Abstract Expressionists with commercially appealing subjects.

In furniture design two important examples of the thin line are Ernest Race's 'Antelope' chair, designed for the Festival of Britain, and American Harry Bertoia's 'chickenwire' chairs. The random graffiti of the American Abstract Expressionists were soon absorbed into the language of the decorative arts. Jackson Pollock's giant canvases formed appropriately modish backdrops to fashion photographs by Cecil Beaton. Pollock, one of the great stylists of American art, provided an inspiration to pattern-makers, as did the lesser names of the new Abstract schools.

The post-war mood of optimism, which

*Left: A large scale painting by Jackson Pollock provides a perfect backdrop in this fashion study by Cecil Beaton c. 1950.
Right: The sparkling lights of Las Vegas, the city described by Tom Wolfe as 'the Versailles of America'.*

explored with such enthusiasm the language of Organic Modernism and which delighted in the magical elements of Surrealism and the decorative whimsy of the 'Festival (of Britain) Style', found perhaps its most symbolic expression in the building of the new Coventry Cathedral, completed in 1962. Basil Spence's design involved the collaboration of Britain's leading artists and craftsmen and forms a setting for such *tours de force* as Sutherland's magnificent tapestry and John Piper's magical stained-glass windows and ·less well-known details such as Elizabeth Frink's lectern or Hans Coper's monumental ceramic candle-holders.

The romantic flush of post-war optimism in decoration and design mellowed into the essential seriousness, the concern with good taste which characterized the more restrained elegance of Fifties Contemporary and which marked the resurgence of International Modernism. Enter Scandinavian design onto the international market. Re-enter Mies Van der Rohe, Bauhaus father of International Modernism, with American architect Philip Johnson holding his coat tails. Mies and his disciples, now based in the United States, were summoned from the wings to build the monuments of post-war prosperity. The towering black steel and plate glass rectangular blocks of Mies's Lake

Shore Drive, Chicago, apartment buildings set the pattern in 1950. The Seagram Building, New York, which he designed in 1958 in partnership with Philip Johnson, is a monument to the continuing influence of International Modernism, as are the countless corporate blocks which line Park Avenue and which now tower over the previously impregnable skylines of London and Paris and almost every major international city. In 1955, Knoll International started the manufacture and distribution of Mies's classic pre-war furniture designs.

As International Modernism, an architectural style for architectural theorists and a domestic style for the design-conscious, reasserted itself, there developed an irrepressible counter-movement, the voice of popular culture which found its brashest, crudest, yet most stylish expression in the post-war architectural phenomenon of the twentieth-century's city of light, Las Vegas. Architect Robert Venturi, a key spokesman and exponent of 'Post-Modernism' has expressed the dilemma in his *Learning from Las Vegas*: 'Modern architecture has not so much excluded the commercial vernacular as it has tried to take it over by inventing and enforcing a vernacular of its own, improved and universal. It has rejected the combination of fine art and crude art ... Naked children have never played in *our* fountains, and I.M. Pei (an architect of the International Modernist School) will never be happy on Route 66.'

The potency of Las Vegas as a symbol of popular culture has been perfectly expressed by Tom Wolfe who describes the city as '.. the Versailles of America.' 'The important thing', he wrote, 'about the building of Las Vegas is not that the builders were gangsters but that they were proles. They celebrated, very early, the new style of life of America – using the money pumped in by the war to show a prole vision ... of style.' And what style!

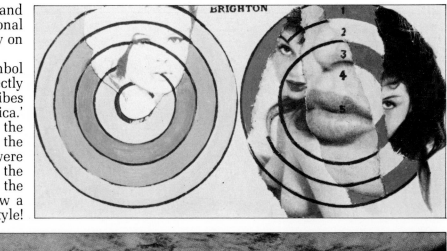

*Above right: Collage by English Pop artist Allen Jones, 1958.*
*Right: 'Just What is it That Makes Today's Homes so Different, so Appealing', collage painting by Richard Hamilton, first shown in 1956 and often cited as the first Pop picture.*

'That fantastic skyline! Las Vegas' neon sculpture, its fantastic fifteen-story-high display signs, parabolas, boomerangs, rhomboids, trapezoids, and all the rest of it are already the staple diet of the American landscape. They soar in shapes before which the existing language of art history is helpless. I can only attempt to supply names – Boomerang Modern, Flash Gordon Ming-Alert Spiral ... Mint Casino Elliptical, Miami Beach Kidney ... Palette Curvilinear.'

The emergence in the States of a truly popular art, a cult of style which was essentially vulgar and, as such, has remained largely anonymous, ignored by 'serious' design history, found its expression in the seeming litter of the urban landscape, in the signs and neon games, distilled to the point of self-caricature in Las Vegas, and in the exaggerated styling of motor cars.

It was this language of disposable, consumer reality which was to fund the image bank of Pop Art, a movement which found its earliest partisans in England, in the Independent Group of the Institute of Contemporary Arts. The crystallization of the 'Pop' ethic came in 1956 with the Whitechapel Art Gallery exhibition 'This is Tomorrow', which introduced many of the key themes of Pop Art: Marilyn Monroe, giant beer bottles, advertising ephemera and presented what is often cited as the first Pop picture, Richard Hamilton's collage *Just What is it That Makes Today's Homes so Different, so Appealing?* In this, a caricature consumer couple, a Charles Atlas-like figure and a sequin-trimmed pin-up, are set awkwardly in a photomontage home surrounded by consumer hardware – on the lampshade a giant shield from the Ford motor company, on the wall a comic-strip frame from *True Romance*. It was too early for them to have a 'genuine' Lichtenstein.

In 1958 film-maker/photographer William Klein made his *Broadway by Light*, a fascinated analysis of one aspect of popular culture. In the 1960s Dan Flavin, with his sculptures in light made from neon tubes, paid fine art's homage to this raw ingredient of popular art. Through the late fifties and into the sixties Pop evolved, found its masters in Andy Warhol, Tom Wesselman, Jasper Johns, Claes Oldenburg, James Rosenquist and Roy Lichtenstein in the United States, Allen Jones and Peter Blake in England.

Pop, which had drawn on popular, consumer imagery, in turn inspired a 'Pop' style in the applied arts, a fad in interior, graphic and fashion design which reached

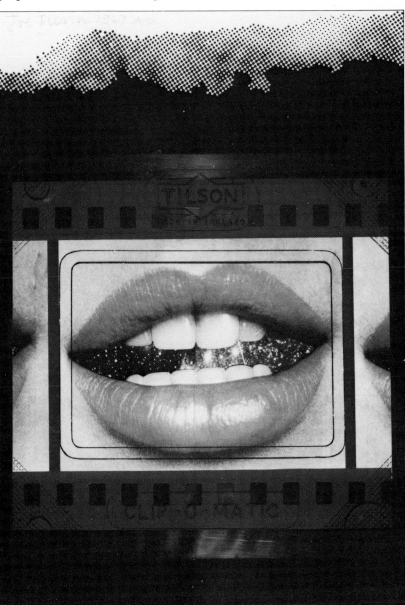

*Below: 'Clip-o-Matic', by Joe Tilson. Screen print with Mylar, 1967. This artist's proof plate is one of a number of variants on the theme.*

Top: Design for shelving
and clothes rails for the
Mr Freedom shop by Jon
Weallans, c. 1970.
Above left: Prototype
models of wardrobes by
Ettore Sottsass, 1966. A
remarkable application
of Fine Art styles to
furniture design by this

brilliant Italian.
Above right: French
plastic bracelet, c. 1970.

# neon

Top: Early seventies
'Neon' sculpture
designed by British art
director, Simon Kentish.
(detail).
Above: London boutique
'Granny Takes a Trip'
with store front painted
by Michael English, one
of a sequence of
frontages which made
this shop a remarkable
manifestation of
disposable street art.
This particular frontage
was published in 'Nova',
April 1967.
Left: Sixties wrapping
paper printed with
pattern designed by
American Pop artist Roy
Lichtenstein.

*'Op Art' scene from the film 'Qui Etes-Vous Polly Magoo' directed by photographer-turned-film maker, William Klein.*

a peak in the late sixties and early seventies. The most enduring legacy, however, of Pop Art and of the concurrent Hard-Edge Abstractionist schools of painting of the sixties has been a dramatic new attitude to colour. The decade of Frank Stella, Ellsworth Kelly, Morris Louis and Kenneth Noland saw the advent of sharp primary colours within the applied arts. These painters found the ideal colours, hard and synthetic for the synthetic materials in which so many objects were now manufactured.

The sixties was a richly diverse decade of stylistic trends. Pop and Hard Edge were dominant influences. Op and Kinetic Art made a short-lived but effective mark. Op Art, notably for a brief season around 1965, enjoyed a considerable influence in every aspect of design, from fashion and interior design to graphics and even film, where it soon lent itself to parody by William Klein in the joke Op Art scenes in his film *Qui Etes-vous Polly Magoo?* of 1967. Bridget Riley's or Victor Vasarely's patterns were never really intended to be worn or lived in.

A notable feature of the sixties was the revival of Art Nouveau, a revival first inspired by the Museum of Modern Art's major 1960 survey exhibition, 'Art Nouveau – Art and Design at the Turn of the

Century.' This was followed in 1963 by a major retrospective of the work of the highly decorative graphic artist Alphonse Mucha at the Victoria and Albert Museum. Mucha's sinuous lines became a major ingredient of poster art in the late sixties and through the seventies reproductions of his work have become best – sellers. Art Nouveau wallpapers by Voysey and the Arts and Crafts designs of William Morris enjoyed considerable popularity. Biba Boutique used Art Nouveau style wallpapers by Anthony Little with bentwood hat stands and Edwardian potted palms to conjure up a fin-de-siècle atmosphere which was much imitated in the late sixties.

Aubrey Beardsley was another turn-of-the-century artist whose work was reappraised with a major Victoria and Albert Museum exhibition in 1966 and his taut, black/white drawings enjoyed a second *succès de scandale*, influencing a new generation of young graphic artists and designers.

Side-by-side, incongruously, with this cult of the decadent age of Art Nouveau came the cult of the images of today, the symbols of speed and the space age. *Vogue* and other magazines illustrated futuristic silver rooms filled with metal furniture and gadgetry, and such fashions as the 'silver paper suit, the ultimate space-age adventure . . .' photographed by David Bailey in British *Vogue* of January 1967. No designer caught this mood more effectively than Paris couturier André Courrèges with his 'Clothes of the Future' which made so forceful an impact in 1965.

Perhaps the most fascinating spontaneous outburst of style of the decade, however, came in the late sixties with the cult, the ideology, but above all the rich imagery of the so-called 'flower children.' The movement took shape in 1967 and combined an endearing *faux-naïf* romanticism with the more sinister exploration of the hallucinatory state, providing. the exotic imagery of psychedelic experience. The cult found its spiritual homes in San Francisco. ('If you're going to San Francisco be sure to wear some flowers in your hair,') or in the remote Indian lairs of self-styled gurus. It found its most richly inspired musical gurus in the Beatles with such songs as *Lucy in the Sky with Diamonds*: 'Picture yourself in a boat on a river,/with tangerine trees and marmalade skies./Somebody calls you, you answer quite slowly,/a girl with kaleidoscope eyes./Cellophane flowers of yellow and green,/towering over your head.'

Despite the Beatles' own protestation to the contrary, the lyrics are pure psychedelic imagery. Such imagery, combined with borrowings from Art Nouveau and with a new palette – the vibrant, acid colours of the so-called acid trip – provided the basis of a highly fertile era in graphic art, most notably in the by-products of the music industry, posters and record sleeves.

A major ingredient of the 'hippie' cult was the fashion for ethnic clothing and interior decoration, the by-product of a naive, if deeply-felt ideological rejection of materialism. The look was perfectly captured by Talitha Getty, wife of the late Paul Getty's son Eugène. Mrs Getty was

*'Courrèges: Clothes of the Future' ran this cover copy in March 1965. Courrèges captured headlines with his stunning space-age styles.*

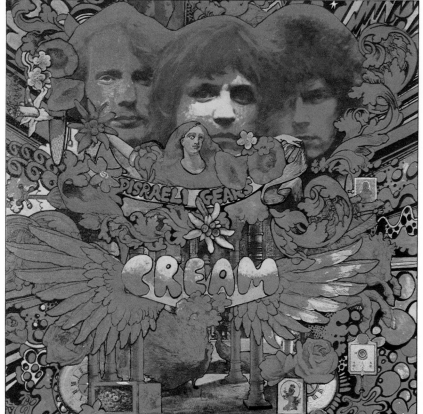

photographed, seated cross-legged in 'rich gypsy' clothes in her Rome drawing room in which '... the atmosphere is even more like that of an Eastern Bazaar: North African antiques are scattered about the room, a shrine to Buddha stands against one wall. The lighting is diffuse ... scented joss sticks burn.' Rolling Stones camp follower Anita Pallenberg was photographed for *Vogue* lying on a fashionable litter of oriental rugs and cushions. Two charming exponents of the hippie style were the couple, Marikje and Simon, who called themselves 'Fool' and painted wonderful, exuberant murals, notably and controversially on the exterior of the Beatles' Baker Street shop 'Apple'. They also contributed to the decoration of the home of Beatle George Harrison.

The young generation eventually and inevitably awoke from this dream and the transition into the seventies was an unsentimental one. The visual arts could not escape the realities of our environment and the 'hippie' cult was seen for what it was, a defiant but futile expression of escapist romanticism.

In painting, the turn of the decade was marked by a strong return to realism with a group of American painters evolving a style variously described as 'Photo-', 'Hyper-', 'New' or 'Sharp-Focus' Realism, a style which met with the almost universal disapprobation of those art critics and commentators who had made so much wordage of the more painterly Pop, but above all of the various post-war abstract movements.

New Realism, however, met with a considerable popularity for it expressed a very real situation. Richard Estes, one of the leading exponents of the genre, expressed his motivation. 'It's funny, all the things I was trained to paint – people and trees, landscapes and all that – I can't paint. We're living in an urban culture that never existed even fifty years ago.' The New Realism was a natural successor

to Pop, but the ethic was quite different. Pop was a painterly probing, a fine art volte-face, an often almost unconscious exploration of as yet half-understood symbols. New Realism was a glossy, lovingly polished interpretation of the imagery of the urban environment. Perhaps the 'serious' critics resented the photographic nature of this realism and the painters' ability to bestow an undeniable beauty on the colours, materials and textures of parking lot or store-front, neon-sign or motor vehicle. The style, beloved of art directors, transformed the American urban landscape into an aesthetic treat, exaggerating the beauty of polished chrome, plate-glass reflections and neon strips. The vibrant colour of Astroturf seemed more appealing than its natural alternative.

It is more difficult to characterize the seventies than the preceding decades, without the advantages of an extended hind-sight, yet certain moods, certain elements already stand out. There is no doubt, for instance, that the New Realists heralded a very positive new aesthetic –

*'Psychedelic imagery ... provided the basis of a highly fertile era in graphic art, most notably in the by-products of the music industry.' Record sleeve for Cream's album 'Disraeli Gears', 1967, by illustrator Martin Sharp and photographer Bob Whitaker.*

frank, hard, cynical, arguably making a virtue of necessity, in fact accepting and enjoying the potential beauty of today's environment and today's materials, seeing the beauty in the man-made, the vulgar, even disposable, enjoying the artifice of the saturated colours, the dynamic primaries which had first appeared in the decorative arts in the late sixties.

The cold polish of chromium-plated steel was enjoyed for its hard chic, without any of the bright-eyed idealism of previous generations. The symbols of the future became available realities in the decade of supersonic travel. The conveyor tubes of Paris' Charles de Gaulle airport were designed for use, not as the space-age set of a futuristic film. The architectural monument to this new frankness is, of course, the Paris Centre Pompidou designed by the Anglo-Italian team of Richard Rogers and Renzo Piano. Its sibling, on a reduced scale, is the British Sainsbury Centre for the Visual Arts, Norwich, designed by Norman Foster and opened in 1978.

The emergence of Post-Modernism as a mode of thought in architecture found perhaps its most iconoclastic expression in the series of Best Products showrooms built across the United States to the designs of the Site Inc. team led by James Wines. Peeling, crumbling walls with piles of fallen bricks and a raw-edged notch in the brick structure to replace the standard entranceway became features of these humorous, controversial but much-loved projects started in 1972.

In domestic design and decoration the appreciation of the intrinsic beauty in the tough serviceability of industrially conceived hardware became a fashion and found a name in the 'High-Tech' style of the late seventies.

The photographer who has best captured the cynicism and the hard chic of the seventies is Helmut Newton. His images are of a brittle, highly-charged and often potentially violent world of harsh-lit swimming pools, anonymous hotel rooms, chic glistening gymnasiums or health-spas. In his gardens, flowers take on acrylic hues.

The other side of the coin, the sinister underside to the chic surface of the super-cool seventies, is the spiritual emptiness

*Left: 'Private Parking VII Americard', by Don Eddy, acrylic on canvas, 1971.*

Interior and exterior views of the Sainsbury Centre for the Visual Arts, Norwich, designed by Norman Foster and opened in 1978. Here is an uncompromising approach to architecture in pursuit of an honest aesthetic appropriate to the demands of the technological age.

which has expressed itself in various brands of nihilistic behaviour, from political terrorism to the savage visual imagery and music of Punk. Andy Warhol expressed this mood of rejection in his usual ironical way, 'I believe that everyone should live in one big empty space. It can be a small space as long as it's clean and empty. I like the Japanese way of rolling everything up and locking it away in cupboards. But I wouldn't even have the cupboards because that's hypocritical.'

The potency and appetite of the commercial machine, however, have come to dominate every aspect of life and transform even nihilistic concepts into marketable commodities. The Punk movement found its true graphic expression in such short-lived minority publications as *Anarchy in the U.K.*, but anarchy must constantly change its spots if it is to survive the inexorable machine of commerce. The apparel of anarchy becomes teenage fashion. Symbol becomes product.

In the face of the commercial realities which have dominated the seventies there has been a strong and not always unsuccessful attempt to revive the crafts, often through government sponsored schemes. This revival, based on romantic notions reminiscent of another age, however unrealistic, is hardly an attempt to go against the tide of modern life. There will always be a role for the hand-crafted object, but more as a romantic symbol for the rich, than as a viable possibility for everyday use.

## The Exhibitions

The story of the contemporary decorative arts would be incomplete without mention of the major national or international exhibitions which have crystalized the mood and styles of particular moments and which in turn have stimulated design by providing major showcases for the best of contemporary work.

Though the post-war period has seen no exhibitions of the importance of the Paris International Exhibitions of 1900 or 1925, or of the original International Exhibition, the Great Exhibition of 1851, several events are worthy of attention, notably, in the United Kingdom, the 'Britain Can Make It' exhibition of 1946 and the Festival of Britain of 1951, the post-war Milan Triennale Exhibitions of 1948, 1951, 1954 and 1957, the Brussels World Fair of 1958 and the Expo '67 held in Montreal.

The title of the first of these exhibitions is self-explanatory. The 'Britain Can Make It' exhibition of 1946 was precisely that: an affirmation of a nation's determination to restructure its arts and its industries after the war years. A symbolic section was entitled 'War to Peace' and showed the adaptation of wartime skills to peacetime usages. The theme was emphatically

'swords-to-ploughshares', but not until 1951 and the far larger concept of the Festival of Britain did the character of post-war design in Britain have the opportunity to show its full colours.

The most exciting architectural features, the focal points of the Festival, were the Dome of Discovery, a discus, perhaps more aptly a flying-saucer shape in aluminium alloy, supported on a slender structure of steel latticework, and the adjacent 'Skylon', a three-hundred foot thrust into the sky, a symbol of optimism which, according to one acid wit, 'like Britain (had) no visible means of support.' Itself a symbol, the Festival created and celebrated a symbolic design style in which heraldic motifs, and motifs derived from the analysis of molecular structure, combined with the whimsical mood of its refined thin lines in structure, flat pattern and furniture and object design. The Festival symbol, a Britannia head on a star sometimes hung with pennants, was a joyous symbol of patriotic enthusiasm.

Molecular structure motifs were used

Verushka photographed in the presidential suite of the Meridian Hotel, Nice, by Helmut Newton, 1975. Newton, perhaps more effectively than any other photographer, captured the cynicism and the hard chic of the seventies.

on a large-scale in the screen at the entrance to the Science Museum Exhibit, designed by Gordon Andrew as an aluminium honeycomb enclosing atom motifs, based on the carbon atom, and in Edward Mills' 'Abacus' screen. The Festival Pattern Group evolved graphic motifs for textiles and other materials from chemical structure patterns. Best-known and highly typical of the 'thin' designs for furniture was Ernest Race's 'Antelope'

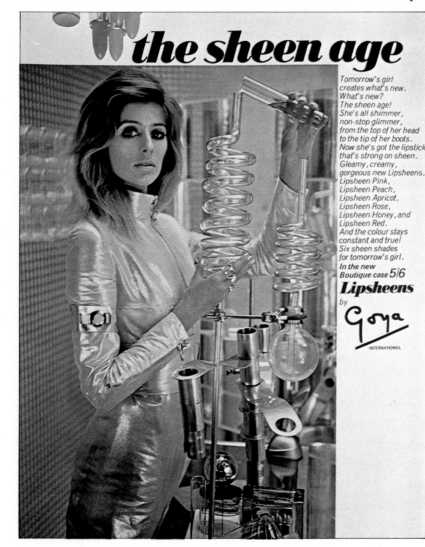

chair, designed for outdoor use on the South Bank.

The Festival mood was so full of hope that few paused to notice that, in fact, many of the new design trends were little more than a reflection of American or Italian ideas. In furniture there were no concepts presented on the South Bank that had not already been explored by Eames and his contemporaries, and it was rightly pointed out by Italian critics that the architecture of the Festival owed a great deal to the designs of Renzo Zavanella for the Milan Exhibition of 1948.

The more impressive Milan Triennale of 1951 demonstrated once again the Italian strength in exhibition design and showed the sophistication of the emergent Italian school of decorative designers, led by the purist Gio Ponti. The entrance hall, grand but with elements of fantasy, was the work of architects Baldessari and Grisotti. The serpentine lines of the ceiling emphasized the deliberate break with rectilinear modernism. Indeed one visitor, Jean Royère, noted as significant pointers the obsessive avoidance of the straight line and the deliberate use of asymmetry to humanize the too-theoretical look of rooms. For the first floor ceiling, above the grand staircase, Lucio Fontana drew an elegant free-form looping arabesque of neon.

A highlight of the 1951 Triennale was the Finnish exhibit, installed by Tapio Wirkkala, and winning much praise and well-deserved prizes for the unity, elegance and restraint of the objects submitted. The Finns, exhibiting again at the 1954 Triennale, and again led by Wirkkala, were once more the centre of attention. Wirkkala has personally accumulated gold and silver Triennale medals and seven Grand Prix.

In 1951 the 'Forma dell'Utile' section, installed by architects Belgroso and Peressutti, was devoted to the increasingly important area of industrial design. The

*The changing face of beauty. Top sixties model Jill Kennington in a space-age sci-fi fantasy lipstick advertisement from 1967 contrasts with the anarchic image of punk as epitomized on the cover of the 'Anarchy in the U.K.'.*

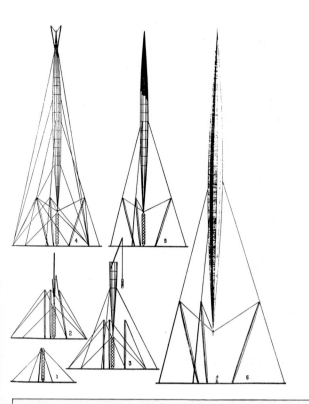

Top: The 'Dome of Discovery' at the Festival of Britain, 1951.
Top right: An artist's impression of the 'Skylon' in the various stages of its construction, 1951.
Right: Lucio Fontana's neon ceiling sculpture for the Milan Triennale of 1951.

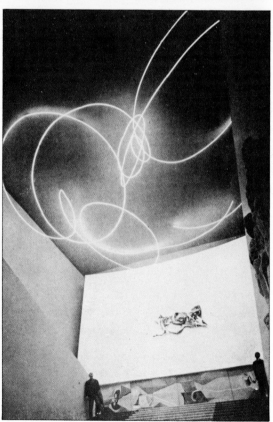

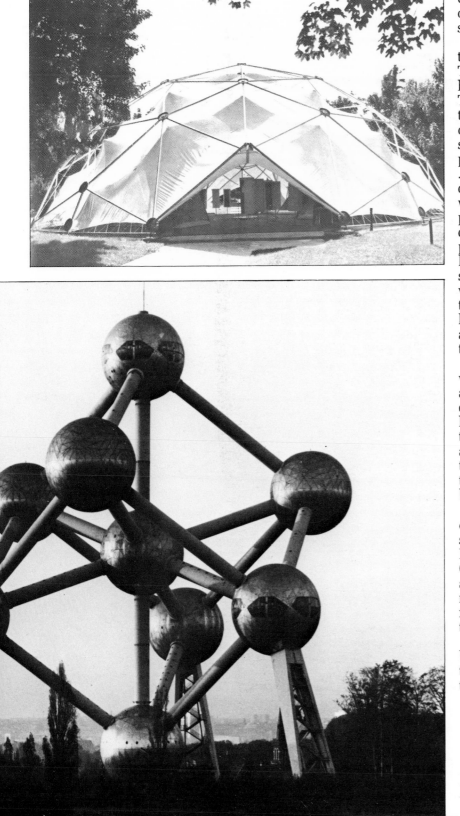

displays were suspended on a criss-cross of steel wire joined by 'molecular' spheres.

The next major exhibition of international importance besides the regular Triennales was the Brussels World Fair held between April and October in 1958. The site was dominated by the 'Atomium', the most important monument to the age of atomic research, an architectural version of the molecular structure. A contemporary commentator wrote that 'Brussels ... will not be remembered for its grandeur and pageantry alone. For all nations will be emphasizing their technological progress, the advances they have made in design ... Indeed, this exhibition should prove to be a scientific and industrial landmark for years to come. Brussels will show that the atom is being adapted to work for peace, electronics and automation have been made beneficial to mankind, and that technical invention advances today hand in hand with industrial design.'

One of the most remarkable pavilions was the pattern of twelve hyperbolic paraboloids conceived in pre-stressed concrete by Le Corbusier for Philips of Eindhoven. Once inside this futuristic fantasy the visitor was exposed to '... a video-aural electronic tour de force spanning the march of mankind from pre-history to the present times, with electronic music, by Edgar Varese, and photo-projections'

Britain's representation included an exhibit of two hundred consumer goods selected by the Council of Industrial Design and shown in a miniature Design Centre. The Finnish exhibit was once again well co-ordinated by Wirkkala, who nine years later was responsible for the fine 'Creative Finland' exhibit at the Montreal Expo '67.

Opening on 28 April, Expo '67 celebrated Canada's centennial year in a spectacular interntional manifestation on the theme of Man and his World.

*Top: Geodetic dome designed by Buckminster Fuller, to house the United States exhibit at the 1957 Milan Triennale.*
*Left: 'Atomium', a remarkable, over-scaled molecular structure which dominated the 1958 Brussels World Fair.*

# FURNITURE & THE INTERIOR

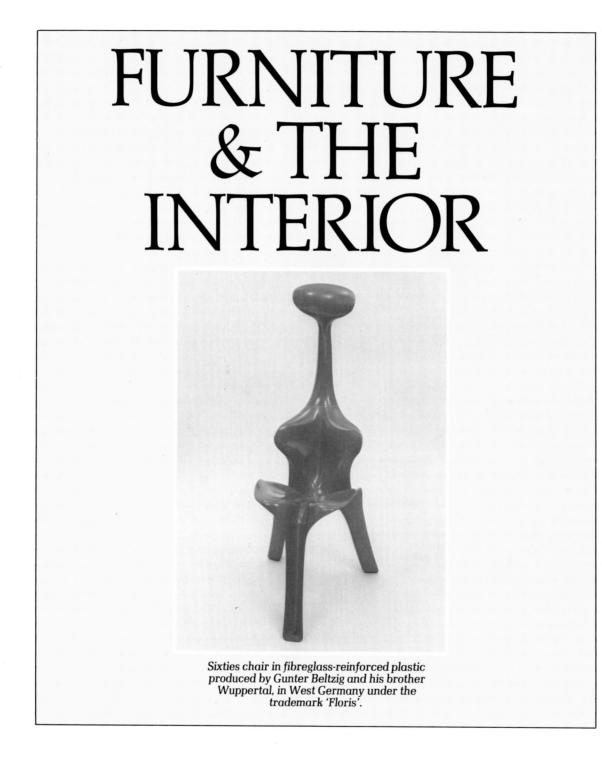

*Sixties chair in fibreglass-reinforced plastic produced by Gunter Beltzig and his brother Wuppertal, in West Germany under the trademark 'Floris'.*

## ———————— 1940 – 1960 ————————
## Utility to Organic Modernism

THE LOOK OF FURNITURE was transformed as the result of experimentation in the early 1940s which established new principles of furniture design. These changes came about in spite of the restrictions imposed by the war; in fact, some were the by-product of wartime experiment in the use of new alloys and new synthetics.

### United States

The conceptual heralds of the new furniture were from the United States, where the arrival in the late 1930s of Bauhaus emigrés Walter Gropius and Mies van der Rohe had encouraged the adoption of German ideas on functionalism. International Modernism had changed its location, but Mies was to remain its guru until his death in 1969. Under the patronage of an enlightened Museum of Modern Art there emerged a new school of designers of whom the most important has been Charles Eames, an architect/designer who created an exciting organic version of International Modernism.

In 1940, the Museum of Modern Art opened an inter-American competition for 'Organic Design in Home Furnishing', sponsored by retailers and manufacturers in search of new design talent. The results were exhibited the following year. The most successful entries were the work of Charles Eames, presented in partnership with Eero Saarinen. Theirs were quite revolutionary new concepts which won them first prize for their seating and other living room furniture designs. In 1946 the same museum devoted a one-man show to Eames's new range of moulded plywood chairs and related designs. Ever to the fore in stimulating and documenting progress, the museum ran in 1948 an international competition for 'Low Cost Furniture Design' organized by Edgar Kauffman Jr. This inspired such advanced ideas as Robert Lewis's and James Pres-

tini's single-unit, moulded plastic chair, the precursor of Verner Panton's elegant design of 1960 and of the plastic and fibre-glass designs which now proliferate.

Eames taught at the Cranbrook Academy from 1936, with Florence Knoll, Harry Bertoia and Eero Saarinen as contemporaries. He became head of the department of experimental design in 1937, a post he held until his move to Venice, California, in 1941 with his wife Ray. It has been said that 'In the 1950s the whole design climate was changed by Charles and Ray Eames. By a few chairs and a house ...' Eames's furniture and interiors explore the idea of 'organic' design in every sense. His schemes have the flexibility and adaptability of living organisms, as can be seen in his designs for storage. Separate container units sit in a variety of positions or combinations on bases which can double as seats, serving a fluid variety of functions. He also explores the 'organic' in his search for ideal forms, notably for seat units, and his solutions are soft, sculptural and essentially curvilinear. Eames's greatest innovations were in chair design, the most dramatic advance being the quite separate consideration of seating shell and supportive sub-structure. He explored new materials, notably injection moulded plastics and new techniques of plywood manufacture to allow multi-directional curvature and flexibility. Amongst Eames's most pleasing furniture designs is his understated serpentine ash plyscreen of 1946, each panel of curved section and joined by a concealed canvas strip. But he is probably most often thought of in association with his now classic lounge chair and ottoman of 1956, a distillation of his ideals, invitingly executed in rosewood ply, hide and cast aluminium.

With the light and open design of his own home, Eames established his role as one of the creators of the California Modern style interior, the most characteristic

feature of which is the fluid interplay between indoor and outdoor space. The *Studio Yearbook* of 1950/51 discusses two homes conceived in this style by leading architect/designer Richard J. Neutra. The first, in Santa Barbara for Mr and Mrs Warren Tremaine, has the characteristic flat, widely overlapping roof slab above walls of plate glass, enclosing minimally decorated inner spaces with 'exterior and interior borderline obliterated ... living areas, covered and roofless terraces ... combined in one flowing space'. The second, a Colorado Desert house for Edgar Kauffman, has similarly fluid indoor/outdoor spaces with vertical aluminium blinds; the sparse furnishings include Eames's 1946 lounge chairs.

The spatial ideals which dictated this

*Above: Installation of furniture designed by Charles Eames and Eero Saarinen in the Museum of Modern Art's 1941 exhibition 'Organic Design in Home Furnishings'.*
*Right: 'Lounging Shape'. Chair design submitted by Eames and Saarinen in the 1940 'Organic Design in Home Furnishings' competition.*

*Left: Dining chair designed by Charles Eames of moulded walnut plywood, steel rods, and rubber shock mounts, 1946.*
*Right: Charles and Ray Eames. 'In the 1950s the whole design climate was changed by Charles and Ray Eames, by a few chairs and a house . . .'*

open-plan style also guided sculptor/ architect Harry Bertoia in his approach to chair design. Given an open brief for furniture design in 1950 by Hans and Florence Knoll, he conceived his celebrated 'chicken wire' chairs of which he wrote '. . . many functional problems have to be satisfied first . . . but when you get right down to it the chairs are studies in space, form and metal too. If you will look at them you will find that they are mostly made of air, just like sculpture. Space passes right through them.'

This sculptural concern in American furniture design found an able exponent in Isamu Noguchi, a sculptor who created a series of refined free-form glass tables on asymmetrical sculpted wood bases, on commission for Herman Miller. Designer Paul Laszlo Inc. took the notion to an eccentric extreme with his sculpted walnut and lucite table published in the *Studio Yearbook* of 1952/3.

Eames's collaborator for the 1940/1 Museum of Modern Art projects, Eero Saarinen, created furniture designs from 1946 for the progressive Knoll International, most notably his refined 'Tulip' suite first conceived in 1953 and put into production in 1956. Made up of white fibreglass seats and marble table tops on white aluminium stems flaring at the base, the elements of this suite have a visual lightness and a consummate elegance in their perfectly balanced proportions and fluid lines.

Organic Modernism found many self-consciously stylish exponents in the United States during the fifties and the free-form table became a symbol of the era. For Keygan Dreyfuss Inc., Vladimir Kagan conceived sculpted tables in fine woods, walnut, mahogany or oiled teak; for the Widdicomb Furniture Co., T.H. Robsjohn-Gibbings designed an impressive free-form stepped-level table in walnut; for Wor-de-Klee Inc., Irina Klepper designed a stylish plate-glass-topped table on a carved wood base. An exception amongst American designers was Tommi Parzinger whose speciality was cabinet furniture in luxury materials, more akin in spirit to the conservative elements amongst French designers. He followed the French fashion for cabinets covered in trellis-tooled hide.

## United Kingdom

While in the United States the Museum of Modern Art was encouraging creative furniture design during the early 1940s, in the United Kingdom the Board of Trade brought furniture design and manufacture under tight and restrictive control through the Domestic Furniture (Control of Manufacture and Supply (No 2)) Order 1942, whereby furniture could only be made under licence from the Board. This order marked the official beginning of 'Utility furniture', almost in exclusive production through the late 1940s, and was not finally revoked until 1952. Gordon Russell saw his role as design consultant as a crusading opportunity to implement his socialist dreams of bringing 'the basic rightness of contemporary design' to the masses. Utility furniture was, certainly, a rational and appropriate solution to wartime conditions. Looking back, however, it stands as a drab symbol of an austere phase in a

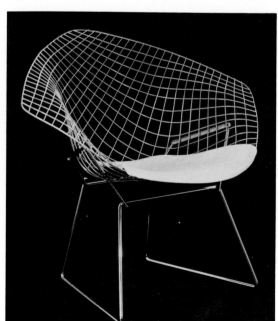

*Right: 'Chickenwire' chair designed by Harry Bertoia for Hans and Florence Knoll. Invited to design furniture in 1950 Bertoia conceived a range of these chairs; '. . . studies in space, form and metal . . .'. Far right: Armchair and marble topped table by Eero Saarinen from the range of pedestal furniture which he created for Knoll. First manufactured in 1956.*

*Charles Eames' most celebrated design, his now-classic Lounge Chair 670 and Ottoman 671 designed in 1956 for Herman Miller. Leather-covered upholstery in rosewood-veneered plywood cradle with cast aluminium brackets and base.*

nation's history and the reaction in the whimsical styles which captured the popular imagination at the Festival of Britain in 1951 would seem to contradict Russell's precept of a constant 'rightness'.

After the war, the trade was anxious for greater freedom of design. The progress of American design was becoming known among a new generation of designers. Robin Day's now classic 'Polyprop' injection moulded polypropylene chair on slender tube base, first manufactured in 1963 and still in production, is the direct descendant of Eames's chairs of c.1950. He, and others of his generation, were fascinated by the visually light substructure of new American designs, by the '. . . strong contrast of weight and thinness.' Day, in collaboration with Clive Latimer, applied this ideal to the design of storage units, the bodies of which were conceived as Mondrian-like compositions, and won first prize for their entry to the 1948 Museum of Modern Art Low Cost Furniture competition. Such storage units became as much the set-piece of the 1950s British home as the cocktail cabinet had been in the 1930s. As free-standing room-dividers they contributed to the new ideal of flexibility in interiors.

The so-called Festival style in furniture design was essentially an opportunity for British designers to catch up with progress elsewhere, notably the United States. Like Day, contemporaries Ernest Race and Dennis Young worked in the shadow of American innovation, often with an element of traditionalism. Race's successful 'Antelope' chair, designed in 1950, reveals an essential conservatism. Here is the traditional Windsor chair interpreted in the newly fashionable steel rod; Young's 'shell' chair of 1947/8, despite the ergonomic concerns which dictated its design, owes its anthropomorphic seatshell and steel-rod base to the Eames/Saarinen 'relaxation' chair of 1940.

Beneath the veneer of novelty of the

*Right: Wall storage unit designed by Robin Day and Clive Latimer for the 1948 Museum of Modern Art 'Low Cost Furniture' competition.*
*Below: Table designed by sculptor Isamu Noguchi for Herman Miller. Plate glass on carved walnut, early 1940,*

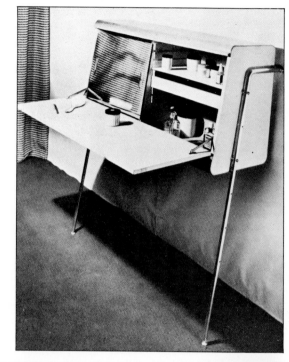

Festival style the conservatism of British taste can be seen in the success of Lucien Ercolani's revamped Windsor chairs, first shown at the Britain Can Make It Exhibition in 1946 and still in production. The pre-war popularity of deep-upholstered seating continued undiminished and found its most fashionable expression in wing armchairs such as those designed by Howard Keith for H.K. Furniture.

On the credit side, there were British designers concerned to exploit new techniques and materials. The *Studio Yearbook* for 1949 illustrates '... one or two interesting results of modern experiment, notably in techniques born of the discovery that dissimilar materials can be firmly bonded together'. In the same year Morris of Glasgow introduced their elegant 'Allegro' suite, designed by Basil Spence, proudly attesting to 'a completely new principle of construction, derived from experimental work on Mosquito fuselages and the manufacture of helicopter blades during the war'.

## France

In post-war France conservatism was very deeply entrenched. Designer/decorator

*Above: 'Shell' chair designed by Dennis Young, 1947/8. Fibrenyle seat shell on steel rod base.*
*Left: Deep-buttoned wing armchair and other designs illustrated in a 1953 advertisement for Ernest Race Ltd.*

Jean Royère wrote in 1953, '... there is practically no furniture industry in France ...' with the reminder that '... the spirit of every Frenchman revolts at the idea of mass-produced stereotypes.' The focus of furniture design was still towards the individual hand-crafted work. With rapid developments in the techniques of series production shaping the future of furniture design in other countries, Royère was able to write complacently that, 'French interior decoration has now reached a somewhat leisurely phase in the history of its development.'

There were, nonetheless, spokesmen of a new rationalism in French furniture design, many of whom were members of the Union des Artistes Modernes, the group which had promoted Modernism during the 1930s and which, in 1955, celebrated a quarter-century of activity. Members René Herbst, Charlotte Perriand, Louis Sognot and Jean Prouvé continued to explore their functionalist ethic,

*Robin Day's most successful design, his so-called 'Polyprop' stacking chair for Hille. First manufactured in 1963, millions have since been produced. This light, sturdy chair with single-unit, moulded seat on steel rod base is a practical design for contract seating.*

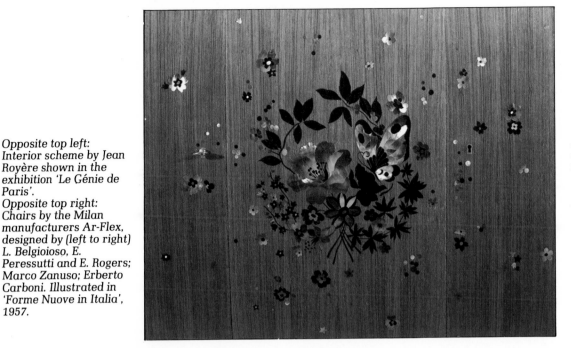

adding new laminates, synthetics and alloys to their repertoire of available materials. But for the most part their post-war work lacks the stylistic confidence either of their American contemporaries or of their own pre-war designs. The 1955 U.A.M. exhibition 'Formes Utiles' included, notably, the results of a 1954 competition for furniture design in fibre-glass reinforced synthetics, sponsored by the Societé d'Encouragement à l'Art et à l'Industrie. Manufacturers took heed and the success of this first competition encouraged another in 1958.

Despite such attempts at a new modernism in furniture design and manufacture, French taste was essentially conservative and ideals of luxury and elegance prevailed over the practical need for a revitalized furniture industry based on new materials and techniques. Favoured materials were novel rather than new. Basketwork, for instance, enjoyed great popularity; Jean Royère devised marquetry decorations in straw and adorned cabinet panels with delicate traceries of dessicated flowers; above all, there was a passion for hide at the most luxurious end of the market. The fashionable saddlers, Hermès, covered the 'functionalist' tubular metal of designs by Jacques Adnet in the luxury of saddle-stitched leather. In 1952 designer-decorator Dupré Laffon

published an elegant bed with soft contoured panels covered in natural vellum and red box-calf. The *Studio Yearbook* of 1950/51 illustrates a chest of drawers completely covered in vellum, made by La Crémaillière to the design of André Renou and Jean-Pierre Genisset, first shown in 1937 but still, in 1951, representative of French taste, and an ash cabinet by Royère with door panels of Havana hide. Both pieces share the same softness of contour. The taste was for pale woods such as ash and sycamore.

Jean Royère created a grand, elegant style, as epitomized in his decoration of the Légation de France in Helsinki, opened on 18 July 1951: full, sober forms for upholstered seat furniture and cabinet furniture in his favoured wood, ash; giltbronze used with judicious restraint in his distinctive open sphere table bases and appliques.

Jacques Dumond found an elegant compromise between tradition and functionalism and won deserved praise for his submission to the reopened Salon des Artistes-Décorateurs in 1951, notably his 'meuble universel', a graceful centrepiece storage/display unit on serpentine base, designed in collaboration with André Monpoix.

Jacques Gadoin, J. Motte, Ramos and P. Pothier each produced interesting designs,

*Furnishings designed by Renzo Zavanella for the Belvedere railcar bar of the 'O.M.da Turismo', 1948.*

often inspired by American innovations.

The lack of direction in French design was noted with regret by Michel Dufet in his introduction to *Décor et Aménagement de la Maison*, 1952. Under the title 'Renaissance Italienne', his praise was mainly directed to the new school of Italian designers, who had presented so strong a front at the Milan Triennale in 1951.

## Italy

Italian design was distinctive, independent and, above all, innovative, reflecting an awareness of technical progress, but also very much concerned with style. The creative centres were Turin and Milan and many of the most important names in furniture design were also trained architects. Gio Ponti reigned as the grand old man of Italian design. Born in 1891 and with his own office in Milan since 1937, he was a purist; his restrained neo-Classical style avoided the almost surrealist forms of certain of his contemporaries. His 'Superleggera Chair 699' of 1956, manufactured by Figli di Amadeo Cassina, is a definitive statement of his purist faith.

The Milan firm of Cassina put into production the designs of leading contemporaries, including Ico Parisi, Gianfranco

Frattini and architect Carlo de Carli, the latter a refined exponent of the Italian School, whose 1951 Triennale exhibit included a characteristic desk and chair, their soft, fluid structure an elegant exercise in discreet refinement. De Carli also designed for the Milan firm of Tecno. For Tecno architect/designer Osvaldo Borsani conceived a fine range of stylish and functional seat furniture, notably his articulated *chaise longue* 'P.40' of 1954.

Other manufacturers of note included Chiesa Arredamenti, Arflex and Fontana Arte of Milan. For 'Way Selecta' designer Carlo Enrico Rava created a sophisticated, somewhat precious range of furniture, characterized by extreme structural slenderness. He conceived delicate chairs and refined tables in gracious curves of carved rosewood, often raised on fine gilt sabots. Renzo Zavanella of Milan was equally individualistic, yet more eccentric in his pursuit of forms, notably in a range of exaggerated wing armchairs which were used in a variety of settings from hotel reception rooms to the Belvedere railcar bar of the 'O.M. de turismo' of 1948.

The most remarkable talent of post-war Italian furniture design, however, was surely Carlo Mollino of Turin. Born in 1905, and trained as an architect, Mollino created a style which combined the melting forms of Surrealism and the aerodynamic curves of streamlining in a baroque, sculptural expression of Italian *brio*. He courted eccentricity yet, even in his most extreme stylistic explorations, was saved by an unerring sense of balance and proportion. His designs were manufactured by the Turin firms of Apelli e Varesio, and Cellerino.

## Scandinavia

If the immediate post-war period in furniture design was notable for the stylishness of Italian work and for the technical progress of American designs it was equally notable for the emergence of the Scandinavian Modern style, which was to have a marked international influence during the 1950s and 1960s.

At the heart of the Scandinavian style was a respect for tradition, for craft and, especially, a respect for wood, perhaps the most valuable natural resource of the Scandinavian countries. Ironically, the wood most closely associated with the Scandinavian style, oiled teak, is not a native wood, but was imported after the war from the Far East.

The roots of the Scandinavian style are to be found above all in pre-war Denmark, in the teachings of Kaare Klint and

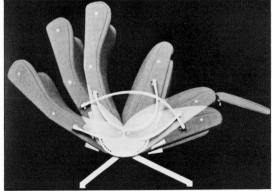

*Far left: Late forties armchair by Carlo Mollino for Cellerino of Turin.*
*Left: Fifties table by Fontana Arte. Plate-glass top on carved walnut base.*
*Bottom left: Forties table by Carlo Mollino for Apelli & Varesio. Glass top, wood side members linked by metal strain rods, sculptured legs.*
*Below: Articulated chaise longue 'P.40' designed by Osvaldo Borsani for Tecno of Milan in 1954. Pressed steel frame, rubber arms, foam upholstery.*

in the work of a small but influential group of craftsmen who revitalized the Danish Cabinetmaker's Guild into an exhibition society whose annual competition shows, started in 1927, set new, high standards and inspired manufacturers. The opening at about the same time of Den Permanente, a permanent commercial display of the best of Danish design provided a similar encouragement, both to designers and to the furniture industry. At the Copenhagen Academy of Art, from 1924, as lecturer then director of the school of cabinet-making, Kaare Klint had promoted a graceful functionalism, imbued with a sense of tradition, quite unlike the hard-edge 'functionalism' of Bauhaus or contemporary French designers. This harmonious ideal was at the basis of the Scandinavian organic modernism of the post-war years.

In Finland, after the stagnation of the war years, the furniture industry was in need of revitalization. Alvar Aalto had made important experiments during the 1930s in the development of plywood and laminates. These designs and the post-war variants on his classic themes assured for Aalto's manufacturing company Artek an important international market. Amongst

his most successful designs was his 1954 stool in which the laminate legs fan out and curve effortlessly into the lines of the seat. The Finnish firm of Asko, with some of Finland's leading talents, including Iimari Tapiovaara and Tapio Wirkkala and later, Eero Aarnio, as freelance or resident designers, asserted itself after the war as one of the most creative, as well as one of the largest furniture factories in Scandinavia. The Finns were open to innovation in the choice of materials for furniture, as was to be most clearly demonstrated during the sixties with Asko's remarkable ventures into fibreglass.

To Danish designers and craftsmen, especially, goes the credit for giving an identity to the mellow, soft-contoured, modest and warmly livable style associated with post-war Scandinavia. No designer better represents this style than architect/designer Hans Wegner, trained at Copenhagen's School of Arts and Crafts and with his own practice from 1943. Grand Prix winner at the Milan Triennale in 1951 and gold and silver medallist in 1954 and 1957 respectively, Wegner designed for a number of firms, including Fritz Hansen and Johannes Hansen, for

*Right: 'The Chair' designed in 1949 by Hans Wegner and made by Johannes Hansen. Walnut, mahogany and cane.*
*Far right: 'Egg' chair designed by Arne Jacobsen in 1958 for Fritz Hansen. Ox-hide upholstered seat unit on cast aluminium base.*

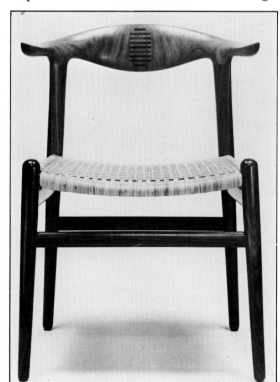

*Stool designed by Alvar Aalto in 1954 and manufactured with a variety of seat finishes by Aalto's manufacturing company Artek.*

whom he created his definitive chair of 1949, a gracious demonstration of the rightness of good design and known simply as 'The Chair'.

Denmark's most distinguished post-war furniture designers, with Wegner, were architects Arne Jacobsen and Poul Kjaerholm. Each has achieved an international reputation for his work and notably for chair designs of great distinction. Jacobsen is known for the confident Organic Modernism of his 'Egg' and 'Swan' chairs; Kjaerholm for his range of designs from the 1950s and 1960s for E. Kold Christensen, which tempered the coldness of steel frames with the natural warmth of cane, carved wood and leather.

Sweden's furniture industry, like Finland's, was in dire need of revitalization after war. The Svenska Slojdföreningen, promoted intelligent collaboration between designers and manufacturers and maintained during the fifties the high standards set by Sweden's pre-war functionalist movement. The leading designers were Bruno Mathesson and Carl Malmsten, both intimately acquainted with wood and both firm advocates of a functionalism based on tradition.

### 1960 – 1970
### New Modernism to Pop

If, in the popular imagination, the fifties will be remembered for their more eccentric stylistic explorations, so, equally, will the sixties be associated with more extreme, eye-catching manifestations in decorative design which have already made of this the 'Pop' decade. Amidst the many fascinating and significant aspects of sixties design, however, one of the strongest threads running through the decade, having taken shape in the late fifties, was the emergence of a new version of International Modernism. The stylistic exuberances of so many post-war designs, the self-consciously organic forms, the graphic whimsies and self-indulgent

*Above: 'Form' seating designed by Robin Day for Hille, 1957.*
*Right: The sixties saw the crystalization of a revived and reinterpreted version of international Modernism in both domestic and contract schemes.*

extremes were ousted by an elegant, cool, classic style, pared down, essentially rectilinear and blending the best of contemporary design with the reappraisal of classics of the Bauhaus era.

## United States

This new rationalism found able advocates internationally. The strongest impetus, however, came from the United States, adopted land of the expatriate giants of pre-war International Modernism. A fine international survey of private houses, published in 1967, by Werner Werdent shows just how pervasive this style had become. The American ideal of open domestic space was now truly international and these elegant, fluid voids were counterpointed with furnishing elements selected with a Japanese sense of restraint and ceremony. The choice of a Bauhaus classic to adorn the home took on a potent symbolism, whilst Eames' lounge chair had already, within the space of a decade, assumed its seminal role in

*Above: Living room designed by Federico Fogh and Inger Klingenberg and presented in the Danish exhibit at the 1957 Milan Triennale.*
*Bottom right: Chair and high stool designed by Roger Tallon for Jacques Lacloche, Paris, 1965. Moulded polyether foam on aluminium pedestal bases.*

the international language of taste. A key element of this new rationalism was the definition of space functions by a bold use of varying floor levels. The 'conversation pit' with built in seating is perhaps the most formal expression of the concept.

The American firms of Herman Miller Inc. and Knoll International played a major role in the propagation of this new Modernism. Knoll International was founded by Eames' contemporaries at Cranbrook, Florence and Hans Knoll. During the fifties they spread internationally, with branches in Germany, France, and the United Kingdom and assumed a

leading role as prestige contract furnishers. In 1955, significantly, they put back into production the pioneering pre-war designs of Mies van der Rohe.

Herman Miller Inc., under the inspired leadership of Dirk Jan de Pree and, from 1947 until 1965, the design directorship of George Nelson, created for itself a position of supreme importance, with Charles Eames as the company's major designer. Nelson started from a position of confidence well expressed in the foreword to the company's 1948 catalogue. He proclaimed his company's confidence in the rightness of its instinct regarding the needs

*Seat and table furniture. All, with the exception of Eero Saarinen's pedestal table and chair were designed in 1967/68 and demonstrate the application of fresh ideas, notably in the use of synthetic materials. The designs include (from left) an inflatable polyvinyl armchair by French team Aubert, Jungmann and Stinco;*

*two cylindrical chairs by Bernard Holdaway for Hull Traders; 'Elephant Armchair' by Rancillac for Galerie Lacloche, in coloured plastic; 'Armchair 300' in molded polyester, by Pierre Paulin; inflatable poufe (top) by Aubert, Jungmann and Stinco and table and chair in rhodoid (foreground) by Jacques Famery.*

and potential of the market for good design.

Although Herman Miller has manufactured classic, rich furnishings for domestic use, the firm's greatest commercial success has been in contract furnishing, from such prestige commissions as the furnishing of Chicago's O'Hare Airport to the more everyday solution of office and other work-space design problems. The latter have been developed since the 1960 establishment of the Herman Miller Research Corporation under Robert Propst whose 'Action Office' and 'Co/Struc' (Coherent Structure) ranges had, by the mid-seventies become the firm's major product lines.

## Europe

The emergence of a new Modernism in Britain is well documented in Dennis and Barbara Young's 1964 survey *Furniture in Britain Today*. In their preface, the authors note that in the preceding few years 'There has been a greatly increased

Joe Colombo inspired a revolutionary approach to furniture design with his novel, experimental concept of foldaway domestic living units.
Right: 'Rotoliving Unit' photographed in the designer's home in 1971 for Nova. The center section pivots to reveal dining table. The unit houses sound, vision, and lighting equipment as well as providing storage space.
Below: Design for three units to serve every domestic function. The prototype was shown in the Museum of Modern Art 1972 exhibition 'Italy: the New Domestic Landscape'.

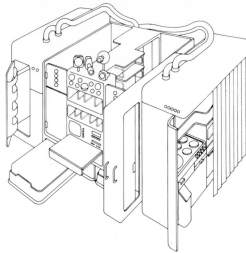

interest in well-designed furniture, by the general public and also by government and local authorities, universities, business organisations, hotels, restaurants and shops.' They appreciate the importance of the contract sector where 'Evidence of new materials and techniques can often best be seen.'

Designer Robin Day emerged as a major talent for the intelligence and understated elegance of his designs. As design consultant to Hille, he created a distinctive new look with his modular seat/table units introduced in the late fifties. Long, low uncluttered lines were the hallmark of his matured style. Although Day and his contemporaries exploited new synthetic materials for contract furnishings and steel had won a universal acceptance in furniture design and construction, natural materials, such as wood and hide, and fabric upholstery were very much in evidence for domestic schemes, giving a natural warmth to otherwise austere designs.

Other firms and designers of note in the British version of the new Modernist ethic include Ernest Race, whose company has become a leader in the contract field; Robert Heritage, designing for Archie Shine, Brooke Marine and Race Furniture; Robin Cruikshank; R.D. Russell for Russell Furnishings; the Conran Design Group; John and Sylvia Reid for Stag. Of these, the name of Conran has become the best-known, though commercial acumen rather than valid achievement in design has been the reason for this success.

Terence Conran opened his first Habitat shop in 1964, with the avowed intention of bringing good taste to a mass market. In fact, the Habitat look is a not always satisfactory blend of fine, classic designs, for the most part standard classics from Thonet to Eames, rather than newly-commissioned designs, and the stripped pine/pseudo-cottage industry folksiness

for which the British seem to have a weakness. The undoubted influence of this brand image, now spreading its operation internationally, should not be allowed to colour judgements as to its importance in the history of furniture and interior design. The Bauhaus style revival of chromium-plated steel and glass was strongly promoted by Habitat. The London design team O.M.K. founded in 1966 rapidly established themselves with Bauhaus inspired furnishings. This cult was international and in Italy found expression in a bizarre design from the Archizoom Studio, the wedge-shaped, flat steel and stretched sheet rubber 'Mies' chair of 1969, conceived in homage to the master of International Modernism.

In marked contrast was the work of Joe Colombo. A furniture designer of note whose background as a sculptor explains the eccentricity of certain of his creations, he set up his Milan design practice in 1961. A great experimenter, Colombo found novel forms for painted plywood, plastics and polyurethane foam for various manufacturers, notably Kartell of Milan, but was to make his most significant mark, before his premature death in 1971, in his prototype living units, a dramatically new environmental concept which superseded traditional approaches to furniture design.

Scandinavian designers were respon-

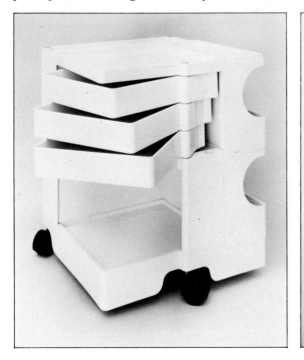

*Far left: 'Boby' trolley, designed in 1968 by Joe Colombo. ABS plastic modular components including pivoting drawers, on three steel rods.*
*Left: Stacking modular storage units designed by Anna Castelli Ferrieri for Kartell, ABS plastic, and manufactured through the seventies.*

sible for some of the most elegant inter-pretations of the new Modernism. Danish designers Arne Jacobsen and Poul Kja-erholm, notably, had established them-selves as exponents of this style and they consolidated their reputations through the sixties with such fine designs as Kja-erholm's 'Hammock Chair 24' of 1965. Finnish designer Antti Nurmesniemi's stool design of 1960 in steel and hide was acquired by the Museum of Modern Art in 1964 as 'an exceptionally harmonious treatment of leading materials of our dec-ade.' Another Finn, Yrjo Kukkapuro, deserves mention for his confident Modernism.

If the essential sobriety of Scandinavian design was well-suited to this mode, the same could not be said of French design. With their essential concern for style, the leading French furniture designers of the sixties, Roger Tallon, Pierre Paulin and Olivier Mourgue, in spite of some explora-tory work in the field of new materials, produced designs which were primarily stylistic rather than functionalist exercises.

Tallon's seatings for Jacques Lacloche, moulded in polyester foam like giant open egg-boxes, are grotesque and eye-catching but hardly inviting. Paulin researched materials for Mobilier National of Paris and acted as design consultant to the Dutch firm of Artifort. Mourgue designed for Mobilier National and for Prisunic, but found perhaps greater freedom of expression in the design of futuristic sets for *2001, A Space Odyssey*. Both favoured a somewhat uninviting jersey stretched over sculptural foam or rubber forms.

The finest traditions of Modernism have been allied with the highest standards of leather work by the Swiss firm De Sede. Established in 1962, this company has earned a reputation as the foremost manu-facturer of classic leather seat furniture and the company's advertising emphasizes the timelessness of the design and manu-facturing perfection which they aim to achieve.

It is perhaps surprising, and certainly disappointing, that the parent country of International Modernism, Germany,

*Opposite: 'Globe' chair designed by Eero Aarnio in 1966 and manufactured by Asko Finnternational. The fibreglass shell, fully upholstered on the inside, pivots on the aluminium base.*
*Above left: Playing card symbols provided the inspiration for these seats designed by Jon Weallans for the Pop boutique Mr Freedom, c. 1970.*

should have failed to re-establish an influential role in furniture design. By contrast, Italy, whose pre-war role was insignificant, was to play an increasingly important role after the war. Indeed, from the mid sixties the laurels for furniture design must surely go without dispute to the new generation of Italian designers whose combination of taste, style, functionalist good sense and quality has made the strongest mark.

### International Pop and Other Styles

Italy produced a confident design move-

*Above: François Lalanne photographed outside his home with his silver leather sardine-can bed. He is holding the two pillows.*

ment when fads and mannerisms seemed to be dominant elsewhere. The mid and late sixties were certainly confusing years in furniture design, years of irreverence, novelty and disposable gimmicks. Pop art had opened the minds of designers to new ideas on colour. For the first time, strong primary colours were used in furniture design with varying degrees of success. Plastics and glass fibre, sleek and shiny, lent themselves to these bright, synthetic colours and a variety of successful designs for chairs, tables or modular storage units in these appropriate materials went into production.

A classic amongst them was Verner Panton's stacking chair, designed in Switzerland in 1960, and put into production by Herman Miller in 1967. Another classic was Eero Aarnio's futuristic 'Globe' chair of 1966, to be followed by his 'Pastilli' chair of 1968, a swollen form of bright fibreglass with scooped seat. Several of the new Italian designers found their own novel formulae in plastics. Studio Artemide manufactured designs by Vico Magistretti, Sergio Mazza, Ernesto Gismondi; C. & B. Italia launched the 'Amanta' range by Mario Bellini in 1967, whilst the Milan firm of Kartell manufactured the designs of Anna Castelli Ferrieri and the everinventive Joe Colombo.

Less satisfactory was the brashly painted wood furniture produced in England. A decade later these relics of 'swinging London' look sadly decrepit. But to the new young markets of the sixties permanence was not a relevant criterion. On the contrary, the sixties became the decade of disposability and built-in obsolescence: furniture printed and stamped from sheet cardboard; Max Clendinnings's painted plywood 'knock-down' range; transparent plastic 'blow-up' furniture.

This was the decade of bright, impractical ideas, stark Op Art or Pop Art interior schemes designed mainly to be photographed for the new newspaper colour

supplements and interior design magazines, and to be promptly superseded and forgotten. In June 1970 *Nova* magazine presented the St. Moritz apartment of playboy industrialist Gunther Sachs, a veritable shrine to Pop Art. Warhol's *Marilyn* was an almost inevitable set-piece; more bizarre was the contribution of anarchic French artist César, a chair modelled as Sachs' open hand and 'the expensive stain on the green nylon carpet . . .' and '. . . a stool with a split in it, which gushes out brightly-coloured sludge.' Bed cover and bath were designed by Lichten-

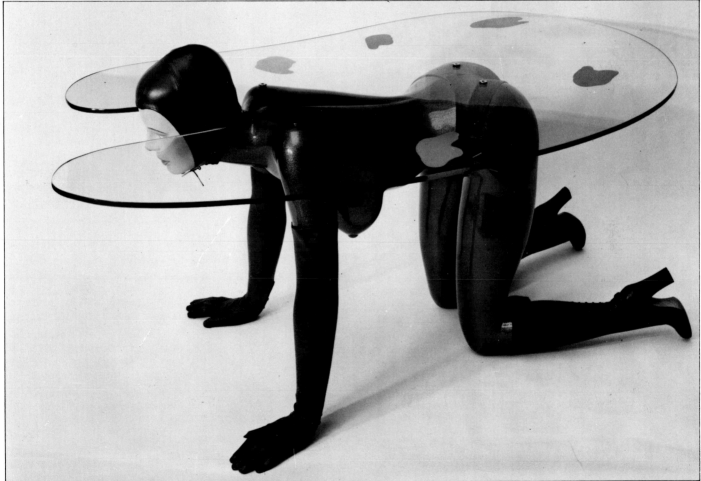

*Top: Chair sculpture by English artist Allen Jones. One of a series of three 1969 fetishistic female figures cast in an edition of six. Fibreglass and leather.*
*Above: Table sculpture by Allen Jones, cast in 1972.*

*Chair '892' designed by
Vico Magistretti in 1963
and manufactured by
Cassina. This now-
classic chair is available
in a variety of finishes of
natural, stained, and
lacquered wood.*

stein, while there was a Pop wall light with giant plastic radio by Wesselman. In the centre of the floor a flock of sheep by French sculptor Francois Lalanne grazed quietly.

Lalanne was one of a number of artists and designers to create furniture which was a mixture of Pop and surreal humour. His ideas issue forth from the country farmhouse where he and his wife, jewellery designer Claude, live and work. They include a bed in slippery silver leather in the form of a giant open can of sardines, with two extra sardines as pillows; a large

leather rhinoceros which breaks up like a three-dimensional jig-saw into a suite of seat furniture; his well-known grazing sheep stools, and his bronze bar, long, slender, supported by two ostriches whose bodies contain the bottles, while a large egg form poised on the bar serves as an ice-bucket. With a typical French concern for quality, the wings and egg are in fine Sèvres biscuit porcelain.

English Pop artist Allen Jones sculpted a disturbingly life-like series of fetishistic leather-clad women, glossy fantasies serving as coat-stands, tables and chairs.

*The 'Cab' chair designed by Mario Bellini in 1977 and manufactured by the Milan-based firm, Cassina. The saddle-stitched hide covering zips into place over the skeletal steel frame.*

Amusing, but of a poor quality of execution, were the Pop furniture ideas to emanate from the short-lived but fertile Mr. Freedom shop, opened in London in 1969, from Lackies in Chelsea's King's Road and from Anderson Manson. These included a giant set of false teeth doubling as a sofa, by Jon Weallans for Mr. Freedom, Liquorice Allsorts pouffes and giant matchstick lamps. In September 1969 *Vogue* illustrated naive 'Rousseau pop' painted wood cut-out trees by Mo McDermott. One is reminded of the flat graphic style of David Hockney's Califor-nia era and it is not surprising to learn that such trees decorate Hockney's home.

Amidst these brash expressions of the Pop culture there developed a strong taste for the ethnic interior, a facet of the hippie sub-culture which manifested itself in a passion for the elimination of all Western furniture, to be replaced by a low litter of Arab tables and deep cushions covered in middle-eastern textiles and rugs. The London home of art dealer Christopher Gibb, photographed by Cecil Beaton in 1968, epitomizes this fad. This has been replaced by an interest in Western culture.

*The 'Pluvium' umbrella stand designed by Gian Carlo Piretti for Anonima Castelli. Moulded in ABS plastic with six eccentrically pivoting umbrella rings. Manufactured through the seventies as a part of the 'PL' range of foldaway furniture.*

## Into the 1970s
### The Italian Influence

Meanwhile, however, the taste and sanity of Italian design were spreading their influence internationally. In 1965 the London *Sunday Times Magazine* had published an interior made up from newly-imported Italian elements, '... the only furniture around that is stylish as well as forward-looking - a welcome change from arty-functionalism.' The Italian designers have had more success than others in lifting new furniture out of modern clichés. Significantly, the magazine article noted, 'They have the advantage ... of manufacturers who are willing to take a chance on an idea.'

Of these manufacturers, the most important is the Milan firm 'of Cassina, synonymous today with the best of contemporary Italian design.

The Cassina image, built up through the sixties and seventies by leading designers such as Vico Magistretti, Tobia Scarpa and Mario Bellini, is of fine materials, both classic and modern, used in designs which are memorably stylish but with an underlying logic and intelligence which could never become parodied. Style is never an end in itself.

Magistretti uses lacquered wood, as in his classic trattoria chair '892' of 1963 or

his Caori table, described by the *Sunday Times* in 1965 as 'a mixture of Italian *brio* and Japanese austerity'. Magistretti has designed ranges of seat furniture in hide which have found a place in the Museum of Modern Art collections, and is active in the design of plastic furniture. Scarpa has designed for Cassina since 1964 and from 1965 date classic ranges of seat and table furniture in fine woods and leather. A large proportion of Cassina's production has been designed by architect Bellini, whose interests range from designs for luxury hide seating, a recent success being his superb 'Cab' chair of 1977, the steel frame cased in saddle-stitched hide, to

*Above: Marble 'Il Colonnato' table designed in 1977 by Mario Bellini and manufactured by Cassina. The free standing legs can be grouped in any number of positions.*
*Left: '925' chair designed in 1965 by Tobia Scarpa and manufactured by Cassina. Walnut and hide-covered plywood.*

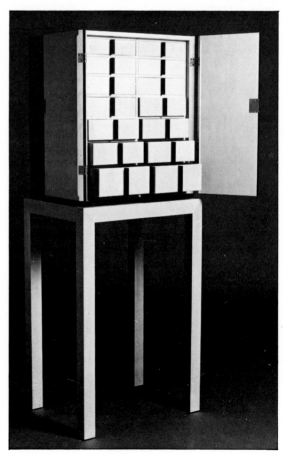

designs for office furnishings, his 'Pianeta Ufficie' range. His marble table 'Il Colonnate' of 1977 shows his perfect marriage of contemporary design ideals and traditional materials.

For the Bologna firm of Anonirna Castelli, Gian Carlo Piretti has designed several modern classics, masterpieces of logic applied to furniture design, notably his widely successful 'Plia' folding chair of 1969, his 'Platone' and 'Plano' folding tables and 'Planta' coat stand.

So strong is this contemporary Italian dominance that it is not easy to list every designer of note. The names of Piero De Martini and Paolo Deganello for Cassina or Carlo Bartoli for Arflex of Milan are a few more to have achieved distinction amongst a talented generation.

### The Craft Revival
The most interesting development during the seventies, outside Italy, has been the British-and American-led revival of interest in fine hand-crafted furniture. Leader in this field, and tutor and inspiration to a

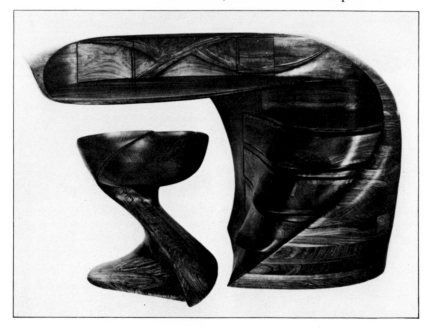

*Above: 'El Morro' desk and 'Matador II' chair designed by Michael Coffey and made in his Vermont workshops. Mozambique wood.*
*Right: Collector's cabinet designed and made by John Coleman and presented by him in his*

*1979 Degree Show at the Royal College of Art. Constructed in sycamore.*

materials, including modern synthetics where appropriate, his prodigious attention to detail and inventive imagination have set new standards for the creation of highly individual luxury furniture, often one-off designs in which the pleasure principle is very much in evidence, furniture lovingly made to be enjoyed.

In his 1975 survey Makepeace lists the achievements of his contemporary American craftsmen, citing Wendell Castle of Scottsville, New York, as one of the most gifted and influential. Castle's is a bold, organic style, as is that of Michael Coffey of Poultney, Vermont, Roy Superior of Connecticut and Peter Danko of Washington. All four furniture-makers carve full, anthropomorphic shapes evocative of the more eccentric extremes of Art Nouveau. The proportions and the craft, however, are faultless. Other North Americans of note are Paul Epp, Stephen Harris and Stephen Hogbin of Canada.

In England, Martin Grierson, Richard La Trobe-Bateman and Rupert Williamson are foremost among a generation of

*Above: Desk designed by Wendell Castle and made in his Scottsville, New York workshops. 1975. Walnut.*

new generation of designer-artisans, is British furniture-maker John Makepeace. In a survey of this craft revival published in 1975, Makepeace quotes Octavio Paz, 'The industrial object (is) the diametrical opposite of the work of art. Craftwork is a mediation between these two poles, its forms are not governed by the principle of efficiency but of pleasure ... Handcraftmanship is a sort of fiesta of the object: it transforms the everyday utensil into a sign of participation.'

Makepeace's perfectionism, his bold choice and mixtures of woods and other

*Above: Desk for two people designed by John Makepeace and made in his workshops. Hollywood and Macassar ebony.*

this genre. Their achievements are well documented in the American bible of interior design, *Architectural Digest*.

This self-conscious aproach to decoration can easily invite caricature. Yves Saint-Laurent presented a prime target in a 1969 London *Sunday Times* article by Francis Wyndham, 'Occupied Paris': 'St Laurent's house in the Place Vauban, on the Left Bank, is an interior decorator's dream which, through sheer excess, has turned out to be a nightmare of *chic*. Egyptian Art, Chinese Art, minimal art and Art Nouveau—the visitor feels like a drowning dilettante as every recent 'good taste' fad swims before his indiscriminate gaze. The only really ugly room, a sentimental shrine to Bernard Buffet, comes almost as a relief, here at least one can smugly identify the démodé. Stumbling out into the garden, one finds an artificial lake on which a gigantic navy blue plastic turd is pointlessly afloat. 'It is by César, you know,'' says a public relations man in reverent tones.'

*Above: Trestle table designed in the Industrial Style by Rodney Kinsman for OMK in 1978. Tubular steel with matt black epoxy finish and wire-reinforced glass.*
*Right: Interior of the Industrial Style London shop 'Joseph', incorporating new and classic Industrial Style elements designed in 1979.*

*Detail of the Paris home of Yves Saint Laurent. The background is Warhol's study of the couturier. Diverse elements include a Roman torso, a 19th century Chinese lacquer chair and a Dunand vase and contribute to the refined eclecticism.*

# SILVER & METAL WORK

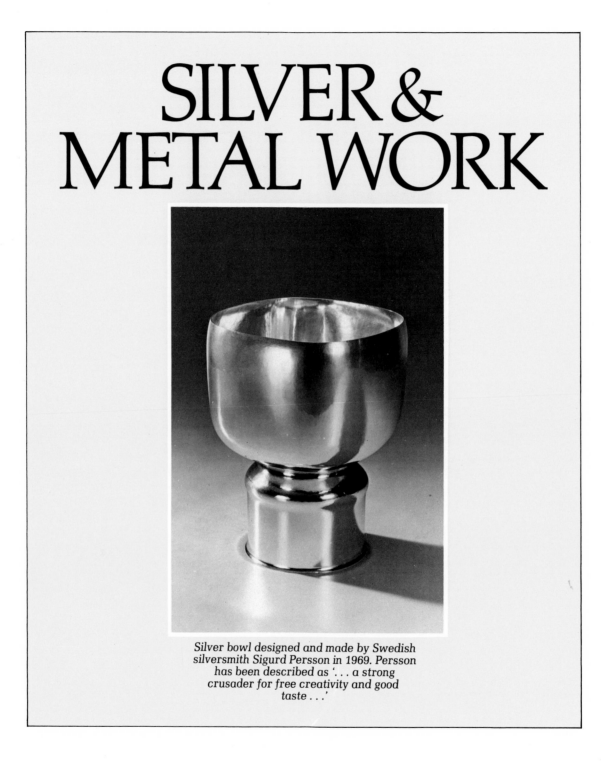

Silver bowl designed and made by Swedish silversmith Sigurd Persson in 1969. Persson has been described as '. . . a strong crusader for free creativity and good taste . . .'

————1945 – Present————
## Innovations in Silver and Metal

THE SILVER CRAFT and the silver and electroplate industries suffered a crippling phase in their history when the Second World War caused workshops, factories and specialized skills to be reoriented towards the manufacture of goods necessary for the war effort. Indeed, in many instances, essential raw materials became unavailable. In Denmark, for example, during the German occupation, silver was unobtainable and the prestigious firm of Georg Jensen was forced to turn its attention to stainless steel. In the States, the large silver manufacturing firm of Gorham won the 'Army-Navy Award for High Achievement in the Production of War Materials', but regular silver production naturally suffered, here as elsewhere.

After the war, the revitalization of both the craft and the industry was made difficult by a vicious circle of conservatism. On the one hand the industry was for the most part reluctant to invest in the unknown. The manufacture of machine tools for the production of new designs involved a measure of risk which most manufacturers were unwilling to take.

The Scandinavians are an exception, but most manufacturers and retailers have complacently accepted the nature of the market and shied away from the relative austerity of largely undecorated modern designs. A glance at the American magazine *Silver,* or at a current catalogue from Garrard & Co., the British Crown Jewellers, will reveal how deeply entrenched is this conservatism in both the manufacture and buying or collecting of silver. Indicative of the public's preference for a conspicious opulence has been the evolution of London-based silversmith Stuart Devlin from elegant, purist beginnings to richly textured, overwrought but, presumably, therefore more saleable designs.

Internationally, however, the major metalware manufacturers have made the innovation of accepting stainless steel as the mass-market contemporary alternative to electroplate. The novelty of the material and the need for new manufacturing equipment and techniques have encouraged a new approach to the creation of designs, with the result that good designs in stainless steel, modern, functional and stylish are now reaching a very wide market. Graham Hughes, artistic director of London's Goldsmiths Hall, writing in 1967, saw as '. . . the pattern for the future: stainless steel and base metal from the big factories for convenience, silver from the small men for beauty.'

The development of a strong modern style in silver and metalware could only profit from competitions such as that for flatware organized in 1960 by the Museum of Contemporary Crafts, New York, and sponsored by the American International Silver Co. to celebrate its sixtieth anniversary. Two years previously, in 1958, the French U.A.M. had exhibited in its 'Formes Utiles' show the winners of a stainless steel flatware competition organized by the Chambre Syndicale des Producteurs d'Aciers Fins et Spéciaux. Sven Gillgren, a Swede, was the winner. In 1967 the Sheffield firm of Viners offered a first prize of £1000 in an open international competition for cutlery design.

The development of truly modern silver design seemed a remote ideal in 1945, but it was to prove attainable, thanks to the self assurance and the good taste of a number of Scandinavian firms, foremost amongst them the Danish firm of Jensen, who set so fine an example after the war, and thanks also, in Britain, to the patronage of the Worshipful Company of Goldsmiths.

## United Kingdom
In the immediate post-war period traditionalism was very strong in British silver, even in supposedly modern designs. In the year of the Festival of Britain, 1951,

the Goldsmiths Hall organized an exhibition of British silver, including 'Ceremonial Plate by Contemporary Craftsmen'. The centrepiece was the magnificent tea set designed by Robert Y. Goodden and made by Leslie Durbin for the Royal Pavilion on the South Bank. This work expressed the popular need for stability and reassurance in its marine symbolism which, according to the catalogue, was '... appropriate to the maritime strength of Great Britain.'

In 1954 the Goldsmiths Hall published a catalogue, *Modern Silver*, illustrating a covered rose bowl designed by J. E. Stapley, a presentation piece from Courtaulds Ltd. to their American subsidiary. The cover had as its finial a phoenix representing the new company rising from the flames of war.

The figurative symbolism of such examples, however, was essentially retrospective in style if not in mood, and the new lead in design was to come from the graceful forms evolved in Scandinavia, the fruit of Functionalist ideas first explored before the war. In pre-war years France had been a leader in silver design, largely through the stylish work of Jean Puiforcat, but his death in 1945 marked a return to conservatism.

The successful evolution of modern silver has depended on patronage and on international competitiveness, encouraged by prizes and exhibitions. British silver has, since the war, proved itself perhaps the most exciting in the world, greatly helped and encouraged by the constant promotional activities of the Goldsmiths Hall and a regular succession of commissions for and from the new universities and colleges and from industry, the church and corporations for important ceremonial or commemorative pieces.

The Worshipful Company of Goldsmiths is a unique organization, the only medieval guild in the world which has kept alive its connections with and influ-

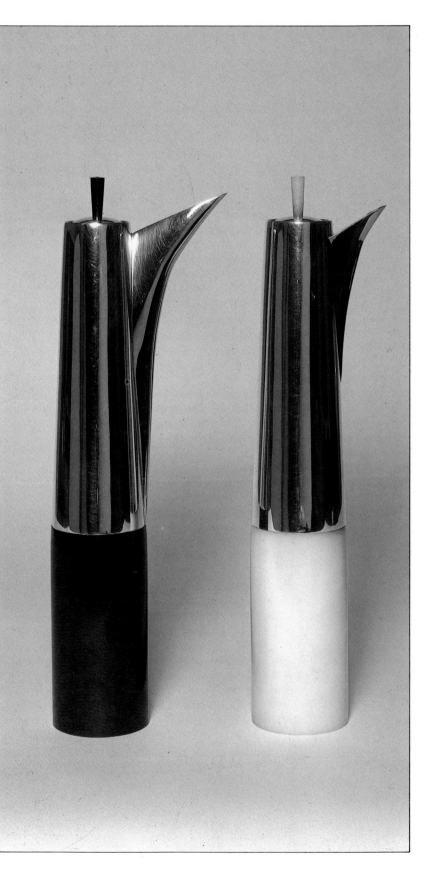

*Coffee service designed by Stuart Devlin while still a student at the Royal College of Art and made by the London firm of Wakely and Wheeler, 1959. Silver and heat-resistant nylon.*

ence on its craft. Its contemporary collection has been seen worldwide and has encouraged good modern design by its example. The Hall, as the Company is popularly known, has made a policy of giving a piece of modern silver to each of the new universities, encouraging them to start their own collections. Fine examples of their generosity include the handsome mace for Bath University, designed by Stuart Devlin in 1966, and the magnificent pair of candelabra for the University of Exeter designed in the same year by Keith Tyssen.

Following the Hall's example, the Wilkinson Sword Co. commissioned a mace for Brunel University in 1966, the design of Alex Styles. Gerald Benney, perhaps Britain's foremost contemporary silversmith, has produced much of his best work for such commissions. He has, since 1958, made a fine series of silver centrepiece bowls with pierced covers for a variety of patrons, including the Bank of England and Courtaulds Ltd; they were commissioned also for numerous colleges, including Leicester University in 1958, London University in 1959 and the Royal College of Physicians in 1962. For the new Coventry Cathedral in 1958, Benney made a fine ciborium with a finial inspired from the symbolic cross of nails.

Benney was trained at Brighton College of Art and the Royal College, setting up his own workshop in London in 1955. He very soon asserted himself with the confidence and originality of his designs, but more particularly with the new language of surface textures which he started to evolve and which have become such a marked feature of contemporary work. Graham Hughes has pin-pointed a parcel-gilt chalice made by Benney in 1956 as '... probably the world's first piece of silver since the 18th Century to be made with an original textured surface of a type now (in 1967) becoming popular not only for beauty, but also to prevent finger

*Pepper mill designed and made by Gerald Benney, 1963. Silver-gilt with the textured surface which Benney was the first to revive and which has become characteristic of contemporary British silver.*

marks.' This textured decoration, often parcel-gilt, has indeed become very popular and provides a richness which relieves the potentially uncommercial austerity of modern, otherwise undecorated forms.

Texturing can, however, all too easily be exaggerated as a saleable decorative feature. When, in the summer of 1979 Stuart Devlin announced the opening of his new shop in London, the publicity showed clearly that a spidery and unconvincing decorative style had proved more commercially attractive than the elegant but bare Contemporary style in which he had shown such promise at London's Royal College of Art in the late fifties. Benney, first to use texturing in silver, has, as design consultant to the Sheffield manufacturers, Viners, extended its use to stainless steel. His 'Studio' range of cutlery, put in production in 1965, was the first use of heavy texturing on machine-made stainless steel. Benney is at his best when given a free hand in commissions for commemorative or ceremonial plate. He clearly enjoys the inherent grandeur of such objects. During the seventies he has turned his attention also to enamelling.

Amongst the most successful exponents of electro-texturing techniques is silversmith Grant MacDonald who opened his own workshop in 1969. He uses texturing judiciously, never allowing it to overwhelm his self-assured forms. Alex Styles, who joined Garrards as resident designer in 1947, has developed strong ideas for commissioned works, achieving a happy compromise between the modern and the traditional in designs for retail sale.

A confident, simple and thoroughly modern aesthetic characterizes the fine work in silver of a group of contemporary British designers, among them notably Keith Tyssen, who opened his Sheffield workshop in 1963, Robert Welch and David Mellor, though both Welch and Mellor have made their more significant contribution in industrial design and design for series-production metalware. 'Explosion', an aptly named retrospective exhibition of post-war British creative silver work, organized in 1977 by the Goldsmiths Hall, was a fascinating showcase for the designs of the many artists who have contributed to Britain's pre-eminence in the field of silverware. To those already mentioned should be added the names of Louis Osman, Gerald Whiles, Leslie Durbin, Desmond Clen-Murphy, Brian Asquith and Jocelyn Burton.

The exemplary work of Scandinavian or British studios, however, is numerically dwarfed by the vast and generally less adventurous production of the major international manufacturing companies – in Britain the companies associated within the British Silverware Group, in Germany the giant W.M.F. and Pott factories, in the United States such companies as Gorham, Kirk and Oneida, in France Christofle and in Sweden the G.A.B. group which, in 1964 absorbed the firm of Gense.

## Scandinavia

The most influential international showcases for the applied arts in the post-war years were the Milan Triennale exhibitions. Here, notably in 1951 and 1954, a

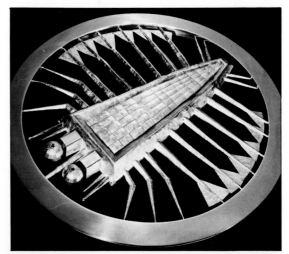

*Right: Large silver bowl with gilt interior designed and made by Gerald Benney, 1962. Below: Rose bowl designed by Jack Stapley for Courtaulds Ltd. as a gift for their American subsidiary. Silver, made by Nayler Bros, 1952. Bottom: Parcel-gilt silver mace designed and made by Stuart Devlin, 1966; commissioned by the Goldsmiths' Company as a gift to the University of Bath.*

Left: Silver candelabra designed and made by Keith Tyssen, 1966; commissioned by the Goldsmiths' Company as a gift to Exeter University.
Below: Parcel-gilt silver tea service designed by Robert Goodden and made by Leslie Durbin, 1950, for the Royal Pavilion of the 'South Bank Exhibition', Festival of Britain.

89

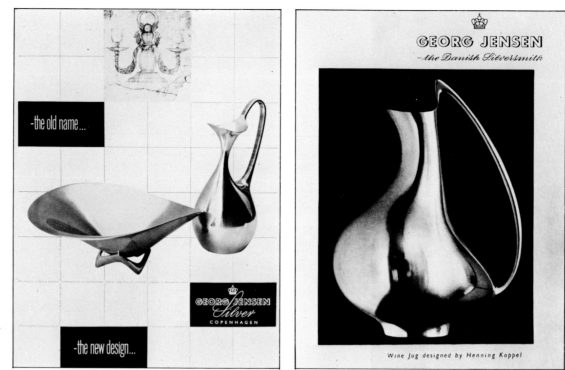

*Two advertisements from the mid-(right) and late-(left) fifties for the Danish firm of silversmiths, Georg Jensen. The elegant free-form pieces illustrated were designed by Henning Koppel.*

wide public saw the elegant forms of Scandinavian silver, in particular those from Jensen, whose designers were well-deserving prize-winners. In 1954 the firm celebrated its fiftieth anniversary with an invitation to Scandinavian artists to submit designs in open competition. Tias Eckhoff from Norway distinguished himself with his designs for flatware which, exhibited in Milan in the same year, won a further award. The influence of the Jensen style and the firm's involvement in the promotion of modern design are central to the story of modern silver.

In 1922 Frederick Lunning had established the American branch of the firm and, until his death in 1952, worked hard and effectively to promote the Jensen style in the States, and indeed, after his death, through his Lunning Prize, was to remain an influential name in the promotion of the Scandinavian style in every aspect of design.

The quality of Scandinavian silver design was just one facet of a mellow interpretation of Functionalist ideas which made so strong an impact on design internationally during the fifties. The Scandinavians approached every material, wood, pottery, glass and of course silver, in a very human way and in silver, as in other media, evolved gracious curves, pleasing soft-textured surfaces and simple designs which reflected the warmth of human concern. Theirs was never, to borrow the words of C. R. Mackintosh, '... the icy perfection of the mere stylist'.

Foremost was the Danish firm founded in 1904 by Georg Jensen. After his death in 1935, the firm's functionalist ideas were developed by Count Sigurd Bernardotte, but the fluid Organic Modernist phase which evolved after the war was due to the sculptural approach of a new generation of designers, led by Søren Georg Jensen, son of the founder, and Henning Koppel, both trained as sculptors. To Koppel are due the most inventive experiments in form: sweeping curves, deliberate asymmetry and elimination of any surface decoration in a pure, sculptural expression.

The more restrained functional curves of designer Magnus Stephensen reflect his architectural background. The modern image of the Danish silversmiths' craft is maintained by a number of other firms, including Hans Hansen and Kaj Bojesen Silver. Bojesen, winner of a Grand Prix at Milan in 1951, worked also in wood and combined both materials in such creations as his silver sauceboat and ladle on a wooden tray of 1949 which has been described as 'one of the most beautiful objects in all of Denmark's silversmithery'. The firm of Hans Hansen was founded in 1906. In 1953 Bent Gabrielsen Pedersen, formerly with Jensen, joined as chief designer and, with art director Karl Gustav Hansen, led the firm to international success.

The versatile Finnish designer Tapio Wirkkala distinguished himself in silver and metalware design as in other materials, especially in his practical approach to flatware design, creating elegantly sculpted and eminently usable designs for various firms including the French firm Christofle. A particularly pleasing design is his 'silverwing' or 'Duo' of 1954, manufactured in Finland and in France. He was one of five preliminary prize winners for his flatware at the New York Museum of Contemporary Crafts competition of 1960.

In Sweden there could be no better example of the worthy maintenance of high craft standards within a practical modern ethic than in the work of the distinguished Sigurd Persson. Graduating in 1943, Persson struggled to set up a small workshop but soon won an international reputation through his participation in the major exhibitions. All the while he kept his operation very small, exploring his craft with considerable inventiveness, style and sparkle and designing for industry. His first major commission was won in 1959 in a competition for designs for flight restaurant ware for S.A.S. He has been called '... a true artisan and sculptor in metals and gems, a serious thinker in many dimensions who is a strong crusader for free creativity and good taste in estimating the real merit of all things in life, both material and aesthetic'. Herein is the philosophy which has assured the contemporary supremacy of Scandinavian design in silver as in other materials.

### Design in Stainless Steel

The most significant post-war ventures by the large manufacturers have been in the exploitation of stainless steel and the evolution of modern styles and finishes appropriate to the new material. First used for domestic wares as recently as the late twenties, stainless steel, now usually with a soft, satin finish, has in post-war years come to dominate the field of domestic metalware. A few designers of note, either working freelance or resident for the large concerns, have found very satisfactory forms and helped create the machinery to manufacture their designs at a low cost.

The British firm of J. & J. Wiggin was

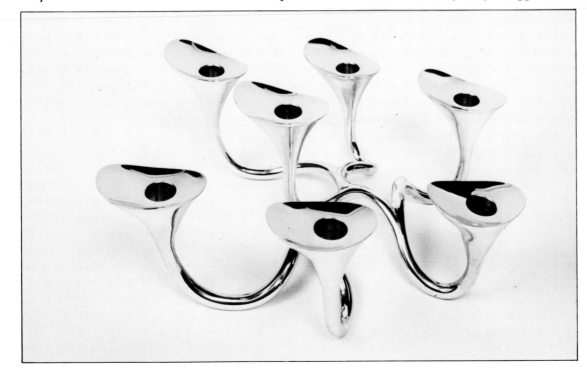

*Parcel-gilt silver candelabra designed by Jeus Andreason and made for Asprey by E. H. Skilton, 1956. The deliberate asymmetry and fluid, melting forms, bare of any decoration, are a perfect expression of Organic Modernism.*

*Silver and enamel commemorative dish and cover, designed by Alex Styles in 1953 to celebrate the coronation of Queen Elizabeth II. Made by Wakely and Wheeler for Garrard.*

a pioneer in the introduction of stainless steel before the war and in Robert Welch found a sensitive and responsible designer. His designs for them and for Old Hall have become much-imitated classics. Gerald Benney's work for Viners included the development between 1958 and 1962 of techniques for flow machine production. David Mellor has acted as consultant designer for Walker & Hall before setting up his own small works in 1974. But the story of such collaborations belongs perhaps more specifically to the history of industrial design.

The Swedish firm of Gense had as head designer from 1940 until 1964 the gifted Folke Arnstöm whose elegant and serviceable flatware designs have been internationally admired. Pott, the German manufacturer, has dominated the international flatware market with designs in stainless steel and in silver, many by Carl Pott, son of the founder. The advent of stainless steel has effectively counter-balanced the conservatism of manufacturers and public alike in the practical areas of domestic metalware design. In many instances stainless steel has inspired a positive new aesthetic. The contemporary designs of the Italian firm of Zani and the Swedish Boda Nova range are particularly stylish examples, while an essentially craft-oriented firm such as Jensen has consistently distinguished itself in both steel and silver by its forward-looking approach to design.

## Contemporary Enamelling

One specialized facet of the metalworker's craft, enamelling, has enjoyed international attention in the Contemporary period with stylish and totally modern work produced with distinction in Italy, Scandinavia and the United States. The work of the post-war Italian enamellists is in a richly decorative vein, in the scratchy

*'Chinese Black' cutlery range designed by David Mellor and manufactured in his Sheffield workshops. Of stainless steel and acetal resin. Introduced in 1975, the range won a Design Centre Award in 1977.*

graphic style so popular in the fifties. Motifs range from purely abstract graffiti designs to animal subjects which combine the stylization of Picasso's *Guernica* period with the bold exaggerations of primitive wall paintings. It is the style of the decorative Italian ceramics of the fifties and was most successfully adapted to enamel by Guido Gambone of Florence, equally adept at pottery decoration. Paulo De Poli of Padua made hand-hammered vessels and enamelled them in rich, plain colours.

In Scandinavia, Norway in particular can boast a long history of fine enamelwork dating from the strong revival of the craft by David Andersen. The firm of David Andersen, founded in 1876, has continued to work in decorative enamels, though, unlike the Swedes, Finns or Danes, the Norwegians are deeply attached to traditional designs and truly contemporary work represents only a

minor part of silver and enamel production. A notable exception amongst conservative Norwegian craftsmen is Sigurd Alf Erikson who, after extensive training in enamelling techniques in Vienna and Paris, has produced attractive contemporary work in enamelled silver for the Oslo firm of Tostrup.

Perhaps the most distinguished Scandinavian enamellist of the Contemporary era is the talented Swedish silversmith Sigurd Persson. By the fifties he had evolved his distinctive style, favouring deceptively simple *cloisonné* decoration for domestic objects but capable also of a strongly expressive figurative style for the ecclesiastical pieces at which he excelled. Swedish designer Stig Lindberg, best known for his elegant fifties Contemporary designs for ceramics for Gustavsberg, turned his talent simultaneously to enamelwork and produced highly decorative enamel on steel panels, including such whimsical extravagances as his giant enamel clock in Stockholm's Skansen park.

Oppi Untracht's 1957 survey *Enamelling on Metal* shows the widespread American interest in enamelwork. Untracht, instructor in enamelling at the Brooklyn Museum Art School in New York, has provided in his own work a foremost example of the stylistic and technical pursuits in post-war America. The predominant style was not dissimilar to the decorative Italian mode, sometimes figurative but just as often favouring an abstract style which owed much to the concepts of Action painting. This contemporary generation included Walter Rogalski, Bernard Fischer, Karl Drerup, Paul Hultberg, J. Anthony Buzelli and Myles Libhart, whose work incorporates a very painterly impasto. Today, decorative enamelwork, like the silversmith's craft, is kept alive purely by and for the luxury market.

## Innovations in Lighting Design

The most basic commercial aspects of domestic metalware design and manufacture are, of necessity, tableware and light fittings and lamps. Just as in the Contemporary era, tableware design has been effectively revitalized by the advent of stainless steel, so, too, have contemporary designers evolved new concepts for lamp design. Italian designers have led the field in the last two decades, with a host of stylish, innovative though usually still quite costly designs.

By the fifties a wide range of novel styles in light fittings was becoming available and distinct trends were emerging internationally. Many designs were whimsical and stylish exaggerations of pre-war ideas for articulated and directional light sources. Immensely popular were the giraffe-like floor lamps with cone shades raised on slender legs of clear-lacquered or painted brass rod which

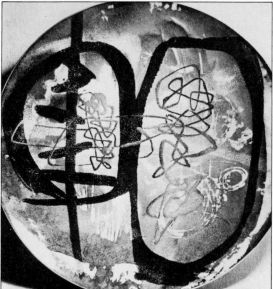

*Above: Clock on top of the tallest building in the amusement park, 'Skansen', in Stockholm. Designed by Stig Lindberg, standing on right. Enamel on steel, Fifties.*
*Left: Enamel on copper dish designed and made by Oppi Untracht. Illustrated in his 1957 survey 'Enamelling on Metal'.*
*Below: 'Tori'. Enamel on metal panel designed and made by Guido Gambone of Florence. Illustrated in 'Forme Nuove in Italia', 1957.*

were manufactured internationally. The *Studio Yearbook* for 1955/6 illustrates a veritable menagerie of typical examples.

Prominent designers and manufacturers included Hans Bergström for Atelje Lyktan of Sweden; Gerald Thurston for the American company, Lightolier Inc; Pierre Disderot for the British Geni Products, and Jacques Bliny for Luminalite of France.

It is this sculptural appeal which particularly characterizes the post-war work of Italian manufacturers. The firms of Stilnovo, Arteluce and Fontana Arte produced eminently stylish forms. It was the Italians, however, who were to lead the return to a self-conscious Functionalism in the sixties. Other fifties designs of note included those by Robin Day for Thorn Electrical Industries Ltd., Paul Laszlo for Laszlo Inc., Paavo Tynell for O/Y Taito AB of Finland and Hildegard Liertz for Hesse Lamps of Germany.

The transition into the sixties was led by the Italian brothers Achille and Pier Giacomo Castiglioni who, as early as the late fifties, were boldly using bare bulbs in a new phase of Functionalist designs. Another key neo-Functionalist design was the 'Toio' lamp of 1962. The light source is a car headlamp pointed ceilingwards and supported on an adjustable metal stem with flex and transformer left exposed: 'High-Tech' *avant la lettre* and a stylish application of the principle of design honesty.

A noteworthy design in the neo-Modernist vein was the aptly called 'artichoke' lamp, the concept of Danish architect Poul Henningsen. This elegant pattern of overlapping thin metal flanges was designed to give a diffused, reflected light, and won international renown for its novel concept and visual appeal.

The Italians have led the way during the sixties and seventies with neo-Modernist and neo-Functionalist designs. The Castiglioni brothers were responsible for

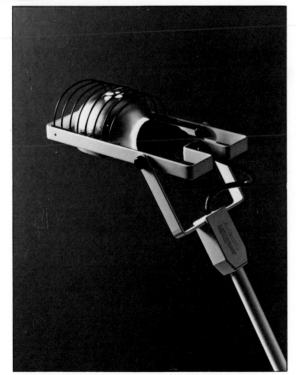

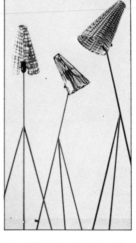

*Top: 'Tizio' articulated table lamp designed by Richard Sapper.*
*Above: Floor lamps designed by Hans Bergström for Atelje Lyktan, Sweden.*
*Left: 'Sintesi' lamp designed by Ernesto Gismondi for Artemide.*

*'Toio' lamp designed by the brothers, Achille and Pier Giacomo Castiglioni for Flos, 1962. Painted steel, nickel-plated brass, exposed transformer and adapted motor-car headlamp.*

the creation of what must rank as one of the most elegant examples of modern design, their 'Arco' lamp first produced in 1962 and still one of the finest on the market. The bowl shade in perforated aluminium is adjustable for angle and position on its telescopic stem sweeping in a gracious arc from the block marble base. This same sophisticated curvilinear Modernism is to be seen in the recent designs by Bruno Gecchelin for Pollux per Skipper and in the designs of Milanese Gae Aulenti, in particular her already classic '620 Pipistrello' for Martinelli Luce and her 'Pileo' range for Artemide. Many of Italy's foremost furniture designers, including Magistretti and Bellini, have designed stylish lamps. The leading manufacturers in this field include Arredoluce, Arteluce, Artemide, Flos, Stilnovo, Martinelli Luce and Pollux per Skipper.

Notable amongst the many fine neo-Functionalist Italian lamps are Richard Sapper's 'Tizio', an elegant exercise in counter-balanced articulation, in matt black finish metal, which has earned a place in the collection of the Museum of Modern Art, New York, and the more aggressively functional 'Sintesi' range designed for Artemide by Ernesto Gismondi. In these the exposed bulb is protected by a metal grille and held within a metal framework painted in bold primary colours.

Future generations of social archaeologists will probably look upon such lamp designs for manufacture in metal, just as they will, surely, regard the best tableware designs in stainless steel, as the true works of art of our Contemporary era, helping to bridge the gap between Art and Industry. The products of the ancient craft of the silversmith, however modern in design, however graciously pursued, will perhaps seem marginal to the main-stream evolution of metalware design and as such will assume the character of an essentially anachronistic luxury.

*'Arco' lamp designed by the Castiglioni brothers for Flos, 1962. Marble base, stainless steel, and aluminium.*

# CERAMICS

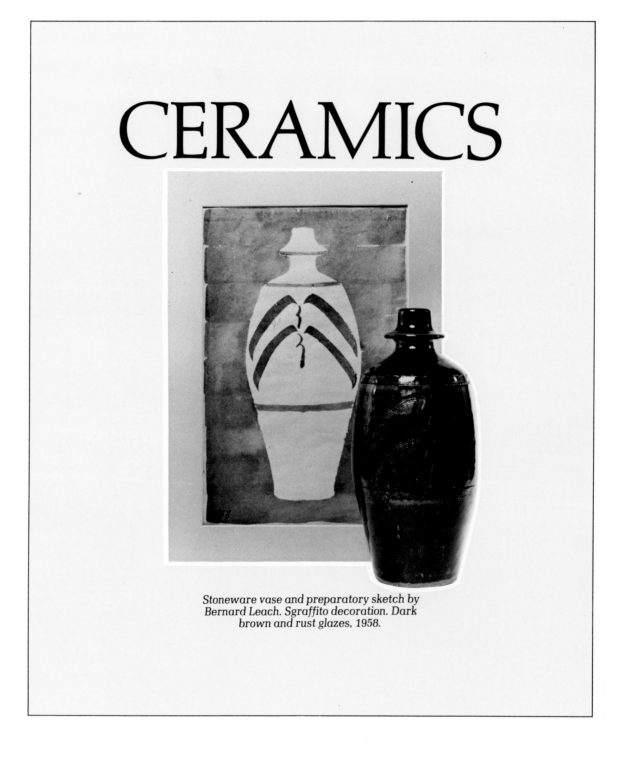

*Stoneware vase and preparatory sketch by Bernard Leach. Sgraffito decoration. Dark brown and rust glazes, 1958.*

## 1940 – 1950
### Origins of Modern Studio Pottery

THE CONTEMPORARY PERIOD has seen novel international exploration, not always successful, in the potential of sculpture in ceramic materials. It has also witnessed the dedication of more than a few manufacturers and individual artisans to the production of domestic wares, both plain and decorative, of considerable beauty and appeal. The central theme of ceramic history, however, is the story of the artist potters who have been driven primarily by aesthetic and emotive factors, though working within the tradition-based limitation of nominally functional vessels. Amongst these, Bernard Leach must take credit as the founding figure of modern 'studio' pottery.

The studio tradition has its origins in France in the last quarter of the nineteenth century. By 1920, the year in which Leach returned from Japan to set up his St. Ives, England pottery with his pupil Shoji Hamada, the craft was in need of new vitality. Leach's deep understanding of the spirit of traditional oriental potting was to affect a whole generation. From 1935 he worked a high-fired stoneware in an austere, dignified and unassuming style which reflects his commitment to principles of 'honesty' towards his *matière*. By the time of his death in 1979 Leach could see the international scope of his influence. His Japanese pupil Hamada had returned to Japan in 1923 and encouraged a renaissance of traditional potting. His contemporaries include, notably, Kangiro Kawai and Kenkichi Tomimoto. Leach's eldest son David has played an important role in the St. Ives pottery and has continued to work in the tradition established by his father.

### United Kingdom

Amongst Leach's pupils perhaps the most notable are Michael Cardew and Katherine Pleydell-Bouverie. Cardew, after three years with Leach, acquired the Winchcombe Pottery in 1926. The forties took him to the Gold Coast of Africa where he started a pottery and spread still wider the ideals of Leach. In 1949 he accepted a post as Pottery Officer in the Department of Industry and Commerce, Nigeria, retiring in 1965 after an influential period in office.

Katherine Pleydell-Bouverie studied for a year with Leach in 1924 before having her own kiln built at Coleshill, Wiltshire. Still active, she produces wares, mostly ash-glazed, of a sturdy, simple beauty and intended for use. The genuine and sympathetic followers of Leach have, regrettably, been gradually outnumbered by the many artisans and indeed manufacturers who have embraced merely the obvious stylistic characteristics of his work, the earthiness, the muted, natural colours and 'rough' glazes, paying only lip-service to the underlying principles.

William Staite Murray is the second father figure of this modern movement and his years as head of the Pottery Department at London's Royal College of Art between 1926 and 1940 were influential ones. His notable pupils included Henry F. Hammond and Sam Haile whose brief career, cut short by his death in 1948, included a few years teaching at New York State College of Ceramics and the University of Michigan during the Second World War.

Unlike Leach, Murray's philosophical approach was not one of artistic humility; on the contrary, he cultivated the notion of the pot as art object and the high prices he charged and the contexts in which he chose to show his work emphasized this distinction. It is a notion which has had the positive effect of encouraging purely artistic experimentation, with the disadvantage of divorcing the ideals of many practitioners from the intrinsic functions and traditions of the ceramic medium.

London's Central School of Art has

provided important practical facilities for studio experimentation and during the fifties played host to several potters of considerable talent. Ian Auld and Dan Arbeid both spent fruitful periods there as technical assistants, the latter becoming senior lecturer in the ceramics department in 1970. Ruth Duckworth studied at the Central, set up a studio in 1958 near Kew Gardens and produced original and refined domestic wares in pottery and porcelain. The acceptance of a teaching post in Chicago in 1964 marked the beginnings of her non-functional work as a ceramic sculptor.

## United States

In the United States, where studio pottery had enjoyed such a success during the Arts and Crafts period, a new phase of studio work developed in the post-war years which showed the mixed influences of Anglo-Oriental work and of the displaced functionalist ideals of the pre-war International Movement. Otto and Gertrud Natzler were foremost amongst the purist potters and, having moved from their native Vienna to settle in Los Angeles in 1939, exemplified this draining of talent from progressive artistic centres in Germany and Austria to the United States. They made fine, classically proportioned vessels, potted by Gertrud and with glazes devised by Otto whose speciality was rich, thick 'volcanic' effects. Karen Barnes and her husband David Weinrib were enthused by the purist studio mode and in 1953, as potters in residence at Black Mountain College, North Carolina, brought Leach and Hamada to an influential symposium.

## Europe

In the Scandinavian countries, the strength of contemporary ceramic work has been in the application of high artistic standards to wares produced in a semi-

*Top: Stoneware dish by Shoji Hamada with tessha glaze on black iron-glaze, c. 1960. Stoneware bottle vase by Bernard Leach, c. 1965. Left: Forties stoneware vase by Katherine Pleydell-Bouverie. Above: Slip-decorated stoneware dish by Michael Cardew, Between 1952 and 1965.*

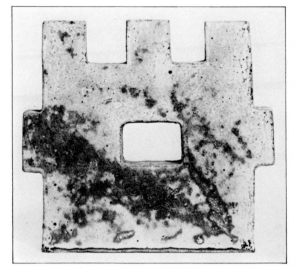

*Left: Rough-textured glazed stoneware vase by Ian Auld.*
*Below: Large rough-textured, ash glazed stoneware free-form vase by Ruth Duckworth, c. 1967.*

industrialized way by the leading factories. In most cases the studio tradition has been promoted as a sponsored offshoot of the factory production.

In Sweden, for example, the leading Gustavsberg factory has employed such talents as Berndt Friberg to make unique stoneware vessels in the purest studio tradition. Similarly Carl Harry Stalhane has made free-form studio pots for Rorstrand.

In Finland, for the leading factory of Arabia, Francesca Lindh has made strong, rough-textured free-thrown vases. Working in a similar rough *chamotte*, Annikki Hovisaari has made handsome turned pots for the Arabia factory since 1949. The head of the Arabia art department since 1946, Kaj Franck, simultaneously head of the art department at Helsinki's Institute of Arts and Crafts and Industrial Design, proved a major influence in allying the artistic and industrial aspects of Finnish ceramics.

The Danish Royal Copenhagen Porcelain Factory has given free rein to the talented art potter Axel Salto. In every case, the Scandinavian factory policy of promoting in-house studio work has served only to raise the standards of commercial design and manufacture.

By the time of the crucial exhibition, 'International Ceramics 1972' held at London's Victoria and Albert Museum, the art pottery ideal was being explored in every corner of the world. The exhibition showed studio work from thirty-eight countries, from the Netherlands to New Zealand, Jamaica to Japan.

### 1950 – Present
### United Kingdom

The Victoria and Albert Museum exhibition showed the influence of the Leach tradition, with its sometimes restrictive emphasis on Oriental precursors. More important, however, was the demonstration of distinct new trends, the sculptural

*Right, Far right:*
*Stoneware vases by Hans*
*Coper.*
*Below: Stoneware bowl*
*by Lucie Rie. Seventies.*
*Below right: 'Farsta',*
*stoneware vase by*
*Wilhelm Kage for*
*Gustavsberg, 1953.*

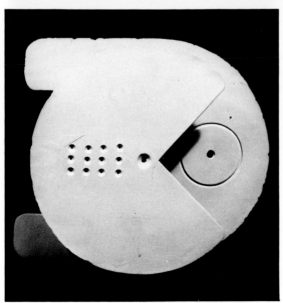

*The ceramic medium becomes a purely artistic form of expression when the potter creates a specifically non-functional object.*
*Above: A late sixties ceramic ball, fragile, precious and feminine, by Mary Kepax.*
*Left: Ceramic sculpture by Eileen Nesbitt, c. 1975.*

tendency developed in the States during the late fifties and sixties and the emergence of a new, lyrical studio style of which Lucie Rie and Hans Coper are the long-established masters and in which newer talents are finding an exciting form of expression. Neither of these artists is British-born, but both have found creative freedom in the enlightened atmosphere of contemporary British craft.

Lucie Rie was born in Austria in 1902 and trained in Vienna under Michael Powolny. When she moved to London in 1938 she was already internationally known, but her encounter with Leach marked the beginning of a new phase in her career. She established her own workshop in 1939 and in 1946 was joined by Hans Coper who had left his native Germany in 1939. It was a fortuitous encounter, each being inspired by the other and, between them, leading the way in a new, elegantly austere but stylish studio mode. It has been rightly pointed out that Rie was '. . . a studio potter . . . not rustic, but metropolitan' and the same might justly be said of Coper. Both have worked throught the fifties, sixties and seventies, creating highly personal and stylish ceramics which have cut the umbilical cord with the self-consciously 'ethnic' Leach school.

Lucie Rie's vessels, all wheel thrown in porcelain or earthenware, are feminine, confident and sophisticated. Coper's pottery has been well described by Tony Birks in *The Art of the Modern Potter:* 'It shares with ancient Mediterranean pottery a relentless refinement, and with Oriental ceramics a search for perfection and rightness, but it carries with it the spirit of the modern world. It is sculptural yet functional, abstract yet endowed with human qualities both in shape and mood. Plain in surface and uncompromising and clean in profile, Hans Coper's readily recognized black, cream and white ceramics have a precision and intensity

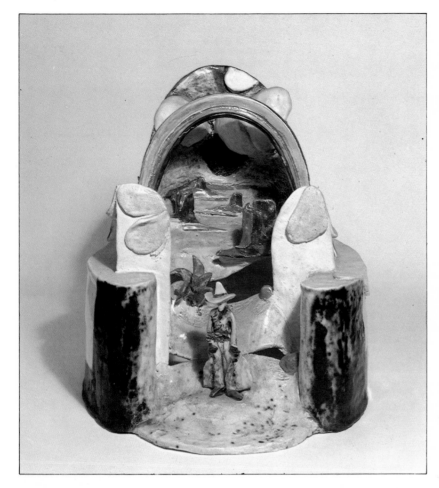

American Pop ceramic sculpture, 'Tom Mix and Rainbow' by R. Carlson. Such 'funky' ceramics were a reaction against the obsessive 'artiness' of the traditional studio potter's approach.

which make other potter's work appear clumsy and crude.'

Notable amongst the younger generation of studio potters working in a similarly sophisticated style are Jacqueline Poncelet and Elizabeth Fritsch, both trained at London's Royal College of Art. Senior of the two, Fritsch creates individualistic and distinctive pots with a deliberate lyricism. They are, in her own words 'pots about Music.' She uses with confidence a light, essentially feminine and seemingly fragile *matière* and her forms are complemented by the crisply drawn graphic decorations. Poncelet's vessels

have an even greater sense of fragility. Perhaps most characteristic are her thin-walled white bone china vases, applied with delicate fins or pierced, like the pots and, subsequently, the Minimalist canvases of the Italian Lucio Fontana. These two lively talents symbolize the rich diversity of contemporary creative potting.

### United States

One major new approach to art pottery which has opened up a new set of aesthetic ideals has been the sculptural approach, originating in the United States, with Peter Voulkos as its most influential early exponent and spokesman, and spreading its influence world-wide. It was during 1950s that American ceramics was finally liberated from the styles of European art and design. In 1954 Peter Voulkos, having majored in 1952 in ceramics after an initial interest in painting at the California College of Arts and Crafts, Oakland, was invited to set up the ceramics faculty at the Otis Art Institute in Los Angeles. The enthusiasm and questioning attitudes of both Voulkos and the students who gathered around him inspired a spirit of experimentation in which the most obviously discernable influences were in the ceramic work of European artists rather than potters - Chagall, Miró, Fontana and, above all, Picasso.

In their study of modern American ceramics, Garth Clark and Margie Hughto stress the developments to emerge from the Otis project, 'First, by imitating the ceramics of Picasso (Voulkos) came to the same realization as the master painter, that the overall painting of the pot surface destroys its three dimensionality...Second, Voulkos began to assemble his vessels from separate elements . . . Third, in this treatment of form, Voulkos began to deal less and less with the pot as volume - a contained space - and more with the pot as mass.' Through the Otis efforts Ameri-

can ceramics found a freedom of form and decoration which drew critical comparisons with prevalent Abstract Expressionist modes in painting.

In the sixties, American ceramics were to take a step forward, again parallelling fine art developments with the application of Pop themes to the liberated *matière*. A key figure in this story was Robert Arneson whose involvement in ceramics began around 1962, 'when he placed a ceramic cap on a handsomely thrown bottle and marked it *no return*'. Arneson, teaching at the University of California at Davis, led a generation of 'funky' Pop ceramic sculp-

tors in the creation of works that were humorous and refreshingly popular in their appeal, while never being merely trite ceramic *pastiches* of a facile Pop visual language. A deliberate roughness in the modelling and a sloppiness in the glazes which characterizes these Pop ceramics underlines their reaction against the obsessive artiness of the traditional studio potter's approach - the Dada element is paramount and the message is shown to be as important as the medium.

These various American approaches have been a major international influence. Ceramic sculptures have, in the

*Vases and dish designed by A.B. Rhead for the Poole pottery of Carter, Stabler and Adams. He joined the firm in 1953 and soon made his mark with a series of wares in the Contemporary style.*

seventies, widened their scope from the abstract, through the commercial application of funky ideas to new, often more polished essays in the figurative, including such tightly disciplined works as Glenys Barton's designs in bone china for Wedgwood or the remarkable verisimilitude achieved by such Super-realist ceramic sculptors as Marilyn Levine of San Francisco.

## Modern Commercial Ceramics

Parallel to the story of aesthetic developments in the work of artist potters is the commercially more important story of the development of styles in wares designed for everyday use and decorative wares in which the appeal is primarily in the graphic decoration of the surface. Scandinavian factories have set a fine example in the contemporary era in the application of high standards of design and decoration to mass-produced wares, though for sheer vitality Italian ceramics of the post-war years have made their mark internationally as an important element within the explosion of Italian talent. The German-based firm of Rosenthal has, meanwhile, consolidated a reputation for a quiet sense of quality in its ceramic products, an image which has been strengthened since the enlisting of Finnish designer Tapio Wirkkala as artistic consultant for their 'Studio' line.

In post-war Italy decorative ceramics became the excuse for a tremendous graphic exuberance. The most characteristic wares were decorated with a seemingly spontaneous boldness with free linear motifs, often on a rough-textured ground. The style of a typical decorator such as Guido Gambone was evolved from a variety of sources - here are the scratchy lines so fashionable in the post-war years, the lines of Bernard Buffet blended with the bold silhouette style of pre-historic cave painting and with more than a passing reference to Picasso's ceramic work,

*Above: Decorative ceramic plate by Nando Farulli for Natale Mancioli e C. Illustrated in 'Forme Nuove in Italia', 1957.*
*Above right: Contemporary style fifties Swedish glazed earthenware vase.*

*Factory mark 'A.L.T.'.*
*Top: 'Woman in Meadow', glazed stoneware sculpture by Dagny Hald. Made at Soon, Norway, in 1972.*

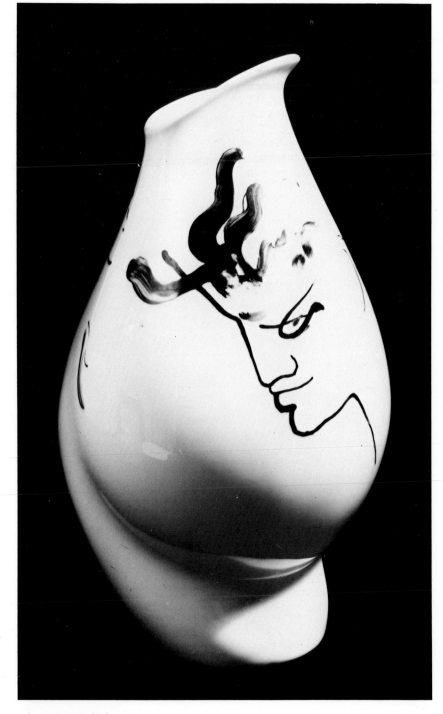

*Above: Rosenthal porcelain vase with decoration by Jean Cocteau, 1952. The asymmetrical free-form could be a sculpture by Arp.*

both in his graphic decoration and in his idea of allowing the lines and demands of the decoration to dictate the form.

A foremost example of the Scandinavian application of high standards to factory production is to be found in the work of Sweden's Gustavsberg factory, notably since 1949 under the guidance of Stig Lindberg as artistic director. Lindberg's designs—disciplined, fluid graphic patterns in restrained colours and applied to gentle, subtle shapes—are perfect exercises in the Contemporary Style and, in contrast to the decorative wares being produced in Italy at the same time, express the self-assured, discreet good taste of Scandinavian design which proved so influential in the fifties.

In Finland, the leading factory of Arabia produced attractive ceramics in the Contemporary Style under the guidance of Kaj Franck. Franck, like Stig Lindberg, was a designer who had not only a sense of style and proportion, but the willingness and ability to translate high ideals, without compromise, into goods that could be manufactured and sold. In Norway, Tias Eckhoff made his mark in the fifties with finely proportioned vessels for daily use designed for the firm of Porsgrund.

In England the Poole pottery of Carter, Stabler & Adams launched a range designed by A.B. Rhead, who joined the firm as design consultant in 1953.

Perhaps the most worthy commercial venture of recent years at the upper end of the market in domestic ceramic wares has been the promotion of the Rosenthal 'Studio' line. The Rosenthal range includes gracious, functional designs by such leading international talents as Timo Sarpaneva, either plain or very simply decorated, and more fanciful designs from an international stable of artists which has included Eduardo Paolozzi and Victor Vasarély, designs which, in the words of the firm's publicity, aim to bring 'great artists to your table'.

# JEWELLERY DESIGN

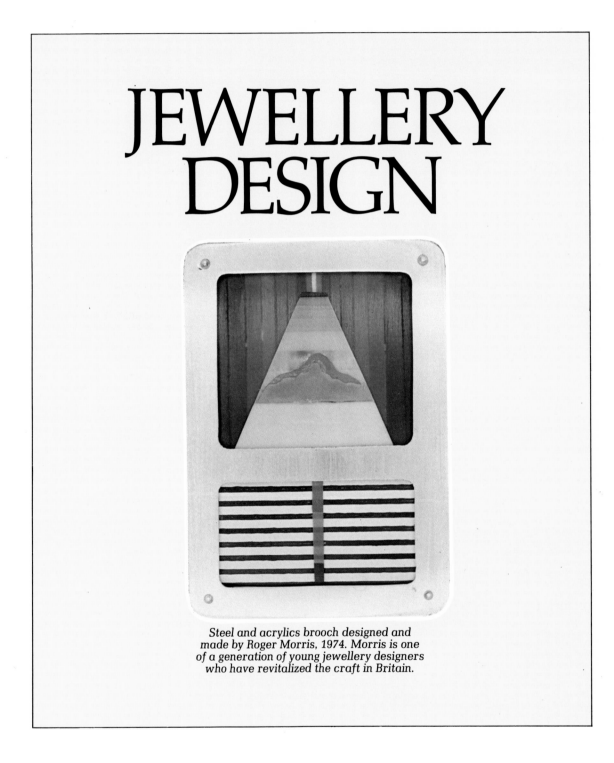

*Steel and acrylics brooch designed and made by Roger Morris, 1974. Morris is one of a generation of young jewellery designers who have revitalized the craft in Britain.*

THE STORY OF CONTEMPORARY JEWELLERY DESIGN follows at least two distinct courses, with price forming the most obviously discernable dividing line. Traditionalism is strong in one side of the jewellery business, especially in the case of the large international companies whose concern is cautiously to evolve commercially safe styles of setting for the high-value stones which are at the basis of their business.

The buyers who invest in expensive baubles from Boucheron, Cartier or Van Cleef & Arpels are not the design-conscious idealists who visit college graduation shows or craft galleries in search of new trends and talents.

The expensive end of the jewellery business is inevitably dominated by the need to display the intrinsic opulence of precious materials. Stone cutting is a well-nigh perfected art and the stylistic evolution of the major international jewellery houses has been largely slow and unadventurous

There has, on the other hand, been a strong flow of new ideas from Scandinavia since the fifties, with an emphasis on simplicity and the exploitation of the intrinsic beauty of silver. During the late sixties and seventies there have also been exciting experimental advances made, especially in Great Britain, in the exploitation of new materials, and in the creation of styles appropriate to these materials.

─────── 1940 – 1960 ───────
### The Great Houses
In the post-war years glamour and romance returned to fashion and the new mood of femininity and extravagance in dress was paralleled by a return to an opulence in jewellery which would have seemed ill-considered during the war years. There was a return to traditional styles, a fashion encouraged by the heavy taxes levied on newly-made jewellery in some countries. Fine cut stones sparkling in discreet settings were the ideal, though few could afford them; the diamond reigned supreme. 'Le Diamant Roi' ran the title of a Paris Vogue feature of June 1951, illustrating a variety of jewels in motifs which have become the clichés of the stone setter's pattern book – formalized flowers, leaves, bouquets, ribbons and free falls of stones. The article featured designs from a number of jewellers who still dominate the world market, notably Boucheron, Cartier and Van Cleef & Arpels. Each French in origin, these firms have based their great success on a policy of internationalism, establishing sales points in the major Western cities, Paris, London and New York and in those centres of wealth, from Palm Springs or Beverly Hills to Monte Carlo, which are the surest catchment areas for the breed of client on whom they thrive.

Cartier, perhaps the most adventurous of the big jewellers, has found considerable success with the range of bibelots de luxe, including lacquered gold lighters, watches, money clips, pens and small leather goods, which, launched in 1976 under the snobbish trademark of 'Les Must de Cartier', now accounts for over half the company's profit. Cartier has managed to make its watches into coveted status symbols and has recently launched its latest design, the 'Santos', on which the exposed screw-heads give an aggressively 'functional' look, a clear expression of the no-nonsense technological aesthetic of the seventies. The revival of the Cartier 'Panthère', so popular during the forties, reflects the more conservative side of a forward-looking company.

In addition to such multi-national operations, several important jewellers have become internationally known through the strength of their national images. The New York-based firm of Tiffany & Co. is one such example, whose symbolic stature was exploited by Truman

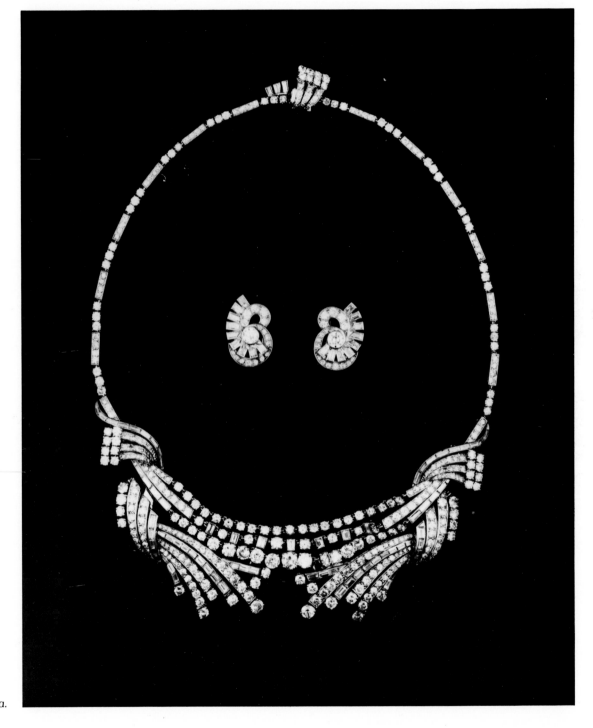

After the war, the big
jewellery houses
continued to sell
traditional styles often
indistinguishable from
designs of the late
thirties.
Diamond necklace and
clips from Boucheron.
The necklace can be
transformed into a tiara.

Capote in his *Breakfast at Tiffany's* of 1958. After the war and in the face of international competition, Tiffany had retreated into an image of aloof traditionalism. The firm's commercial reawakening came in the mid fifties with the arrival of French jeweller Jean Schlumberger in 1956 as chief designer and vice-president. Schlumberger soon revitalized the firm's reputation with exciting jewels and the precious *bibelots* in which he specialized. Tiffany learned also the value of display and, with a large frontage in central Manhattan, deliberately reduced the size of the window displays, creating intimate settings for the precious objects on view. Tiffany now has branches across the States from Houston to San Francisco and has found in Elsa Peretti a designer who has brought today's underplayed chic to jewellery in a more widely accessible price range.

The Italian firm of Bulgari, Garrard of London, Crown Jewellers since 1843, and Swedish court jewellers Bolin are major names in the world of jewellery, but principally as dealers in traditional precious objects, hardly as design innovators. Harry Winston's name has, similarly, acquired an international prestige by association with the undeniably magical qualities of the diamonds in which he is perhaps the world's leading specialist jeweller.

Diamonds and good, modern design are far from incompatible, however, and the two have been brought together by the promotional activities of the diamond merchants De Beers. In 1954 they instituted their annual Diamonds-International Awards. No prizes are given but the competition encourages a high standard of design and inventiveness and commended designers are assured of highly beneficial publicity.

--------- 1960 – 1970 ---------
### United Kingdom
One of the greatest innovators in the design of precious jewellery in the Contemporary era is Andrew Grima, a British jeweller who, since opening his first shop in London in 1966, has spread his operations with outlets in New York, Sydney, Tokyo and Zurich. Grima's career as a jeweller started in the immediate post-war period when he soon became known for his novel style. He was one of the first jewellers to break the tradition of disciplined and restrained lines in jewellery design. Taking his inspiration from natural textures and patterns, crystalline structures or rock formations, his jewels have a distinctive liveliness of surface and silhouette and often incorporate rare and uncut mineral samples, exquisite shells and other natural elements.

Grima has won the international recognition which his adventurous approach to jewellery design deserves and he has accumulated numerous awards, including the Queen's Award for Industry, and a record eleven Diamond-International

*In the fifties traditional jewellers evolved a less rigid style than had been prevalent before the war. Above left: Two diamond brooches of the fifties. Left: Pair of gold, ruby, and diamond clips from Cartier, c. 1950.*

*Above: Enamel and gilt metal earring by Ken Lane.*

*Brooch designed by
Andrew Grima and made
in his workshops 1975.
Shell, textured gold and
pavé set diamonds.*

Awards. Nominated crown jeweller in 1970, Grima designed and created the brooch presented by the Queen on her state visit to France as a personal gift to Mme Pompidou.

John Donald, who studied jewellery at London's Royal College of Art and set up his own workshop in 1961, has distinguished himself in his personal interpretation of this 'crystalline' style and has earned a reputation as one of Britain's foremost jewellery designers. Another influential name in British jewellery has been that of Gertrude Flockinger, a much admired artist in surface texturing in her distinctive gold jewellery.

### United States

The sixties saw distinct new developments in the middle-range luxury jewellery market. American jeweller David Webb found instant success in 1963 with a formula which was soon much copied. His designs were baroque and colourful and though he exploited the rich look of precious metals, he avoided the prohibitive cost of high-value stones, adding colour with bright enamels and favouring semi-precious stones.

Foremost amongst the copyists of this richly decorative style were the countless Italian jewellers whose natural talent with enamels found a new direction. It also provided the inspiration for the New York jeweller Ken Lane who became perhaps the most influential figure since Chanel in the history of costume jewellery. Ken Lane's creations are colourful and rich-looking extravagances, accessible and more fashion-conscious versions of ostentatious jewellery in the 'grand' manner. Lane is an unrepentant plagiarist whose style is a decorative amalgam of the fashionable and the traditional and acknowledges the truth that the majority of women want jewellery with sparkle and connotations of luxury.

### Scandinavia

From Scandinavia in the fifties and sixties came a refreshingly new approach to jewellery design, eschewing the gaudy tradi-

*Pendant on neck chain.
Ivory and yellow and
white gold set with
diamonds. Designed by
Steven Behrens and
chosen for the De Beers
Diamond Collection '79.
This photograph was
used by De Beers in their
publicity for 1978/79.*

*Silver link bracelet designed by Henning Koppel for the Danish silversmiths Georg Jensen in 1947. The fashionable amoeboid forms of c. 1950 were elegantly adapted to jewellery by the talented Koppel.*

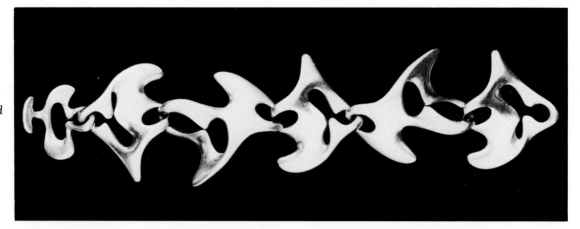

tion of conspicuous opulence and evolving a style in which, in the words of leading Finnish jeweller Bjorn Weckström, 'Jewellery is sculpture. . . with a human background.' The new generation of Scandinavian jewellers generally had little interest in expensive materials, favouring silver and the haphazard beauty of semi-precious stones.

The prominent names in jewellery design were often the same names that appear in the internationally influential story of post-war Scandinavian silver. Foremost is the Danish firm of Georg Jensen which in Nanna Ditzel found a sensitive designer with a totally contemporary approach to jewellery. She came to prominence in the fifties with her unadorned shapes, softly contoured in silver and occasionally set with plain *cabochons* of polished semi-precious stones. The Ditzel style was the inspiration to a whole generation of designers. Henning Koppel designed a stylish series of enamelled silver brooches in the fashionable free-forms of the fifties but found a more satisfactory expression of his sculptural approach to silver in his holloware for Jensen. The fifties and sixties saw Jensen's exploration of sculptural themes in a stylish series of silver link bracelets and necklaces from designers Koppel, Søren

Georg Jensen and Ibe Dalquist.

Bent Gabriel Pedersen emerged in the fifties as one of the leading Danish exponents of the new style, designing for Jensen, but he is best known for a range of jewellery for Hans Hansen, including his celebrated necklace in silver with fire gilding of 1968. The Copenhagen jewellers P. Klarlund retail the work of some of the foremost Danish jewel artisans. Prominent among them are Jane Wiberg, who sets *cabochons* of amber or semi-precious stones in deceptively simple silver settings of considerable beauty, and Åge Fausing, whose workshop produces strongly designed jewels in the simple contemporary Scandinavian mode.

Sweden can boast several very talented exponents of the simple, sculptural style of jewellery, not least the versatile craftsman and gifted artist Sigurd Persson, whose seemingly simple jewellery shapes have a perfection of proportion and finish that is not easy to emulate. Two women jewellers, Torun Bülow-Hübe and Inga-Britt Dahlquist, have explored the relationship between simple, gracious metal shapes and counterpoints of semi-precious stone or crystal. Bülow-Hübe settled in France in 1958 and in 1960 won a gold medal at the Milan Triennale for her fresh, contemporary approach to silver.

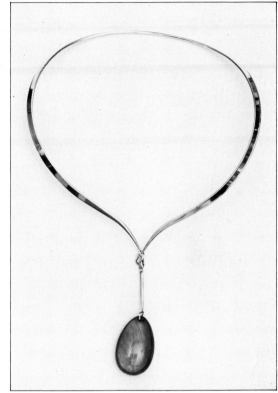

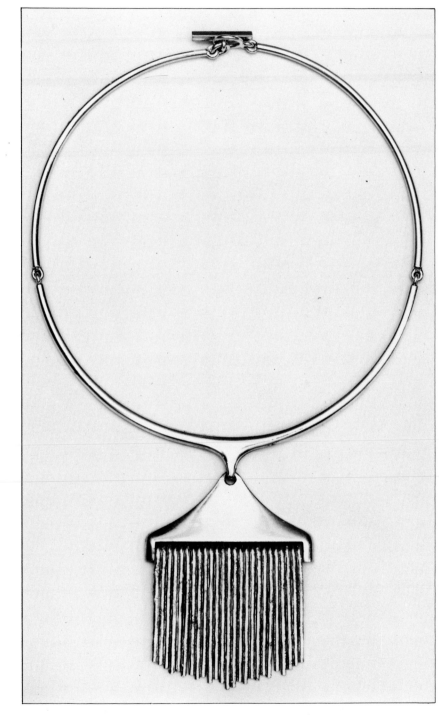

*Above: Silver necklace with fire-gilded pendant fringe, designed by Bent Gabriel Pedersen for Hans Hansen in 1968. Top right: Silver necklace with polished semi-translucent quartz drop. Designed by Torun for Georg Jensen, c. 1960.*

She won the Lunning prize in the same year. Dahlquist, a younger jeweller, carries on the Scandinavian tradition in her Malmö workshop.

Bjorn Weckström, who graduated in 1956, ranks as perhaps Finland's leading contemporary jeweller, though his approach differs from the soft but austere Scandinavian image. Weckström, like others of his generation, has explored free-forms and has exploited the beauty of uncut semi-precious stones, but his is a rather more richly decorated style than the Scandinavian norm. He has worked in gold in preference to silver and explored effects of surface texture inspired from nature. In comparison with the more worldly creations of Grima, however, Weckström's style shows the restraint of the contemporary Nordic approach to

*Silver and titanium necklace designed and made by Edward de Large. De Large, a graduate of the Camberwell School of Art, London, rapidly earned wide acclaim as an innovative jeweller for his remarkable experiments in making images on titanium by a complex variety of techniques. Late seventies.*

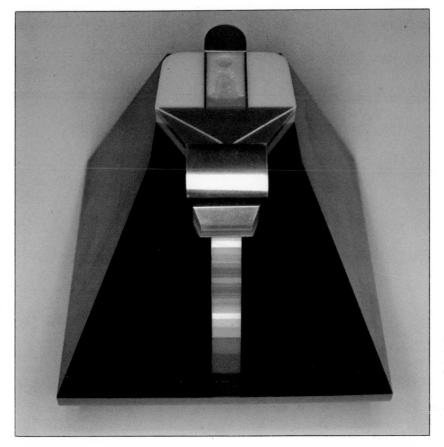

*Ring and pyramidal mount designed by Roger Morris. 1975. Morris, one of the inventive jewellers whose work is handled by the Electrum Gallery, London, has made a speciality of working in bright-coloured acrylics.*

design. In 1968 he won the coveted Lunning Prize and in 1970, a slightly belated commemoration of man's conquest of space, launched his 'Space Silver' bracelets, fanciful concepts on the space theme with such titles as 'Dance in the Galaxy' and 'Near Eruption'.

---

## 1965 – 1970
### Couture and Fine Art Influences

In its attitude to materials and its evolution of elegant, modern forms, the Scandinavian influence has been a purifying force in contemporary jewellery, as it has in other media. It has been left to others to design the shock items which have captured the attention of the fashionable, but often just as soon discarded.

In the late sixties Paris couture led the way with a variety of jewellery ideas, in particular the concept of body jewellery launched so spectacularly by Paco Rabanne in 1966 and ably taken up by Emmanuel Ungaro. Rabanne presented his clothes of metal and plastic as designs for an age when 'cities will be, like Manaos in Brazil, completely covered over by a dome, entirely air-conditioned. There will only be one kind of covering, and of necessity it will be ornamental.' His exciting and inventive designs are conceived primarily as body adornment and as such preclude the wearing of any accompanying jewellery – they are in

*Body jewellery by
sculptor Gustin worn
with feather trousers by
Emmanuel Ungaro from
1969.*

themselves futuristic notions of body jewellery.

Ungaro peppered several of his collections from the late sixties with publicity-winning metal body jewellery. In 1969 he showed a remarkable necklace/ breast-plate *cum* belt, wrought and welded by French . sculptor Gustin and worn with feather trousers. Another eye-catcher was a stainless steel necklace-corsage by sculptor Joe Pomodora.

The ever-inventive Yves Saint-Laurent responded with a memorable series of dresses incorporating body jewellery conceived in collaboration with Claude Lalanne, wife of the fanciful furniture artist Francois Lalanne. These integral parts of

dresses were cast from moulds made directly from parts of the body and in turn adorned in gilt metal the parts of the body, waist, neck or breasts, from which they were modelled. Claude Lalanne has made many surprising jewels, as inspired and disarming as her husband's furniture.

Couturier Pierre Cardin joined the body-jewellery fad with his personal vision in metal and plastic of futuristic erotic adornment for a space-age environment, in which traditional clothing becomes superfluous.

The sixties and early seventies saw a fertile variety of novel Pop and other fine art-derived jewellery, in several instances the creations of painters and sculptors. Roy Lichtenstein adapted his cartoon imagery to a series of enamelled brooches; sculptor César put his signature to expensive rectangular blocks of compressed scrap metal. Saint-Laurent made Pop brooches – such as his bright red or black hearts pierced with rhinestone arrows – to complement his flirtation with Pop in his fashion collections. A far broader influence came in the sixties from Pop and Hard-Edge attitudes to colour, and mass-market plastic jewellery was made in the hard, bright colours appropriate to the material, no longer feeling the need to imitate other more precious substances.

––––––––––––– 1970 – 1980 –––––––––––––
### The British Renaissance
The story of creative jewellery in the seventies belongs to the young British talents who have revitalized the concept of the individual artist/craftsman jeweller and have led the field internationally with the variety and inventiveness of their work. They have evolved new modes of expression diametrically opposed to the traditional styles associated with jewellery as a display of wealth and to the flashy costume jewellery which is the by-product of this type. Theirs is a visual language which seems more truly contemporary

*Left: Silver and titanium lapel brooch designed and made by Janet E. Robinson. Late seventies. Below left: Silver brooch designed and made by John Plenderleith, 1971. Below right: Silver, gold and titanium brooch designed and made by Celia Mannheim, 1973.*

than the inventive, but nonetheless specifically opulent, creations of jewellers such as Andrew Grima or John Donald. For opulence has little meaning to this young generation – theirs is a lively and often humourous approach and an important aspect of their collective image is the exploration of new and often intrinsically valueless materials. Young British jewellers have enjoyed the support of the Crafts Council and of the Worshipful Company of Goldsmiths whose regular 'Loot' exhibitions, inaugurated in 1975, have shown the feasibility of truly creative design at accessible prices.

Whilst it may seem invidious to single out individual names among so many and such diverse talents, certain artists nonetheless seem representative of the prevalent trends. David Watkins, trained as a sculptor, has brought a sculptor's way of thinking to jewellery design and has worked to great effect since the late sixties in the acrylics which have become so characteristic a part of the contemporary jewellery vernacular. His wife, Wendy Ramshaw, designs lively jewels, setting semi-precious stones in precious metal in novel ways and presenting them in groups as sculptures on distinctive sand-blasted stands of striped perspex. Roger Morris, a graduate of the Royal College of Art, is another talented designer to use acrylics to great effect in jewellery of distinctive

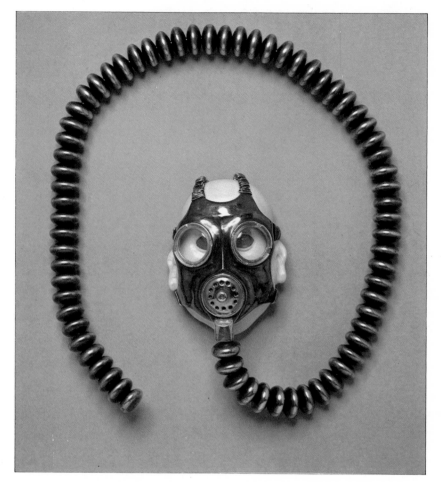

*Necklace designed and made by Susan Vavadi. Carved ivory, moonstones, partly oxidised silver, and gold. 1972.*

and highly personal design.

Caroline Broadhead started her career in 1973 and has proved herself a great experimenter using such novel materials as clustered strands of fluorescent-coloured nylon. Julia Manheim works in silver, ebony and ivory in purist designs which have the lines of chic French Modernist jewels of the late twenties and the strong presence of primitive African tribal jewellery. Susanna Heron has used synthetic resins in cheerfully naive designs.

One of the most interesting innovations has been the use of titanium and this cannot be seen to better effect than in the work of Edward De-Large. A graduate of Camberwell College of Art and the Royal College, De-Large has learned to create extraordinary three-dimensional pictorial effects by painting with heat on this metal. His work is shown, together with the creations of many of the foremost artisans of this British renaissance of the jewellery craft, in London's Electrum Gallery.

## Watches and Accessories

Watches have been the object of particular attention from jewellers in the past ten or fifteen years and identifiable designs from the most prestigious firms are inter-

*The stainless steel and gold 'Santos' sport watch, launched by Cartier in 1978. The design has established itself as an instant classic.*
*Left: Pendant watch. One of the range of watches designed for Omega by Andrew Grima. Textured gold, smokey quartz and pavé set diamonds.*

national status symbols. Cartier has led the field for understated elegance with the variants on their classic 'Tank' watch. The most truly exciting contemporary watch from Cartier has been the 'Santos', a luxurious yet functional design for both sexes. The same fashion for a rational but chic look which inspired the 'Santos' has transformed Rolex's avowedly purely functional watches into high fashion items. These watches, most distinctive in a matt black finish, are designed to resist all adverse conditions and incorporate numerous added technical features. The fashion-conscious have appreciated in their design the same frank but stylish functionalist aesthetic which inspired the building of the Centre Pompidou in Paris and wear them as symbols of the modern technological age.

In 1970 Andrew Grima was invited to design a watch collection for Omega and the results, in the jeweller's distinctive style, introduced exciting new concepts in the luxurious packaging of the functional timepiece. Prominent amongst the luxury watch makers has been the Swiss firm of Piaget.

It is a curious feature of the past ten years or so that the fashion in expensive accessories should be for the recognizable rather than the unique, hence the success of such expensive set-piece status symbols as the Cartier watch, the distinctive cigarette lighter from Dupont in France or Dunhill in London. Hence also the vogue for accessories emblazoned with the monogram of the designer. French luggage-ware manufacturers Louis Vuitton, who for many decades have been selling the same products covered with the 'L.V.' monogram, have come into vogue with this fad and been much imitated. Paris saddlers, Hermès, have similarly exploited their easily recognized equestrian motifs on a wide range of luxury products including, jewellery and the leather goods for which they are best known.

# GLASS DESIGN

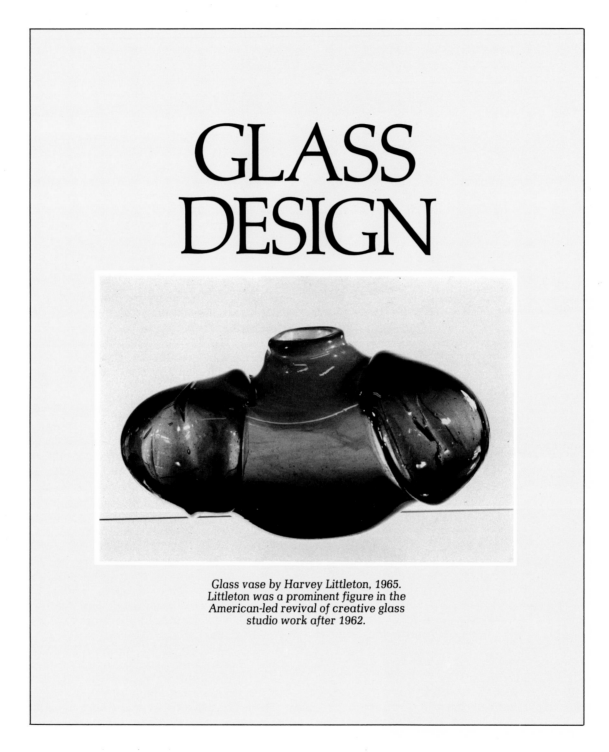

*Glass vase by Harvey Littleton, 1965.
Littleton was a prominent figure in the
American-led revival of creative glass
studio work after 1962.*

## 1945 – Present
### Experiments in Style

IN PRE-WAR EUROPE, France had emerged as the undisputed leader in the manufacture of high-quality decorative glass, and in the work of *artistes verriers*. France's supremacy was successfully challenged, however, after the war by the vitality of the glass emanating from Italy, Sweden and Finland.

The characteristics of the new glass were an emphasis on form, often asymmetrical, functionalist in its simplicity of silhouette, yet sensual and sophisticated; and on largely abstract decoration, again of a refined simplicity. The figurative moulded decoration of Lalique, the decadent elaboration of Art Noveau glass, were very much of the past.

The newly emergent styles found an international showing at the Milan Triennale Exhibitions. Here the Murano group of glassworks asserted the renewed supremacy of Venetian glass, while the Scandinavians earned wide acclaim. Here were displayed the techniques and styles which dominated the late 1940s and 1950s. The successes of these years were summed up and defined in the exhibition 'Glass 1959' held in that year at the Corning Museum of Glass, New York.

This American résumé of post-war achievement was followed in 1962 by a major American breakthrough which has significantly influenced contemporary art glass work. Under the auspices of the Toledo Museum of Art, craftsmen and technicians sought and perfected 'glass from a new formula that could be melted at a temperature low enough to be workable in the average studio or class-room situation.' Dominick Labino and Harvey Littleton were at the forefront of this experiment. The opening of small workshops and the ensuing expansion of the glass craft was a direct result of their successful endeavours.

The revival of interest in Art Nouveau during the 1960s and 1970s has influenced contemporary glass perhaps more than any other craft and the trend has been away from the simple stylishness of post-war 'modern glass' and towards experiments in texture and colour inspired above all by the works of L.C. Tiffany.

The emphasis in the post-war period has certainly been on furnace and blow-pipe work, the *travail à chaud* which Maurice Marinot and, indeed, L.C. Tiffany had so ably demonstrated as perhaps the purest approach to creation in glass. The traditions of cutting and engraving have been maintained, however, and have found distinguished exponents in a contemporary idiom.

In 1979, twenty years on from the 'Glass 1959' exhibition, the Corning Museum brought the story of glass up to date with a major international survey, 'New Glass', featuring over four hundred entries, selected by jury and constituting a complete panorama of glass achievement

## The 1940s and 1950s
### Italy

The international success of post-war Italian glass was achieved by a number of glassworks, experimenting yet with a common stylistic thread. The most notable of these works were the Murano ateliers of Paolo Venini, whose death in 1959 marked the closing of a significant phase in glass history; Seguso Vetri d'Arte, where head designer Flavio Poli showed an extraordinary mastery of proportion, achieved the effortless, monumental grace of sculptures by Arp or Hepworth in its blown glass; Barovier & Toso, inspired by the experiments of Ercole Barovier, used exciting new techniques in decoration.

Venini had become head of his own glassworks in 1923. By the 1940s he was a master in his chosen craft. His works are characterized by a confidence of form and design and the delicacy and refinement of decoration which have traditionally typi-

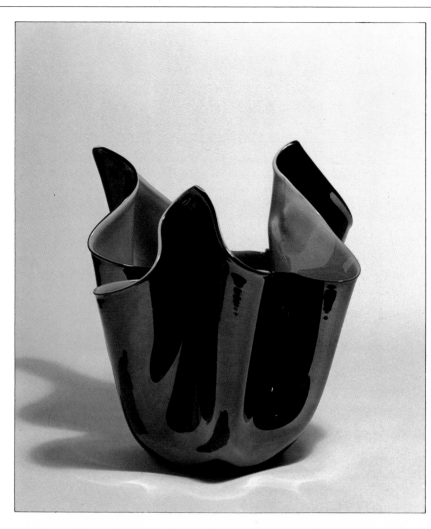

Left: 'Handkerchief' vase
designed by Paolo
Venini. The Murano
glassworks of which
Venini had been head
since 1923 produced a
variety of these vases
through the forties and
fifties, the most complex
using elaborate lattacino
techniques.
Below: Internally
decorated (patchwork)
vase from the Barovier
and Toso glassworks, c.
1950.

fied the best of Venetian glass. He revived some traditional techniques, notably the *lattacino* decoration, which found its most perfect expression in his 'handkerchief' vases introduced in 1940. Innovations in decoration included his *vetro tessuto*, glass inlaid with fine lines in contrasting colour, his patchwork inlay *vetro pezzato* technique on appropriately dubbed *vasi arlecchino* (harlequin-pattern vases) and his *vetro murrina*, opaque glass with tight festooned decoration.

Venini was his own best designer, but he enlisted a variety of outside talents including Falvio Bianconi, Carlo Scarpa and Gio Ponti. The filigree work which Venini popularized was ably exploited by Carlo Scarpa for Mazzega I.V.R., by Archimede Seguso and by Dino Martens, whose own patchwork *lattacino* vases for Vetreria Aureliano Toso are *tours de force* of delicacy.

For the Murano decorating firm S.A.L.I.R., designer Vinicio Vianello produced noteworthy models, ranging from wafer-thin, slightly iridescent vases of bizarre silhouette, to heavy, blown vessels cut with abstract patterns of geometrically perfect, intaglio, scooped circles.

Ercole Barovier, born in 1889, inherited the family firm, Artisti Barovier, after the First World War. In 1936, with brothers Artemi and Decio Toso, he founded the Barovier Toso workshops. A great experimenter, he devised new techniques of surface decoration and was still active as head designer during the 1970s. His son Angelo, born in 1927, entered the firm to become both designer and export ·manager. Barovier found his own variations of the *pezzato* technique, but made his mark with the more personal skills of surface texturing and decoration.

The designs of Flavio Poli differ from

*Fifties heavy-walled, free-blown glass vase of the type associated with the designer Flavio Poli working for the Murano studio, Segusi-Vetri d'Arte.*

Vicke Linstrand, designer in chief of Kosta Glassworks, instructs master blower Heintze

those of the other Murano works by the heaviness of the *matière*. In his heavy-walled, free-blown vases, he used tints to emphasize the lines of the inner wall, often an asymmetrical counter-balance to the outer silhouette. The maximum effect, a sculptural perfection, is achieved through the most sparing and disciplined use of colour and mass.

## Scandinavia

In modern Scandinavian glass the most important names are perhaps those of Orrefors and Kosta, the foremost Swedish glassworks, which created glass both stylistically and technically significant in the Contemporary idiom.

The success of the Orrefors works dates from the pre-war era of designers Simon Gate and Edward Hald. They laid the foundations for the high standards of the post-war design studios. Gate died in 1945, but Hald continued as head of the design studio and the 1950s found him refining the *graal* and *ariel* techniques introduced before the war. Orrefors' next generation of designers included, most notably: Sven Palmquist and Nils Landberg, both with the firm since before the war; Edvin Ohrstrom, part-time with Orrefors since 1936. and one of their most important designers till 1957, when he left to concentrate on glass sculpture; and Ingeborg Landin, with Orrefors from 1947 till 1970.

Palmquist was the great technical inno-

*Above left: Fifties advertisement for Kosta showing design director, Vicke Lindstrand supervizing the creation of a piece.*
*Above: Fifties heavy-walled blown glass vases from the Orrefors glassworks.*
*Right: Orrefors glass vase with 'Ariel' decoration of stylized zebra heads by Ingeborg Lundin.*

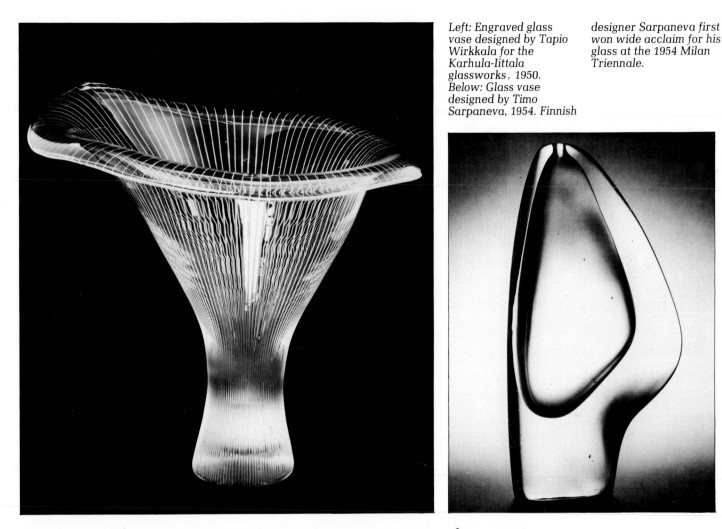

*Left: Engraved glass vase designed by Tapio Wirkkala for the Karhula-Iittala glassworks, 1950. Below: Glass vase designed by Timo Sarpaneva, 1954. Finnish designer Sarpaneva first won wide acclaim for his glass at the 1954 Milan Triennale.*

vator, responsible for a variety of new decorating skills. His 'Ravenna' glass, developed in the late 1940s, was a rich variant on the *graal* technique of internal decoration, in which brilliant, jewel-like pieces of glass were trapped within massive glass walls of another tint. His 'Kraka' was a further variant, while his 'Fuga' designs were a novel application of the principle of centrifugal force to spin glass into a pre-formed mould. Landin and Landberg were both concerned as much with form as with decoration and were responsible for free-blown vessels of considerable refinement, the contours emphasized, on occasion, by a restrained engraved design. Both won gold medals at the Milan 1957 Triennale, where Palmquist won a Grand Prix for his exhibit.

The principal influence at the Kosta works was Vicke Lindstrand, who had worked as a designer with Gate and Hald at Orrefors during the 1930s. In 1950 he joined Kosta as director of design, taking over from Elis Bergh on his retirement. Lindstrand continued to use the tech-

Right: Glass vase
designed by Kaj Franck
for the Wärtsilä Arabia
glassworks, Nuutajärvi-
Notsjö, of which he was
artistic director from
1950 to 1973.
Far right: 'Flamme',
1956. One of a series of
blown crystal/glass
vessels and sculptures
introduced by the Daum
studio in 1945.

niques learnt at Orrefors—*graal*, *ariel* and engraving—refining and perfecting them and creating an important body of work. He sculpted glass in thin-walled, free-form blown vessels, pierced like the sculptures of Henry Moore or Barbara Hepworth. His heavy-walled, yet visually light, asymmetrical crystal vases with spun thread decoration are frozen kinetic sculptures. He produced many significant designs for the engravers at Kosta, such as his elliptically-patterned 'construction', illustrated as an experimental design in the *Studio Yearbook 1955/56*, as well as variants on his classic pre-war subjects.

Bengt Orup, designing for the Johansfors glassworks, was a masterful exponent of the spare asymmetrical style that so characterized glass design during the 1940s and 1950s.

In Finland, the first significant steps towards a contemporary style of artistic glass were made by Gunnel Nyman. She developed her bold and distinctive style between 1945 and her death, at the age of forty, in 1948. Her free-form 'folded' and cut vessels, usually in colourless glass, emphasized the clarity and brilliance of the *matière* and captured the contemporary mood of sophisticated neo-Functionalism. She designed for the leading Finnish works of Riihimaki, Nuutajarvi and Karhula Iittala.

The impetus given by Nyman was taken up by a group of Finnish designers who were soon to find international acclaim at the Milan Triennale in 1951. There, within the pavilion designed by Tapio Wirkkala, Finnish designers won numerous prizes.

Wirkkala had graduated in 1936 from Helsinki's Institute of Industrial Arts and was soon to establish his reputation as one of his country's foremost all-round designers. From 1947 he designed glass for the Karhula-Iittala works and up till the mid-1950s created a variety of works that have become classics of the Contemporary neo-Functionalist style, notably his asymmetrically blown and cut vessels in the tradition of Nyman, and his elegant, thin vases, enhanced with light engraving. He also conceived more elaborate figurative designs for engraving.

Wirkkala continued to design glass on a free-lance basis for Iittala and other firms, notably for the Rosenthal 'Studio Line.' His ice-blocks of 1960 for Littala were a step into a new era of art glass design, away from the neo-Functionalist ethic, towards the more experimental, freer mood of the 1960s and 1970s.

The other exciting designer of the Finnish group was the talented Timo Sarpaneva. Graduating from the Institute of Industrial Arts in 1948, he first designed glass for Iittala in 1950 and won considerable acclaim at the Milan Triennale of 1954 for the sculptural beauty of his designs. A fine and typical example of his confident style is the vase of 1954 examples of which are in the collections of the Metropolitan Museum of Art, New York, and in the Victoria and Albert Museum, London. The free-formed, asymmetrical yet finely balanced mass of clear blown glass is lined with an inner wall of milky white. Conceived as a vase, this is pure sculpture in glass and parallels the work of Italian Flavio Poli. In the 1960s Sarpaneva, like Wirkkala, found a new mode and made a speciality of forming glass vessels and extraordinary baroque abstract sculptures in textured moulds.

**Europe**

Few other glassworks in Europe or America could rival the masterful creations from Italy, Sweden or Finland during the 1940s and 1950s. In the Netherlands, the Leerdam works, under the design directorship of Andries Copier, produced interesting experiments in free-form work, in light lustre texturing and in engraving. Copier's pupils, Floris Meydam, joining in

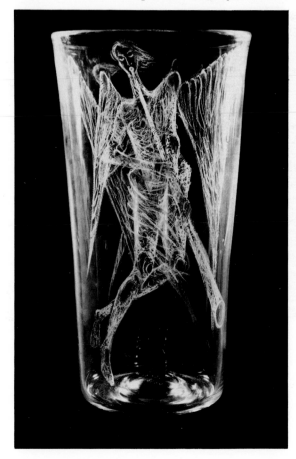

*Far left: 1960 Whitefriars glass vase stipple engraved with a design by John Hutton of figures from his glass panels for Coventry Cathedral.*
*Left: 'The Tree of Life', engraved glass vase by Stephen Rickard, 1958.*

1935, and Willem Heesen, in 1943, added individual talents, the former creating impressive blown and cut sculptural forms during the 1950s, the latter reviving diamond-point work.

In France, the most significant innovation was the range of crystal sculptures introduced by the Daum glassworks in 1945. After decades devoted to the elaborate colouring and decoration of glass, Michel Daum returned to basic principles, to the beauty of colourless, high-grade glass blown and pulled into forms which a contemporary critic, writing in *Le Monde*, described as '*L'affirmation pure du cristal . . . inventions fluides, souples et presque spontanées, . . . "coulées de lumières"*' ('A pure statement in crystal . . . soft, fluid and near-spontaneous creations . . . "liquid light"').

### United States
In the United States, this ideal of a return to the exploitation of the most basic qualities of high-grade glass was nurtured by Arthur Houghton who took over the Steuben glassworks in 1933. In 1936 he set up a design department under Sidney Waugh, chief designer from 1933 until 1963. Steuben glass has achieved an enviable status through the quality of the *matière* workmanship, notably in the field of engraved decoration and through the reflected glory of the many artists of international stature who have been commissioned to submit designs for engraving. These include Pavel Tchelitchew, Jean Cocteau, Salvador Dali, Raoul Dufy, Giorgio de Chirico, Eric Gill and Georgia O'Keeffe.

### United Kingdom
British glass manufacture of the forties and fifties was characterized by a conservatism of design, and a reliance on the commercially safe, traditional forms of decoration, predominantly cutting. The equally traditional craft of engraving has

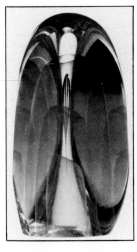

'Triangular Fountain', multiple overlay-glass sculpture by Dominick Labino. Created in 1978 and included in the Corning Museum exhibition 'New Glass 1979'.

however found a few notable and innovative exponents. Most significant, perhaps, in view of the scale of his work is New Zealand-born John Hutton, whose *chef d'oeuvre* is the great west screen of Coventry Cathedral which he undertook in 1952. He employed a distinctive, spontaneous shallow-engraving technique and used a variety of wheels on a flexible drive, giving the ease of movement necessary for his monumental panels.

Laurence Whistler started his diamond-point work before the war and has earned an international reputation for his charming and whimsical creations. Stephen Rickard, Peter Dreiser, June Majella, Dorothy Brown and Harold Gordon have all produced attractive engraved work. Jane Webster, a Stourbridge College of Art and Royal College of Art graduate, is probably the leading engraver in England today.

---
## 1960 – Present
### New Directions
A turning point in the story of contemporary glass was the Toledo Museum of Art's sponsorship of research into formulae for a new low-temperature melt *matière*. These experiments, started in March 1962, were led by Dominick Labino, formerly vice-president for research with the John Manville Fiber Glass Corporation, and Harvey Littleton. They sought new formulae for new colours, but at the root of their work was the ideal of creating the practical possibility for an individual craft-work situation in which students could set up a simple furnace and come to terms directly with their chosen medium – the art glass designer was to be his own craftsman, glass a living material. The Toledo seminars were to have a far-reaching influence and Labino and Littleton are today justly regarded as the force behind the current studio glass revival.

A noteworthy feature of much of their own work, and a significant indication of

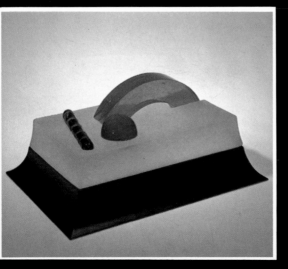

*Above left: Blown glass vase by Sam Herman, one of the most successful graduates (1965) of Harvey Littleton's University of Wisconsin course.*
*Top right: Glass vase made by the Venini glassworks for the Belgian firm, Philips.*
*Left: Pâte de verre sculpture, 'Le Billard' made by the Daum glassworks from the design by Del Pezzo, 1970.*
*Above/Above left: Glass sculpture by Seide, U.S.A. Blown glass tubes containing neon, argon and mercury gas. Made in 1978 and included in the Corning Museum exhibition 'New Glass 1979'.*

the increased regard for glass as a medium of purely artistic expression, has been the lack of any pretence at function. Even the most refined sculptured forms of Poli or Sarpaneva, from the fifties, were generally conceived as vases. Labino and Littleton were sculptors in glass and encouraged an international trend. By the mid- to late-sixties Sarpaneva was casting baroque abstracts in glass; leading Finnish glass artist Oiva Toikka was making sculptures such as his Pop coloured 'Lollipop Isle' of 1969, and Littleton's pupils, Sam Herman and Marvin Lipofsky, were blowing organic free-forms.

A significant influence on this new generation of studio glass artists has been the major international reappraisal of Art Nouveau since the mid-sixties. The extraordinary, inventive creations of leading Art Nouveau glass artists, such as Emile Gallé and L. C. Tiffany, had explored colour, texture and internal reactions in unprecedented depth. The works of the Tiffany Studios in particular, with their magical lustres and almost exclusive concentration on furnace as opposed to cold bench work, have provided a major source of inspiration. Numerous glassworkers today have leaned too heavily on

this source and are producing *pastiches* of Tiffany or its Austrian counterpart, Loetz glass.

The more talented, however, having learnt the chemistry of lustres and internal colouring in the Tiffany mode, have developed a personal style. A part of this re-awakening of interest in the skills of Art Nouveau glassmakers has been a revival of the technique of *pâte-de-verre*. The subject of recent study and experiment at the Royal College of Art in London, *pâte-de-verre* was first revived by the Daum works, where the necessary research was undertaken from 1965. During the late sixties and into the seventies, Daum issued limited editions of *pâte-de-verre* sculptures commissioned from a variety of prominent sculptors, including Salvador Dali, César, Pedro Ramirez Vazquez and Maurice Legendre. Amongst the most striking, for its Pop colours and crisp, Hard-Edge design, was Del Pezzo's 'Le Billard' of 1970.

The work of Labino and Littleton was carried on by their pupils, notably by those who studied with Littleton at his University of Wisconsin course. Among the most prominent were Marvin Lipofsky, who took his Master's degree in 1964,

*Right: Glass sculpture by Marvin Lipofsky. Opaque white and coloured glass cased in clear glass, partly mould-blown. Made in 1978 with the assistance of Gianni Toso and included in the 'New Glass 1979' exhibition. Far right: Mould-blown textured glass vessel designed by Timo Sarpaneva. Sixties.*

'Lollipop Isle'. Sculpture
in glass, on a Pop theme.
Pop colours, by Oiva
Toikka, 1969. Toikka is
perhaps the most
prominent figure in the
story of creative Finnish
glass today. In 1973 he
became artistic director
of the Arabia works.

*'Judges' vase, made by Steve Newall at The Glasshouse, London, 1979. Blown and etched glass with a slightly iridescent surface.*

and Mexican-born Sam Herman, who graduated in 1965. Lipofsky moved to California where he set up a glass course at the University of California, Berkeley. He has travelled extensively, demonstrating his skills by invitation to glassworks in Finland, Italy, and the Netherlands. His approach to colour and decoration is more disciplined than the fluid style of contemporary Sam Herman.

Herman came to Britain after graduating from Wisconsin and his creative energy revitalized British glass. Working first at Edinburgh College of Art under Helen Monro Turner, he moved to London in 1967 on a research fellowship at the Royal College of Art where he soon became tutor in charge of the glass department. Perhaps the most important legacy of his stay in London was the foundation

of The Glasshouse in 1969 for the commercial promotion of young talent. Herman was joined in this project by Graham Hughes, artistic director of the Goldsmiths Hall, and remained a director of The Glasshouse's activities until his departure for Australia in 1974. His Brussels patrons and agents, L'Ecuyer, have recently invited Herman to experiment at the Belgian glassworks, Val Saint Lambert.

The establishment of The Glasshouse has proved an exciting step in the promotion of the art of glass. Pauline Solven, trained at Stourbridge College of Art and the Royal College of Art between 1961 and 1968, became its first studio manager

The American Charlie Meaker is one of the more exciting young talents attracted to the craft by the inspiration of The Glasshouse. It was there that he saw Steve

*Internally decorated glass vase made by Annette Meech at The Glasshouse, London. Late 1970s. This small studio, set up in 1969, provides a young generation of glass artisans the opportunity for creative experiment.*

Newall blowing glass. In an interview in 1979 he recalled, 'I had never seen anything like it. It was so graceful to watch, so fluid. He was controlling and shaping it without touching it. It was as though he was dancing with it. I knew then it was the medium for me.' Annette Meech and Dillon Clarke are actively pursuing the beauties of fluid internal decoration and their work is now on permanent exhibition at The Glasshouse. The experiments of their American counter-parts are exhibited at the Contemporary Art Glass Gallery in New York.

Scandinavian supremacy has been kept very much alive by a new generation of artists. In Sweden, the Kosta works have found able exponents of a modern idiom in Goran and Ann Warff and Bertil Vallien, with Kosta since the early 1960s.

Goran Warff's vessels in bold primary contrasting colours are very much a product of the post-Pop consciousness. Vallien's forté is pure sculpture in glass, either emphasizing the fluid beauty of the *matière* in free-form creations or exploring the versatility of glass through a variety of colouring and decorating skills.

In Finland today the most prominent figure is Oiva Toikka, artistic director of the Wartsila Arabia glassworks since the retirement in 1973 of his able predecessor Kaj Franck. Working in glass since 1963 Toikka designs domestic wares for factory production but is known internationally for his purely artistic creations. These range from delicate works in clear glass, decorated with particles of precious metal, to substantial, sometimes humorous sculptures in clear coloured glass.

# TEXTILE DESIGN

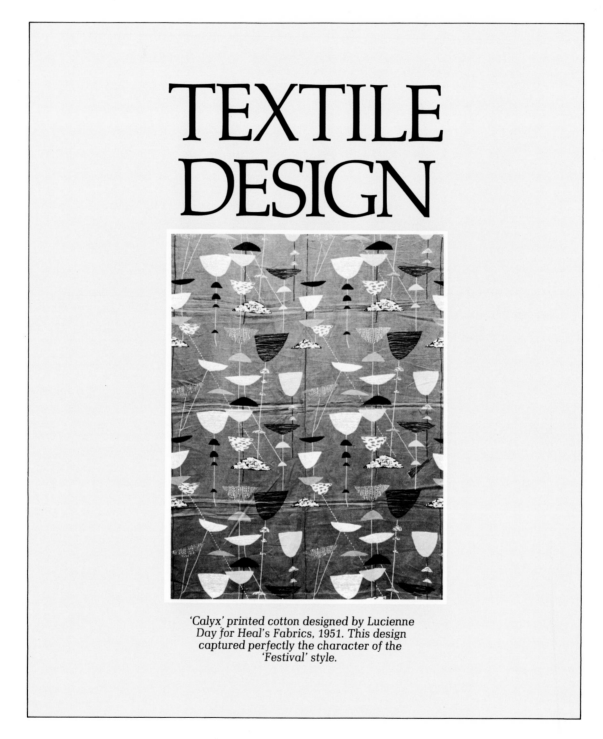

'Calyx' printed cotton designed by Lucienne
Day for Heal's Fabrics, 1951. This design
captured perfectly the character of the
'Festival' style.

FASHIONS IN FURNISHING FABRICS have been subject to considerable changes within the contemporary period, a constant process of stylistic development which parallels and reflects changing tastes and influences in other areas of decorative art. Perhaps the most significant developments, however, in the story of contemporary fabric design have been in the increasing exploitation of man-made fabrics, the intrinsic characteristics of which have in many instances dictated quite new directions for furniture design. A prime example is in the synthetic stretch jerseys which suggested new forms in the sixties. Nylons, rayons and the countless other synthetic yarns now available have transformed the industry, isolating natural materials as a generally more costly luxury.

------------------ 1940 – 1960 ------------------
### Figurative to Abstract

Tastes in the forties were predominantly oriented towards figurative motifs and traditional floral themes enjoyed wide popularity. The post-war years saw the exploration of a whole new repertoire of figurative motifs which were at once lively, joyful and re-assuring – typical is a selection illustrated in the *Studio Year Book* of 1949 which included 'Maytime', a charming restrained floral pattern by Swedish designer Stig Lindberg, 'Carnival', with motifs based on traditional Polish peasant costume, by Costan Niau, 'Pegasus' by Marion Mahler and other designs of birds, leaves and the popular mermaid motif.

A significant shift in taste occurred around the turn of the decade with an exciting and very inventive exploration of abstract themes. Not that floral or other figurative motifs were abandoned. Indeed, one commentator, Annette Reilly, discussing British textiles in 1955 wrote, 'The British textile tradition is rooted in the garden.' The fashionable fabrics of the early fifties, however, owed their inspiration to trends in abstract art and few designers captured the spirit of the moment more successfully than British artists Marion Mahler, Jacqueline Groag, and, most notably, Lucienne Day, wife of furniture designer Robin Day.

Lucienne Day has detailed some of the most specific painterly or sculptural influences on her own work and on that of like-minded contemporaries. Miró, Calder and Klee were strong influences, each having a style which lent itself easily to translation into flat repeat patterns. Day's 'Perpetua' design was a very specific homage to Calder in its refined balance of abstract masses of colour joined by thin, bowed lines. Her 'Calyx' design of 1951 for Heal's Fabrics is her most celebrated exercise in the genre. It was featured in the Festival of Britain, won a Milan Triennale Gold Medal and was the starting point for many inferior imitations. 'Silver Birch', created for Heal's, was amongst the most refined patterns from this gifted fabric designer.

Day, Mahler and Groag were talented designers with fresh ideas, but credit must go also to the fabric manufacturers who were prepared to promote their exciting new work, notable among them being the firms of Heal's, Edinburgh Weavers and David Whitehead. An important body of work in dress and furnishing fabric, carpet and paper design was created by the Festival (of Britain) Pattern Group. This team evolved a whole new vernacular of abstract motifs derived from diagrams of crystalline and molecular structures.

The new abstract styles derived from new schools of painting were by no means restricted to Britain. Notable designs were produced in the United States, while from Italy came exuberant abstract painterly patterns of considerable vigour. One remarkable American fabric was 'Pirouette' a cotton gabardine designed by Azia Martinelli for Morton Sundour Co. Inc. Its trailing lines of colour would seem

*Above left: Early fifties 'Pirouette' cotton gabardine designed by Azia Martinelli for Morton Sundour Co. Inc.*
*Above right: Printed Rayon designed by Marion Mahler for David Whitehead Ltd. Early fifties.*
*Right: Late forties Woven fabric designed by Marion Mahler for Edinburgh Weavers ltd.*

to be copied directly from the Action Painting canvases of Jackson Pollock. Ruth Adler was responsible for pleasing designs for Adler Schnee Associates. Her 'Lazy Leaves' is typical of its time with its balances of abstract forms and fine lines.

The vitality of Italian fabrics was just one facet of the renaissance of Italian decorative art in the post-war period. Italian patterns, from such designers as Elena Cristofanetti, Roberto Crippa, Renato Birolli and Fede Cheti suggested a distinctive sense of spontaneous energy in their creation. The Milan manufacturers Socota produced fabrics of particular interest in the Abstract Expressionist style.

Looking back in 1957 over the story of

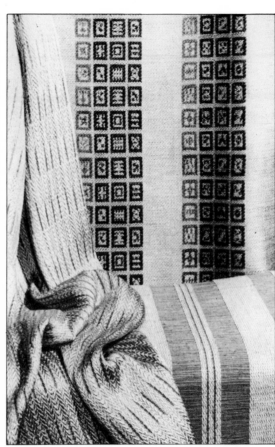

*Far left: 'Giotto' printed satin furnishing fabric designed by Roberto Crippa for Manifattura Jsa-Busto Arsizio, fifties.*
*Left: Three handwoven 'Contemporary Style' fabrics designed and made by Alice Lunds Textilier, Sweden. Mid-Fifties.*
*Bottom left: 'Lazy Leaves' printed fabric designed by Ruth Adler for Adler Schnee Associates. Early fifties.*

fabric design since the war, Lucienne Day defined the changes in taste. 'In the very few years since the end of the war, a new style in furnishing fabrics has emerged. Thinking back and seeing this period as a whole, I suppose the most noticeable thing about it has been the reduction in popularity of patterns based on floral motifs and the replacement of these by non-representational patterns – generally executed in clear, bright colours, and inspired by the modern abstract school of painting.' Already, in 1957, however, she was able to define a further evolution: 'In the last year or two', she wrote, 'there has been a definite move among some designers towards greater simplification and there-

*Above: Carpet design by Antonio Boggeri for Polymer Montecatini Edison, Italy.*
*Right: 'Stones' cotton-velvet designed by Wolf Bauer for Knoll Associates. Both fabrics were illustrated in the 1970/71 edition of 'Decorative Art in Modern Interiors'.*

fore more dignity; more attention to detail and to colour relationships, less colour in a single pattern, and above all for designs of a more diffuse and textural nature . . .'

The Contemporary look in furniture and decorative design was evolving its formulae for fabric design – less interest in pattern and a greater concern for texture. Muted, natural colours, beiges, oatmeals, creams, enjoyed considerable popularity and perfectly complemented the mellow woods, notably the oiled teak of Contemporary interiors. Weave patterns, often

knobbly-textured, played an important part in a new style in which Scandinavian designers and manufacturers had taken an influential lead since the early fifties. Pattern was kept to a subdued minimum in the creations of manufacturers such as the Swedish firms Textil Kammaren, Nordiska Kompaniet of Stockholm and Alice Lund Textilien or the Danish Frederick Fiedler A/S. Astrid Sempre, Viola Grasten and Stig Lindberg produced restrained designs for Nordiska Kompaniet, Bent Karlby similarly for Frederick Fiedler. British designer Tibor Reich for Tibor Ltd. explored deep textured fabrics to considerable effect in the Contemporary manner.

The 'Rya' rug, a deep-textured rug or wall-hanging, is a Norwegian traditional craft which has enjoyed a renewed popularity in the contemporary era.

Open- and textured-weave rugs and hangings have attracted increasing attention since the fifties and the genre has found a masterful exponent in British artist Peter Collingwood. Collingwood has made an art of the craft of the hand loom and is perhaps the most prominent figure in a craft which through the sixties and seventies has considerable popularity.

*Left: 'Maze' printed cotton by Tamesa from their 1978 collection. Bottom left: 'Nuts' designed by Yuki Odawara for Isetan Co. Ltd, Japan. Below: Wall hanging by Peter Collingwood.*

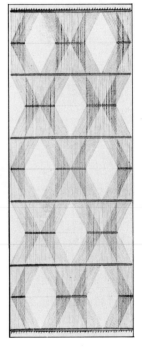

----------- 1960 – 1970 -----------
### Art Nouveau and Pop
The sixties saw many new trends and fads in textile design. One very specific fashion was the revival of Arts and Crafts and Art Nouveau designs, in particular those by William Morris and Charles Annesley Voysey. Morris's fussy floral designs covered walls and seat furniture and hung as curtains. They have been succeeded by a fashion for pretty miniature floral designs, generally in a limited colour range, which are still popular today. Pattern returned to textile design in the sixties after the dominance of the neat, self-effacing, textured fabrics of the Contemporary Style and in many instances was a

'Space Walk' designed by Sue Thatcher for Warner's in the spring of 1969. The Space Race of the sixties provided a vivid source of imagery.

reflection of fashionable styles in painting. The colourful Op Art of painter Victor Vasarely was enormously influential in suggesting styles for fabrics, papers and carpets. Vasarély's tightly disciplined geometric canvases were translated into crisp graphic repeat patterns. Decorator David Hicks designed distinctive carpets in this style. The optically disturbing black/white paintings of Bridget Riley were adapted to a repeat pattern for a carpet designed by Antonio Boggeri as a project for Polymer-Montecatini Edison of Italy.

A consistent theme of sixties pattern-making was a boldness of scale, this usually combined with a crispness of motif and a limited palette, a trend which maintained its popularity internationally into the seventies. *Decorative Art in Modern Interiors 1970-71* illustrates a prime example, 'Stones', a cotton velvet designed by Wolf Bauer for Knoll Associates. The 1975-6 volume illustrates two further good examples, 'Nut' designed by Yuki Odawara for Isetan Co. Ltd. of Japan, and 'Fronde' by the leading London/Brussels firm Tamesa Fabrics. 'Maze', 'Odyssey', 'Iliad', 'Bamboo' and 'Ritz' are but a few in the fine range manufactured by Tamesa in a bold but disciplined style.

The late sixties saw a number of isolated but interesting examples of the

*Printed cotton scarf from Fiorucci. In stock in 1980 this design captures the mood of the moment just as 'Calyx' so perfectly caught the flavour of 1951. Designer Ettore Sottsass has recently been employed by Fiorucci to preserve the freshness and spontaneity of the company's image as it expands its operations worldwide.*

influences of Pop Art and Pop culture on textile design. The conquest of space was celebrated by the manufacturers, Warner's, with designs in Pop/cartoon style. Designer S. Thatcher created a 'Space Walk' pattern, Eddie Squires produced a pattern 'Lunar Rocket'. Warner's had been amongst the firms to manufacture Vasarély-derived Op designs earlier in the decade.

For that extraordinary phenomenon, the London shop Mr. Freedom, Jane Weallans, wife of Jon Weallans who created the furniture and decor, designed a whole range of fabrics under the trademark O.K. Textiles. These fabrics and the cushions,

blinds and other soft furnishings also by Mrs Weallans derived their themes from souped-up Odeonesque motifs and Pop imagery. Such blatant homage to Pop was a short-lived indulgence. More lasting has been the influence of Pop in colour, in textile as in other areas of design. Pop has set a seal of approval on the bright, primary colours which many designers have confidently exploited through the seventies. Fresh colours, clean lines have been the dominant themes of recent years with the exploration of delightful, light abstract geometric motifs providing new decorative ideas in the endless process of renewal.

# FASHION DESIGN

*A 1950 image of the changing face of beauty.
Portrait of model Jean Patchett by
photographer Erwin Blumenfeld.*

## 1945 – Present
### Fashion and Style

FASHION IS THE MOST ELUSIVE and, by its very nature, the most ephemeral of the applied arts. The creations of dress designers may survive, but only as symbols; for the mood in which they were conceived, the manner in which they were worn and the gestures and attitudes which accompanied them are intangibles which can never be recaptured. Only the increased sophistication of fashion photography has made it possible to capture the perfect concoction of dress, accessories, make-up, model and mood, so that there might survive in two dimensional form an idealized record of a moment in time.

The art of fashion lies in the perception of the ideal appropriate to the age, the creation of the symbol to which the age will wish, if only for a season, to conform. The great couturier or designer does not impose, he responds, adding an ingredient of individuality, of novelty and invention.

Fashion is an art, and an industry, devoted above all to the cult of an idealized Woman. It has cynically been remarked that male fashion has undergone only two noteworthy, and those virtually imperceptible, changes since 1913 — the suppression of a particular jacket seam and the introduction of the trouser crease. Apart from a gradual move away from formality, and aside from such localized exceptions as the garish outburst of male peacockry provoked by Carnaby Street shops in the sixties, it is true to say that male dress is the subject of only the most marginal changes and differentiations.

Fashion has long played a secondary role in histories of the applied arts, but the expansion of the fashion industry in the post-war decades has made it the most immediate and widespread reflection of changing life-styles, of shifting tastes and influences. Fashion has been, in some ways the victim, in others the beneficiary, and at all times the mirror of the extensive upheavals which have brought about a new social climate if not a new society.

The war years and the immediate post-war period were lean times for fashion. Not only were quality materials, indeed any materials, in extremely short supply, but the mood was hardly conducive to indulgence in any kind of ostentation. Amongst the most memorable fashion photographs of this austere era was Cecil Beaton's image of Balmain's plain trouser suit of 1945 photographed on a sad boyish model in a shabby courtyard. One year later, however, fashion regained its self-confidence and Christian Dior, whose New Look was an overnight sensation, became a household name. Unashamed luxury was welcomed back and Dior became synonymous in the public mind with the exclusive image of the grand couturier, the semi-divine master in the world of fashion catering autocratically to the wealthy few. Seldom, if ever before, had the precious world of couture, the ivory towers of Paris' XVIème *arrondissement* enjoyed such a position as that attained by Dior in 1947 and shared by others in his wake over the next ten years. The breath-taking Paris collections of autumn 1950 consolidated the position of Dior and Balenciaga, Fath and Balmain, as the new gods of fashion. The photographs from this period by Irving Penn and Richard Avedon are imbued with the excitement of a reawakened post-war Paris.

Just as surely as Paris couture had flowered exquisitely in the late forties, so, inevitably, was it destined ultimately to wilt and die. The war had swept away so many social barriers and customs that couture re-emerged to cater to an already moribund society. New voices could be heard in the arena of fashion, above all the voice of the young, who were to take over from the wealthy as the dictators of

*Above: Trouser suit by Pierre Balmain photographed in 1945 by Cecil Beaton.*
*Above right: The 'New Look', launched by Christian Dior in 1947. Dior sensed the need for an expression of extravagance and romance and his 'New Look' made his name into a household word.*

style. Couturiers beat a slow retreat. Some accepted the need to go down-market and create ready-to-wear ranges, others maintained the prestige of unprofitable couture collections, finding commercial success in the manufacture of perfumes and accessories. The new tycoons of fashion catered unashamedly to the young, satisfying a vast market for the inexpensive, the amusing, the throwaway. A key date in this reversal was the opening by Mary Quant in 1955 of her first Bazaar boutique in the King's Road in Chelsea, London.

The emergence of youth as an independent cultural group was a post-war phenomenon. The beginnings during the fifties of a new affluence in a generation rela-

tively unfettered by traditional class distinctions, created a new market for classless fashions that were above all an expression of the new independence and vitality of youth. Fashion became polarized and the sixties was a decade of extremes.

Despite the decline in the market for couture clothes, a number of new couturiers found success in the mid-sixties with remarkable new ideas. Notable among these were André Courrèges, with his space-age look, and Paco Rabanne, with his creations in metal and plastic. Their appeal was aimed at the young but, despite their relatively new affluence, the young were not prepared to pay couture prices, and the designers found that survival would entail breaking out of the exclusive couture mould. Courrèges found commercial success by the marketing of diluted ready-to-wear versions of his original uncompromising styles; Rabanne based his commercial success on his Eau de Calandre perfume and *eau de toilette*.

Youth, meanwhile, was making itself felt in a veritable fashion revolution. Young fashions were anarchic, often shoddy and vulgar, relying on novelty, gimmickry and shock value. The mini-skirt was the great shock garment of the decade. The young wore a succession of new looks, derived amusingly in some cases from fashionable styles in painting. The Op Art look of the mid-sixties was typical of the aggressiveness of so many of these fads. The bright colours of Pop Art, too, were soon absorbed into youthful fashions. In the hands of the self-consciously classless new youth fashion could take on a socio-political significance. The liberal, pacifist hippie sub-culture of the late sixties evolved an international fashion uniform.

Youth has, above all, demanded an end to rules in fashion. The trend towards casualness has been a key feature of youthful dominance of the market and the most successful garment of the post-war era is undoubtedly blue denim jeans, a market originally dominated by Levi-Strauss, but today catered to by a host of other manufacturers. Not that this casualness has precluded the vanities of display and it is typical of today's inverted snobbery that a brand of denim jeans and jean-style trousers should be photographed and advertised worn with elegant shoes and costly jewellery from Graff.

After the revolution of the sixties, a decade which pursued style rather than elegance and for which impact was more important than quality, the seventies emerged as a period of rationalization. Couture now played a token, background role and the ready-to-wear industry achieved far greater sophistication, attracting talented and highly professional designers. The ready-to-wear collections in Paris, London and Rome became the hub of the industry, while in the United States a group of designers found success with an easy, uncluttered, elegant style of dress.

Fashion must keep moving. It is a creative art in a perpetual state of flux and kept alive by regular injections of anarchy

*Below left: Levi Strauss blue denim jeans have become the most widespread and democratic fashion of the contemporary period.*
*Below: Black leather version of the classic jeans style. Manufactured by 'Midnight Blue' in 1978.*

and innovation. Among the most interesting fashion manifestations of the late seventies, serving as a reminder to the industry of its origins in the youth revolution, was the influence of the Punk sub-culture.

———————— 1940 – 1960 ————————
### The French Revival
When the world of Paris couture reawakened after the war, it seemed, on the surface, as if little had changed. A few new names appeared on the scene. A few old ones failed to return or rested on their pre-war laurels. Jean Patou had died in 1936; Madeleine Vionnet, so important in the early thirties for her use of the bias cut, had retired in 1939; 'Coco' Chanel had closed her couture business in 1939. She staged a come-back in 1954 but essentially with a reinterpretation of her classic pre-war styles. Pierre Piguet died in 1953 and Elsa Schiaparelli did not close her couture business until 1954, but theirs are names firmly associated with the pre-war years.

The exciting new talents included Pierre Balmain, who opened his salon in October 1945, having worked at first with Molyneux and Lelong; Jacques Fath, who had started to design immediately before the war and finally opened a new salon in 1944, the Spaniard Cristobal Balenciaga, who had opened in August 1937 and who was to emerge as the genius of post-war Paris couture; and, of course, Christian Dior, who rose to fame on the success of his first collection, only a few months after the establishment of his business in October 1946. Nina Ricci, who had opened in 1932, enjoyed a lasting success with her luxurious understated style. This group was soon joined by Hubert de Givenchy, who opened his own salon in 1951 after working with Piguet, Schiaparelli and Fath, and Antonio Canovas del Castillo, who gave a new vigour to the house of Lanvin when he joined it in 1950. He opened his own salon in 1963.

Dior and Balenciaga are the two out-

*Above: Renée, one of Dior's favourite models in one of his frothy and romantic evening gowns, 1955.*
*Right: Christian Dior at work with members of his staff including Mme Bricard on his right and Mme Marguerite on his left.*

standing figures of their generation and provide an interesting comparison. Cecil Beaton nimbly expressed the contrast in *The Glass of Fashion* when he wrote, 'If Dior is the Watteau of dressmaking – full of nuances, chic, delicate and timely – then Balenciaga is fashion's Picasso. For like that painter, underneath all his experiments with the modern, Balenciaga has a deep respect for tradition and a pure classic line.'

## Dior

Christian Dior provided the magical blend of femininity, froth and romance so sorely needed after the war years. His wealthy family background had enabled him to indulge his artistic interests by backing a new modern art gallery in the late 1920s, but a reversal in his fortunes following the 1929 crash forced him to seek a more profitable career. He created his first fashion sketches in 1935, selling them over the next couple of years to a number of well-known houses. In 1937 he was invited to join the house of Robert Piguet as *modéliste*, moving from there to Lucien Lelong. *Vogue* correspondent Bettina Ballard recalled the summer of 1946 when '... Christian Dior was a much-talked about personality owing to the extraordinary news that Marcel Boussac, the cotton king of France and a great racing figure, was to back him in a couture house of his own that would open the next season. Lelong told me sadly that he could not help encouraging his star designer to branch out on his own with the talent that he had.'

On the morning of 12 February 1947 crowds jostled for admission at the grey-canopied entrance to Dior's new 30 avenue Montaigne premises. Those fortunate enough to reach the inner sanctuary were not to be disappointed. After years of imposed restraint, women were invited by Dior to indulge in full skirts, extravagantly using many yards of fabric in tight pleat-ing. This new femininity, emphasized by tight-nipped waists, was rapidly dubbed the 'New Look' and broadcast on both sides of the Atlantic. Overnight Dior became the high priest of fashion and his success continued as, season after season, he proposed one line after another to women still willing to conform to a dominant look, such looks as his 'H' line or his 'ligne flèche', which set the pace during the fifties.

Dior, the dilettante, became a shrewd business man, capitalizing on the name that was his most valuable asset. In 1947 he opened a department specializing in furs and in the same year founded the Société des Parfums Christian Dior. In 1949 he launched an American subsidiary, Christian Dior New York, and in 1951, as if sensing the direction which fashion was ultimately to follow, created a special department to develop and co-ordinate the world-wide spread of the Dior trademark. Dior died in 1957, after only ten years in the limelight, and his mantle fell on the nervous young shoulders of his brilliant protégé, Yves Saint-Laurent. In those brief ten years Dior had created a fashion empire which continued to flourish after the death of its founder and which, in 1977, thirty years after his first collection, could boast a gross turnover of some £200,000,000.

## Balenciaga

Unlike Dior, who became a couturier almost by chance, Balenciaga knew his vocation from a very early age. It was not until the age of forty-two, however, that he opened his Paris salon. He launched himself in 1937 with a neo-Victorian style which enjoyed a brief popularity. Around 1950 a new Balenciaga was in evidence showing a complete mastery of his personal fashion idiom – bold, classic, severe, yet sumptuously elegant, a peak of sophistication achieved through a rare instinct for form, fabric and cut. Balenciaga was

Above: Cristobal
Balenciaga
photographed in 1962 by
Cecil Beaton.
Right: Black silk taffeta
evening cape by
Balenciaga from his
autumn 1950 collection.
Photographed by Irving
Penn.

the unequalled master of cut. He worked his fabrics, notably his favourite plain pink and black silk taffetas into light, dancing shapes, sculptures in cloth which combined daring with a classic simplicity, often belying the subtle complexity of the cut. And always, running through his work and deeply rooted in Balenciaga's Spanish background, was a finely tuned, masterfully controlled blend of fiery grandeur and exquisite simplicity.

Diana Vreeland wrote a perceptive appreciation of the couturier, acknowledging this background: 'Cristobal Balenciaga was the true son of a strong country filled with style, vibrant color, and a fine history. He remained forever a Spaniard and his inspiration came from the bullrings, the flamenco dancers, the fishermen in their boots and loose blouses, the glories of the church and the cool of the cloisters and monasteries. He took their colours, their cuts, then festooned them to his own taste and dressed the Western world for thirty years.' He cut clothes, she continued '. . . with such gusto and flair of tailoring as the Western world has never known. He was the master tailor, the master dressmaker.'

Surrounded by couturiers anxious to court a broader market, Balenciaga refused to compromise and continued to work exclusively in haute couture until his retirement in 1968. He shunned publicity and in 1957 decided to exclude the press from his shows. Balenciaga, the *grand seigneur* of Paris couture, died in 1972, but his influence is very much alive.

### Fath, Rochas, Dessès and Balmain

Amongst the post-war Paris couturiers Jacques Fath emerges as one of the more fascinating talents. Born in 1912, Fath started modestly in couture in 1937 with a small showing of some twenty designs in cramped premises in the rue de le Boëtie. His luxurious, imaginative, feminine clothes and his lively colour sense soon attracted attention. His own elegantly frothy life-style drew a glittering clientèle to his salon. Success was assured and there was every indication that his shrewd business sense and awareness of the potential of licencing the manufacture of his designs for ready-to-wear international retail would have placed him at the very top in the industry. His career was cut short by his death in 1954.

Marcel Rochas was, like Fath, a great socialite as well as a gifted designer. Jean Dessès, who had opened his Paris salon in 1937, is remembered for his seductive, feminine evening dresses in softly draped sheer fabrics.

Pierre Balmain had started his career with Molyneux in 1934. Opening his own salon in 1945 he was prompt to exploit the new field of international ready-to-wear marketing, establishing links with such major retailers as Nieman-Marcus and travelling with his collections and designs as far afield as Argentina and Australia.

### United Kingdom

Although Paris was the undisputed centre of fashion in the post-war years, English couture enjoyed, nonetheless, the unique advantage of the royal court, its ceremonies and its patronage. The oldest established royal dressmaker was Norman Hartnell who had the distinction of royal warrants from two Queens, Queen Elizabeth II and Queen Elizabeth the Queen Mother, formerly Duchess of York, for whom he had created an image inspired by the grand gowns of the court of the Empress Eugénie. His designs, for such occasions as the Elysée Palace banquet on the State Visit of Queen Elizabeth II to France in 1957, are truly royal in their timeless grandeur. Hartnell's hallmark was spectacular embroidered decoration.

Hardy Amies opened his couture house at 16 Savile Row in 1946 and has held a royal warrant as Dressmaker to Queen Elizabeth II since 1955. Hartnell and Amies are perhaps the best known

'Mermaid' evening dress by Jacques Fath. Velvet. Photographed in 1951 for the 'Daily Express' by Richard Dormer and modelled by Barbara Goalen.

amongst the designers to have grouped themselves formally in 1942 as the Incorporated Society of London Fashion Designers, which was formed initially to promote export.

It was not until the sixties, however, and then from a quite different style of designer, that English fashion began to have a strong international impact. Among the more talented members of the I.S.L.F.D. were John Cavanagh, who opened his salon in 1952 after working with Molyneux and Balmain, and Victor Stiebel whose salon, reopened in 1945 and closed finally in 1963, became known for romantic evening dresses.

## United States

In the United States, as long as Paris ruled, the most influential figures in fashion were the buyers for the big retail stores such as Bendels, Nieman-Marcus and Magnin. Their buyers descended twice a year on the Paris collections and their collective response spelt success or disaster.

America's strength has been in the promotion of casual clothes, but one designer working in the grand manner is worthy of special attention. Charles James was a brilliant master of cut, as original as Balenciaga and, like Balenciaga, devoted to the principles of haute couture. In an article published shortly after James's death in 1978, John Duka wrote, 'James did not want to acknowledge that the ready-to-wear industry was helping couture into an early grave. He continued to devote himself to his art, spending several months to perfect a sleeve...'

James, an Anglo-American, started his career before the war, working in Chicago, London, Paris and New York. After the war, he settled in New York where he began to create fabulous gowns, constructed like sculptures with complex draperies, full skirts, elaborate panniers of tucked cloth. He boldly mixed satin with

Left: Evening dress by Victor Stiebel, 1952, with a full skirt and tight-fitted bodice and shaped bustline typical of the era.

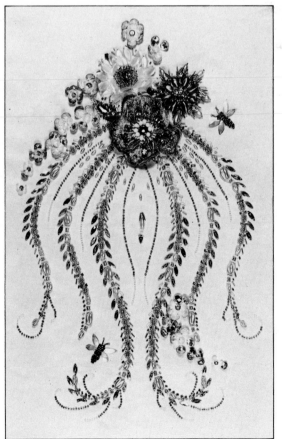

Left: Detail of the elaborate embroideries on the ball gown designed by Royal dressmaker Norman Hartnell for her Majesty Queen Elizabeth II's state visit to France in April 1957.

*Above: The virtuosity of designer Charles James is eloquently expressed in these spectacular evening dresses photographed in 1949 by Cecil Beaton.*
*Right: Charles James at work fitting a model. Photographed by Cecil Beaton in January 1948.*

velvet as in the spectacular clover-leaf skirted gown created for Mrs William Randolph Hearst Jr. for the Inaugural Ball of 1952. Eleanor Lambert, promoter of the Coty Awards and the Best Dressed List, conceded that 'Everyone in the fashion world agrees that Charlie was a genius.' But he was no businessman and his paranoia over the plagiarization of his designs led to costly lawsuits during the mid fifties in defence of his copyrights which broke him and effectively ended his career.

## 1950 – 1960
### New Directions

During the fifties there was no doubt that Paris ruled the world of fashion, though the autocratic and sometimes seemingly arbitrary nature of her rule attracted regular criticism. 'Coco' Chanel, returning to fashion in 1954, condemned the power of the couturiers to impose successive looks, shifting a hem or a waistline and making last season's clothes instantly démodé. Chanel was the advocate of continuity, of clothes in which a woman might feel at ease. Although her designs were in no way revolutionary, her classic style, shunning all extremes, was precisely the reason for her success in a world of rapidly changing looks. Chanel promoted a shorter length for cocktail and evening dresses and designed a charming series of short black lace cocktail dresses in the late fifties.

Although the trend for evening wear was moving away from the full-skirted romantic look of the early fifties towards a sleeker line, the trend with day dresses, suits and coats was towards a looser outline. In 1956 capes and bulbous, enveloping coats were prominent in the collections. Nineteen fifty-seven was the year of the sack and also the year in which sleeves became looser, shoulders more rounded and dresses bulbous around the hips. By 1959 the balloon look was consolidated in puff-ball skirts and in the 'suspense-jupe', its fullness constricted at the knee.

Big, rounded, sloping shoulders on coats and jackets, wide, wide necklines with stand-up or roll collars and bold, deceptively simple seaming created a new, highly stylized look that bore little relation to the female form. These new proportions were emphasized and exaggerated by the newly-fashionable stiletto-heeled, finely pointed shoes.

The prominent new materials included overblown tartans, tweeds and hound's tooth checks, plain, smooth wools, often in flame orange, red or yellow with broad welted seams and a few giant buttons. Pierre Cardin made his mark during this period with the superb confidence of his cutting. It was not until the mid sixties, however, that he widened his field and gave free rein to his creative abilities.

Around 1960 beading enjoyed a renewed popularity, decorating the bod-

*Far left: Evening dress designed by Pierre Balmain from his autumn 1961 collection. Photographed by John French.*
*Left: Evening dress from Nina Ricci. Early sixties. Photographed by John French.*

*Right: André Courrèges breathed new life into Paris fashions with his fresh, youthful, and thoroughly up-to-date 'Space Age' collections. Day suit from his most forceful collection spring 1965.*
*Below: André Courrèges in his clinically white salon. Photographed in 1968.*

ices of slim evening dresses. Around this date also hair enjoyed a return to prominence. Worn close to the head for over a decade, hair was now piled on the head or worn loose. By the mid sixties this was to reach its apogee in the back-combed, tawny mane as sported by Pop-cult heroine 'Baby' Jane Holzer.

## Courrèges

The youthful undercurrent which became so potent as a fashion force in the sixties demanded a new direction from Paris couture and the first to respond with a revolutionary new style was André Courrèges whose collections of 1964 and the following year introduced a 'space-age' look for a new woman, the woman who '. . . wants to work, travel, even run . . . we are experimenting to find a new way of dressing which fits the age.' Courrèges had enjoyed an apprenticeship chez Balenciaga since 1950 and when he opened his own salon in 1961 in the avenue Kléber.

By the spring of 1964, however, he had found his own formula and was ready to launch his dynamic new ideas. In this and the following two collections he made what he described as 'my strong statements', his spring '65 collection being his most perfect, and most publicized. When his tanned athletic models came bounding into his clinically white salon to the sound of jungle music those present could be in no doubt that they were witnessing a turnabout as significant as Dior's New Look of 1947.

The Courrèges style was architectural, with skirts and dresses crisply cut in white or pastel fabrics, a favourite being double-sided wool/cotton gabardine. He lifted skirts above the knee, proposed white leather flat-heeled boots, white plastic goggles and space-helmet hats and designed trousers for every occasion. 'The engineer of clothes', 'the Le Corbusier of the Paris couture' was internationally plagiarized and decided not to show in autumn '65, devoting himself instead to the problems of manufacturing his designs for international ready-to-wear distribution. He returned to the seasonal showings in 1967, but was never again to capture the headlines as he had in his eighteen months as a trail-blazer.

## Ungaro

Following in Courrèges' footsteps came a second advocate of the crisp, pared-down look, Emmanuel Ungaro. The Italian-born Ungaro had taken Courrèges' place in the house of Balenciaga, then spent a season with Courrèges before his first show in 1965. The cut was similar to that of Courrèges, both designers having learned Bal-

*Emmanuel Ungaro rose to fame with a crisp tailored look. By the late sixties he was more open to experiment with remarkable designs which were an amalgam of clothing and body jewellery. This design is from 1969.*

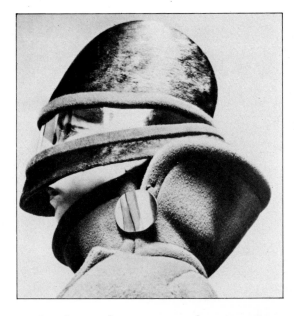

enciaga's perfect sense of proportions. Ungaro showed short, trapeze skirts, folding back to reveal shorts in fabrics designed by his close collaborator Sonja Knapp, vivid clashing stripes and abstract splashes of colour. After his first impact with couture, Ungaro based his commercial success on his 'Ungaro Parallèle' ready-to-wear range launched in 1968.

## Cardin

Pierre Cardin, a dynamic businessman who has succeeded in selling his designs in Russia, came to prominence in the mid sixties. He is credited with reinventing the bias cut and displayed his mastery of this and other skills in the gorgeous evening dresses which were his forte. Pastel chiffon creations trimmed with feathers or beaded at collar and hem, tight sunray pleats flaring out from the neck, asymmetrical cuts baring a shoulder, dipping hems, tight, shimmering sequined sheaths won Cardin deserved acclaim. Bursting with ideas, anxious to add his personal piquant to the space-age idiom, Cardin made brief tunics or skirts over knitted

*Above left: Pierre Cardin was responsible for a number of designs in a futuristic, 'Space Age' style in the late sixties, Above: Cardin has also proved his mastery in such classic designs as this, photographed in 1970.*

body suits; he used metal, shiny vinyl and giant zippers to give a modern, functional look to clean-cut shapes. At the height of the space fad his models wore helmets with perspex viewing slits, vinyl skull caps and visors, but these were mere gimmicks and should not be allowed to overshadow Cardin's ability to cut cloth with unerring confidence. Cardin is perhaps the most versatile of the Paris couturiers. His talent as a designer has expanded well beyond the realm of couture and successfully embraced both industrial and domestic design.

## Rabanne

Only the sixties, the decade of extremes, could have launched Paco Rabanne, quoted in a 1967 interview in *Life* as claiming, 'My swimsuits are not for bathing. My dresses are not for sitting in. Shoes, if I did them now, wouldn't be for walking.' Rabanne, a Spaniard trained as an architect, rose to instant fame with his first Paris collection in the spring of 1966. There is no denying the impact of his designs. Provocative, timely, aggressively new and epitomizing the futuristic fantasies of the era, they attracted international attention, though few could find occasion to wear them. Rabanne's materials were metal and plastic, cut into discs or small plaques and linked with wire. He similarly used leather in silver or sharp, flourescent colours. Perhaps the most wearable of his designs were his evening dresses in plaques of transparent rhodoid decorated with ostrich feathers. Rabanne's keenest admirers were surely the photographers who exploited the shock value of his creations in a neophiliac age which nourished itself on visual imagery. Salvador Dali thought fit to pose coloured model Donyale Luna in Rabanne's shimmering metal.

## Italian Fashion

The success of Italian couture in the six-

*Above: The exotic model Donyale Luna as posed by Salvador Dali in a late sixties metal dress by designer Paco Rabanne. Above right: Paco Rabanne, one of the most original talents to emerge in the world of late sixties fashion.*

ties was based on a stylish pursuit of luxury and elegance. The trim, tailored, easy day clothes pioneered by Courrèges were elegantly reinterpreted in the Italian collections by Mila Schön, Valentino and others. The Italian forte, however, was in the sumptuous fabrics, embroideries and extravagancies of evening wear and the bold colourful fabrics typified by Emilio Pucci. Federico Forquet used sophisticated Op Art stripes and patterns, 'dynamic geometric prints and colour combinations like Neapolitan ice creams.'

―――――― 1960 – 1970 ――――――
## The Youth Explosion

When David Bailey published his 'saraband for the sixties', *Goodbye Baby and Amen*, he bid farewell to a decade of youthful, irreverent upheaval in social life and in fashion in which he had been both chronicler and archetypal anti-hero. Much of the momentum of youth's counter-culture had come from America, the cradle of consumerism. From the United States came rock 'n' roll, a new slang, new heroes and, of course, blue jeans. But the explosion of this culture was centred in 'Swinging London', focal point of the frenetic imagery of the sixties.

The fifties had been a poor decade for young fashions. An expanding potential market yearned to emulate the casual style of film or music idols but was inadequately catered for. The beatnik look was

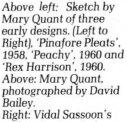

*Above left: Sketch by Mary Quant of three early designs. (Left to Right), 'Pinafore Pleats', 1958, 'Peachy', 1960 and 'Rex Harrison', 1960.*
*Above: Mary Quant, photographed by David Bailey.*
*Right: Vidal Sassoon's mid sixties '5-point' cut.*

Left: 'New RCA talent',
Ossie Clark, aged twenty-
three, with Chrissie
Shrimpton modelling his
1965 'Op Art' quilted silk
coat.
Above: Sketch for a zip-
up, hooded mini-dress by
Barbara Hulanicki for
Biba.

an ugly anti-fashion protest from a young, self-conscious intelligentsia.

## London Boutique Styles

Changes were on their way. As early as 1948, the Royal College of Art in London had founded a fashion design course under Madge Garland. Mary Quant came on the scene in 1955 and a year later John Stephen opened his first, pre-Carnaby Street shop. Mary Quant found the right formula, fun and above all inexpensive, to appeal to the young market. In 1963 she set up her Ginger Group to market her designs on a wider basis. Quant, whose name is now more closely associated with cosmetics than with fashion, is credited with the popularization, if not the invention, of the mini-skirt.

London in the mid sixties became the city of boutiques. Biba was perhaps the most representative and seemingly the most successful, growing from a mail order offer in 1964 of a gingham dress and scarf for twenty-five shillings. It was the brain child of fashion illustrator Barbara Hulanicki, who opened her first Abingdon Road Biba shop to sell cheap, well-designed young fashion. Granny Takes a Trip symbolized the more esoteric extremes of boutique-land; situated at the World's End, Chelsea, with at one time a gaudily-painted car bursting through its window, its name and atmosphere heavily redolent of hippie drug-culture, the boutique sold above all an idea. Ossie Clark, one of the bright young stars of the Royal College of Art, opened his Quorum boutique in the mid sixties, starting in the Op Art idiom and moving to a softer look with

*Opposite: Late seventies poster for the Milan-based fashion firm Fiorucci. Fiorucci have preserved the freshness and vitality of Pop through the seventies. Above: Pop fashions published in Nova, May 1970. The satin jacket and 'Elvis' waistcoat were designed by Mike Rogers for Mr Freedom.*

*Above: Rudi Gernreich's 'Thong' swimsuit, 1974. Photographed on models Lisa Taylor and Jerry Hall in Miami by Helmut Newton.*
*Right: The late sixties 'ethnic' fashion as worn by model Kelly.*

satins and the light printed fabrics of his partner Celia Birtwell.

Fashion and Pop Art came together in the Mr. Freedom boutique opened in 1969 by Tommy Roberts. His Pop colours, bright reds, acid blues, gaudy satins, Pop symbols of comic-strip space-rockets or cartoon characters enjoyed a brief but significant success. A more lasting success has been that of Elio Fiorucci, a Milan cobbler's son, whose name today is synonymous with a gaudy but chic Pop style of dressing. Skin-tight trousers, shiny fabrics, animal skin prints and brash colours are his hallmark.

The incursion of youth gave a new freedom to fashion in more than one sense. The young demanded a new freedom for the body, discarding restrictive

undergarments and making increased bareness acceptable, notably for beachwear. American designer Rudi Gernreich proposed the first topless swimsuit in 1964. In 1972 the miniscule G-string became fashionable on the permissive beaches of Saint. Tropez and was publicized internationally.

Most significantly, the young demanded a freedom of choice and encouraged an anti-fashion, anything-goes look described by Tom Wolfe as Funky Chic and first noticed by him '. . . one night in October 1969 in London in a club called Arethusa . . . only the waiters wear white shirts and black ties. The clientèle sit there roaring and gurgling . . . in a rout of leather jerkins, Hindu tunics, buckskin skirts, deerslayer boots, duelling shirts, bandanas

*Above: Portrait by Beaton of couturier Yves Saint Laurent, perhaps the most influential figure in fashion through the late sixties and seventies.*
*Left: Yves Saint Laurent's 1969 version of the mini with thigh-high ocelot-trimmed boots.*

*Exotic model Verushka collaborated with Franco Rubartelli to create some of the most exciting fashion spreads of the late sixties, notably for Paris Vogue, Queen and the Daily Telegraph Magazine. From a series published in the Telegraph, June 1968.*

*The return to romantic, exotic fashions in the late sixties exemplified in a 1969 design from the house of Dior.*

knotted at the Adam's apple, love beads dangling to the belly, turtlenecks reaching up to meet the muttonchops at midjowl, Indian blouses worn thin and raggy . . .'

The ethnic looks pinpointed by Wolfe had their roots in the hippie sub-culture and in a reaction to the cold space-age look promoted by Courrèges. The young demanded the option of fantasy in fashion.

In England the ethnic cult had been greatly promoted by the pilgrimage of the Beatles to the supposed mystic revelations of an Indian guru. The romantic reaction to the crisp space-age and brash young fashions of the mid sixties was spearheaded by two of the most talented products of art college fashion courses. Bill Gibb, trained at St. Martin's College of Art and set up a business in 1968. Zandra Rhodes, trained at the Royal College of

Art, started her career as a textile designer and began to design professionally in 1968-9. Both had a strong feel for pattern and fabric and brought a new softness and richness to English fashion. Bill Gibb trimmed evening dresses with feathers and fur, Zandra Rhodes described her creations in 1970 as 'dream clothes'.

This exotic mood of the late sixties was exemplified by the model Verushka who teamed up with photographer Franco Rubartelli to produce the most exciting fashion spreads of the day, notably for Paris *Vogue's* 'Jungle Look' issue of July/August 1968 and for *Queen* and the *Telegraph Magazine* in England.

### Yves Saint-Laurent

The need for the exotic, for fantasy, for romance and above all for variety in fashion was perhaps best understood by

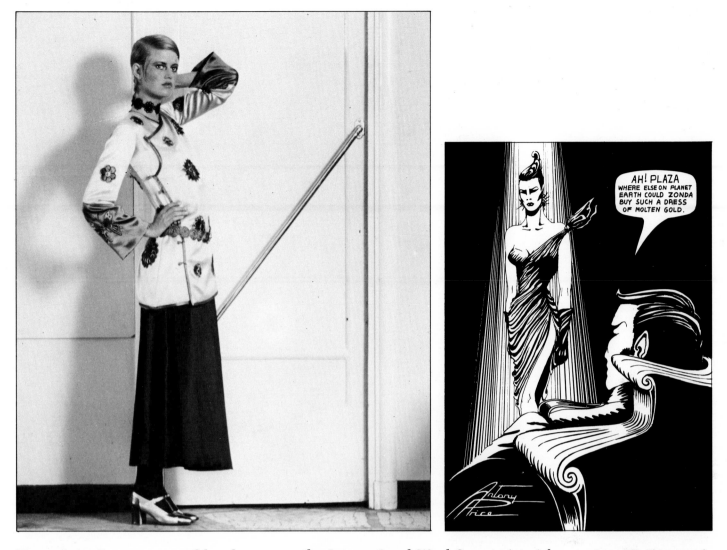

Yves Saint-Laurent, possibly the most important contemporary couturier/ designer. The Saint-Laurent style is sophisticated and eclectic, at times supremely practical, at others fabulously rich and theatrical. Saint-Laurent is a designer of considerable culture and the wide variety of styles in his designs is matched by the eclecticism of his taste in the furnishing and decoration of his Paris home. His passion for the theatre can be seen in the magical touch, the *imprévu* of his glamorous and extraordinary creations for evening wear. His ventures into theatrical design include costumes for a lavish revue for the Casino de Paris in the best traditions of Bakst's designs for *Schéhérazade*.

Yves Saint-Laurent's talent first won recognition with a first prize in a fashion design competition organized in 1953 by the International Wool Secretariat. Adopted by Dior, the young Saint-Laurent was soon to take on the most prestigious job in Paris couture, designing the entire spring 1958 Dior collection after the master's death the previous year. His most significant collection chez Dior was the 'Beat' collection of 1960 in which he took his ideas from young Left Bank trends - pale make-up, leather suits and plenty of black.

Escaping the restrictions of the Dior organization, Saint-Laurent launched his own couture house in the rue Spontini in 1962. The first couturier to take his ready-to-wear collections more seriously than his haute couture he regarded the popularization of his ideas not as a compromise but as a challenge. The original Rive Gauche boutique was opened in 1966 and within ten years there were over a

*Above left: Chinese-style, embroidered satin tunic jacket from Yves Saint Laurent's collection for autumn 1970.*

*Above: Advertisement for Plaza, the London shop of designer Anthony Price, an influential figure with a small but impressive clientèle, 1979.*

*Opposite: Yuki demonstrates his flair for draping and pleating fabrics in the skirt of this outfit, photographed by Lorenz Zatecky.*

*Right and far right: Claude Montana emerged in the late seventies as one of the new young stars of Paris fashion. His style was dramatic, somewhat sinister and featured exaggerated broad shoulders, as in these leather coats from his autumn 1979 collection.*

hundred others throughout the world.

Saint-Laurent's fashion message is for freedom and variety, for practicality where necessary, but for luxury where possible. His collections are pot-pourris of ideas, some presented with tongue-in-cheek, which have enlarged the scope of fashion. In 1966 he made the first dresses on Pop Art themes; in 1968 he caused a sensation with his see-through evening dress in sheer black chiffon and ostrich feathers. His important contributions to fashion include the pea jacket of 1962, the safari suit, seductive black, tailored trouser suits for evenings but, above all, the various 'ethnic' looks which provide him

with the opportunity to indulge his love of opulent combinations of colour and texture. Thanks to Saint-Laurent, from the late sixties a woman could freely adopt the colourful styles of Cossack, Turk, Arab, Mandarin, Spanish dancer or Ukrainian peasant.

———————— 1970 – Present ————————

**Ready to Wear and the American Look**
During the seventies the ready-to-wear industry attracted designers of considerable talent. In Paris, Karl Lagerfeld, designing primarily under the Chlöe label, has emerged as one of the most gifted. Full of ideas, he has remained hard to

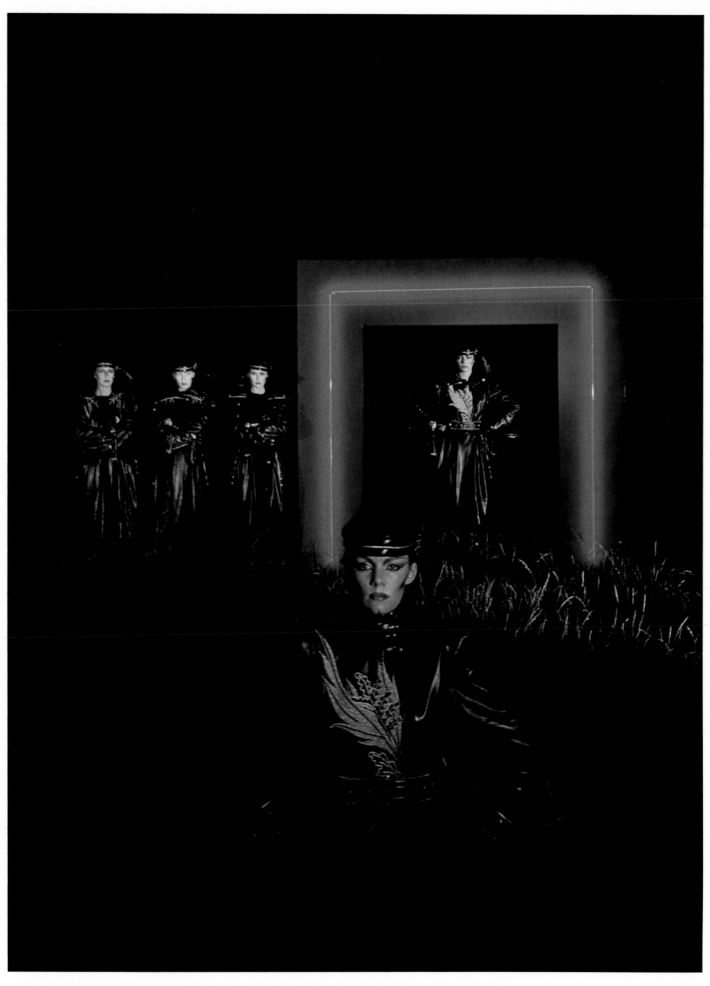

Sleek and aggressive, a certain facet of the late seventies was well expressed in a range of clothes designed in 1976 under the pseudonym 'Miss Mouse' by Rea Spencer Cullen. This skin-tight evening bodysuit is in shiny black ciré trimmed with pink maribou feathers.

define, believing that a designer should not impose an identifiable style or restrictive formula. Kenzo Takada, designing under the Jap label, has been consistently inventive. New names to emerge in the late seventies in Paris ready-to-wear include, most notably, Claude Montana and Thierry Mugler. Both have successfully promoted a broad-shouldered look, Montana cutting magnificent coats, jackets and taper-trousered suits in soft, often bright-coloured leathers, Mugler promoting the same silhouette in a variety of shimmering fabrics. In spring 1979 Mugler created a stunning, sequinned, skin-tight body suit with pointed fins running up the length of the sleeves, a space-heroine look, but tougher, sleeker, more sophisti-

cated than the space-age styles of the sixties.

In England this same look had been promoted since the early seventies by designer Anthony Price, though it did not find acceptance until the second half of the decade, adopting certain elements from the aggressive Punk style. In autumn 1976 Rea Spencer Cullen, working under the pseudonym Miss Mouse, designed a timely collection of fantasy clothes in pink and black skin-tight ciré, wide shouldered and subversive. Punk inspired notable eccentricities in make-up and hair-styling, and fashion caught up with the extraordinary hair-colours and war-paint that Zandra Rhodes had been sporting for years. London hairdresser Heinz Schummi pro-

*Above left: Punk haircut by Heinz Schummi as published in Ritz, May 1978 in an advertisement for his salon.*
*Above: Punk dress by Zandra Rhodes, silk jersey and safety pins, 1977.*

moted spiked 'electric shock' cuts. Punk heroine Jordan attracted considerable publicity in 1978 for her bizarre asymmetrical make-up, whilst the most daring, or misguided, had their hair dyed in fluorescent colours or patterned like wild animal skins.

In 1977 Zandra Rhodes made news with her sophisticated interpretation of the Punk look, creating a series of dresses in black and pink silk jerseys with slashes and tears held together by chains and jewelled safety-pins.

London-based, Japanese-born designer Yuki has earned a reputation as a talented designer in a more traditional mould. Trained with Cardin, he is a master of pleating and draping and has brought an echo of couture elegance to ready-to-wear fashions. Another Japanese-born designer,

*Above left: 'Sleeping Bag Coat', designed by Norma Kamali for her New York shop 'O.M.O.' ('On My Own), 1979.*
*Above: Outfit designed by Halston and inspired by the Playboy costume. Photographed in 1975 by Helmut Newton.*

*Outfit by Calvin Klein from his spring 1980 collection. Cotton knit sweater-jacket, cream crêpe de chine silk blouse, and linen trousers.*

Issey Mujake, has achieved an international reputation through the seventies with stylish, easy-to-wear clothes, their elegance and sense of style rooted in Japanese tradition.

From America during the seventies came the cult for fitness and it became more typical for the newer stars to be photographed in running shorts than in glamorous evening wear. The new look was described by *Time* magazine in 1976 as 'cleanly functional, fluid, soft, supple, sexy and unstuffy.' A *Vogue* editor called it 'the effortless look.' These American clothes were easy to wear, emphasizing the body, yet leaving it free to move, using plain, strong colours in easily mixed ranges. American *Vogue* of the late seventies was full of cool tunic dresses over trousers, slit dresses and light wrap skirts, leotards and body suits. Halston is the best known of this generation of designers, the first to make his mark, selling his label in 1973 to Norton Simon for twelve million dollars. His clientèle has included Marisa Berenson, Mrs Gianni Agnelli, Raquel Welch and Jacqueline Onassis. Other designers of note include Geoffrey Beene, Bill Blass Ralph Lauren, and the *enfant chéri* of American fashion and master of the new easy styles, Calvin Klein. Norma Kamali is an inventive individualist who specializes in synthetic stretch fabrics and has helped transform 'bodywear (into) a whole new way of dressing.' The strong international influence which these American designers enjoyed towards the close of the seventies has inspired the prediction that theirs would be the look of the eighties.

# INDUSTRIAL DESIGN

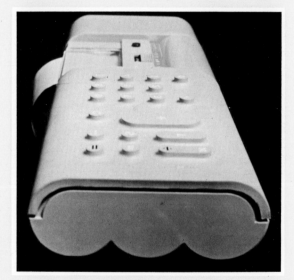

*'Divisumma 18' adding machine designed for
Olivetti by a team led by Mario Bellini, 1973.
ABS plastic and rubber.*

——————1940 – Present——————
## The Role of Consumerism

INDUSTRIAL DESIGNERS have been aptly dubbed 'The Practical Idealists'. The description was coined by John and Avril Blake as the title of their 1969 twenty-five year retrospective of the work of the Design Research Unit and expresses the twin talents required of those designers, many of whom remain anonymous, who help shape the urban and domestic environments of our world.

Ours is an age in which the mass-produced has finally asserted its supremacy over the individually hand-wrought; the crafts, though far from dead and, indeed, enjoying a strong revival in many areas, are nonetheless kept alive as a minority luxury and for their symbolic values. The appearance of our environment, the nature of the objects which surround us, reflect the inexorable progress of industrialization. The story of design in the twentieth century is very much the story of the resolution of conflicts in the relationships between art and design and industry.

The history of these conflicts is well documented in Nikolaus Pevsner's *Pioneers of Modern Design*. It is only since the Second World War, however, that consumerism has really taken root as a way of life, though by 1980 the image of a wish-fulfillment world of consumer-oriented production has already lost much of the gloss which it certainly had in the fifties to a generation emerging from the austerity of war.

Looking back on the fifties as the beginnings of a golden age of consumerism, artist Richard Hamilton, whose own work is littered with the symbols of industrialization, made the following remarks, 'The 1950's have seen many changes in the human situation; not least among them are the new attitudes towards those commodities which affect most directly the individual way of life – consumer goods. It is now accepted that saucepans, refrigerators, cars, vacuum cleaners, suitcases, radios, washing machines – all the paraphernalia of mid-century existence – should be designed by a specialist in the look of things. . . William Morris and Walter Gropius realized the potential. What is new is the increased number of exponents, their power and influence upon our economic and cultural life. Design is established and training for the profession is widespread.'

Hamilton was well justified in emphasizing the two sides of the story of design for mass-production – both the appetite, affluence of the consumer market, and the increasing emphasis on specific training for the industrial sector as a major area of design creativity. A report published in 1937 by the Council for Art and Industry on 'Design and the Designer in Industry' underlined as key factors slowing the improvement of design standards in industry the low status accorded to product designers within manufacturing companies, their often inadequate training and the blindness of many manufacturers to the sales efficacy of good product design and brand image, assuming rather grandly, like Sir Kenneth Clark that 'on the whole the public prefers ugly objects.'

Industrial and commercial design has become an increasingly important feature of art college and technical college curricula and the Contemporary period has witnessed a considerable expansion of the role and activities of freelance design groups. The 1937 report already cited emphasized the value of the consultant designer, 'The fresh mind of these craftsmen and artists and their experience in other and freer fields may bring to industry a revelation and an inspiration not otherwise obtainable.' While most in-house designers, as members of a team with a corporate identity or, for that matter, most members of freelance design groups, rarely achieve wide personal rec-

*Right: Project for a motor car by leading American industrial designer Raymond Loewy, 1950. Above: The Queen's Award emblem symbolizing Royal recognition of export achievement and technological innovation.*

ognition, subordinating their own images to the images of the products on which they work, a few notable talents have achieved reputations outside their specialized circles, either by sheer force of talent, their personal flamboyance, or their polemical activities.

Perhaps the best known of all industrial designers of the contemporary period, although he was already successful before the war, is American Raymond Loewy, a talented man with a tremendous sense of style and a shrewd ability to put into words the problems and demands of his chosen profession.

In 1979 Loewy celebrated fifty years of work in industrial design and published a survey of his career littered with pithy comments which suggest he would have been as good a copywriter as he was a designer. He started in the twenties from the simple maxim which he printed on a card and sent to everyone he knew that 'Between two products equal in price, function, and quality, the better looking will outsell the other'. Loewy was a key

influence in shaping the glamourous styles of the American consumer products which seemed so magical to post-war Europe.

In his survey, entitled simply *Industrial Design*, Loewy wrote of the fifties, 'By this time the principles of industrial design and the efficacity of a concern for both aesthetics and function were well established. No firm of any size or sophistication in the United States was unaware of them or could do without them.'

## Design for Mass-Production
With a few notable exceptions, such as Raymond Loewy, industrial designers are the unsung heroes of modern design, wielding an enormous influence on our environment. In the tidal wave of post-war consumerism, certainly, there has been a good deal of shoddy thinking and manufacture. The post-war decades have, nonetheless, seen the increasing application of sophisticated standards to the creation of designs for mass-production and to the training of designers for the task.

The most tangible symbols of industrial

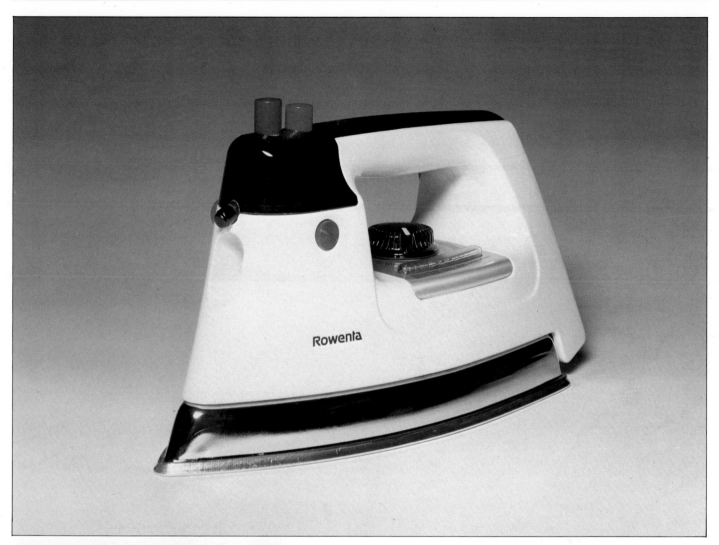

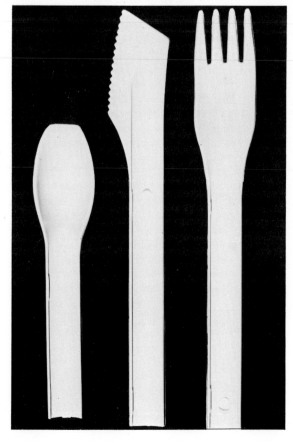

design progress are the everyday items of hardware on which we have come to depend. The motor car industry is a foremost example of a manufacturing area strongly dependent on design image. Much thought has gone, similarly, into design for other forms of transport, especially airplane design and its related areas, including airport and in-flight utility-ware design. Clever packaging transformed the Vespa scooter into a status symbol of youth. The lesson so clearly demonstrated is that style in itself fulfills a function and serviceability alone is not always an adequate selling point. Considerable care has also gone into the design of hardware for domestic and personal use. The list of product types involved is a long one and must include kitchen equipment; from refrigerator to

*Above: Steam iron designed and manufactured in the late seventies by the German firm Rowenta.*
*Left: Seventies disposable white plastic cutlery designed by the Studio Joe Columbo for Alitalia.*

electric kettle, entertainment equipment, televisions, tape or record decks and every kind of appliance from hair-dryer to steam-iron, instant camera to pocket calculator. Equal attention has been given to the designing of hardware for the work situation, from duplicating machine to filing trolley, machine tools to typewriters.

## Europe

The co-operative approach encouraged by a team such as the D. R. U. in England has found considerable favour in the Scandinavian countries in the Contemporary era. Though by no means heavily industrialized, the Scandinavian countries — especially Denmark, Finland and — Sweden have made a strong mark with their manufactures in the international markets by their high standards of design and execution, the fruit of collective efforts to uphold demanding, self-imposed principles. In Finland Ornamo, in Sweden the Svenska Slöjdföreningen and in Denmark the Society of Arts and Crafts and Industrial Design helped set and maintain the highly competitive standards of contemporary Scandinavian design and manufacture.

In other European countries, in Germany and Italy in particular, product design leadership is most frequently associated with specific, pace-setting companies. In the case of the former no one company better symbolizes the achievement of international respect and commercial success through design consciousness than the Frankfurt-based electrical goods manufacturers Braun A.G.

The Braun design programme was a practical application of the ideals of the Modern Movement. From the mid-fifties it won international acclaim for the firm and, from 1958, the accolade of a permanent exhibition of a range of Braun products at New York's Museum of Modern Art. It was Dr Fritz Eichler who, with Arthur and Erwin Braun, brought to the

*The German electrical goods manufacturers Braun have achieved international respect for their high design standards.*
*Right: 'TFG 2 Cylindric' table lighter designed in 1969.*

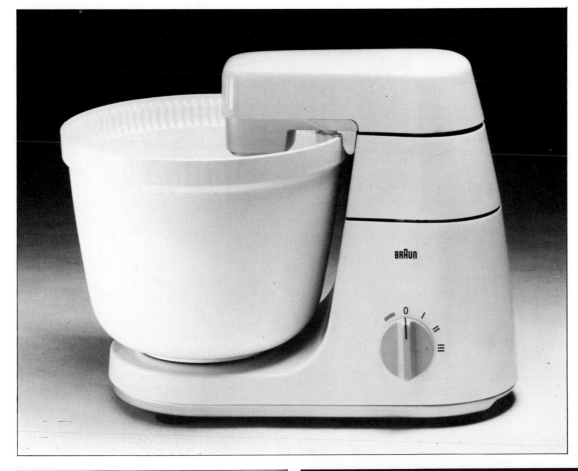

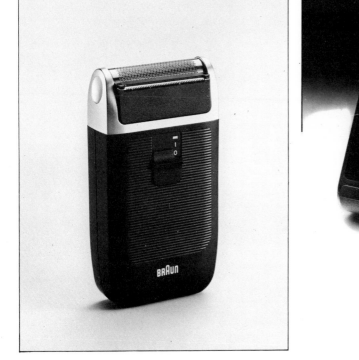

Left: Braun food mixer
'KM 3' designed in 1957.
A good, early example of
the firm's developing
house style of sleek-
packaged electrics.
Bottom left: Braun
'Sixtant 8008' electric
razor, designed in 1974.
Below: Braun digital
clock.

company the ideology of the Hochschule für Gestaltung at Ulm. He enlisted Hans Gugelot as designer in 1954 and Dieter Rams as head of the design team in 1955 to translate principles into products. Rams, above all, has been responsible for the rigidly disciplined style now so strongly associated with Braun – a style in which the mechanics are always well-concealed, their presence merely implied by the clinical, strictly geometric lines of the casing – a hard and uncompromising minimalist aesthetic.

### United Kingdom

If the British government involvement in industrial design has been exemplary by international standards, design development in Britain has been slowed all too often by the caution and conservatism of manufacturers in the styling and packaging of their products. On the other hand the strength of industrial design in Germany, the United States, Italy, and as far afield as Japan has been in the adventurous attitudes of manufacturers, their open-minded approach to the marketing situation and their appreciation of the commercial value of design both sound and appealing.

It is fitting that Britain should have so strong an official lead in industrial design, for it has perhaps a longer history than any other country of concern for the design problems of the machine age. Among the important landmarks in the

pre-war years had been the appointment in 1931 by the Board of Trade of a Committee on Art and Industry under Lord Gorell which, the following year, submitted a report on art and education. In 1934 the Board of Trade set up the Council for Art and Industry with Frank Pick as chairman. Ten years later the more effective Council of Industrial Design came into being. The opening of the Design Centre in 1956, the institution of Design Centre Awards in 1957 and of the coveted Queen's Awards to Industry in 1965 each permitting the use of a graphic symbol which has come to be regarded as a seal of approval, are symptomatic features of a healthy official involvement.

The Design Research Unit, first formulated in 1942 by Herbert Read, Misha Black, Marcus Brumwell and Milner Gray, was a pioneering British experiment in design consultancy work, larger in scope than any comparable body in Europe.

Gray and Black had been collaborating since 1934, and in 1935 were founder members of the Industrial Design Partnership. Black was to be an influential figure in a variety of roles which included the post of professor of Industrial Design at the Royal College of Art. The Industrial Design Partnership was to set a pattern for the more ambitious D.R.U. An early pamphlet explained the Unit's aims, 'Like every aspect of modern industry, design

*Below: Station interior for the Hong Kong underground railway, designed by the Design Research Unit.*
*Below right: Public area on the P & O liner 'Oriana', designed by the DRU in 1959.*

The Franco-British, supersonic jet 'Concorde' streaks elegantly through the sky as a superb example of industrial design and as a symbol, albeit a costly one, of the technological age and of Franco-British collaboration. The Air France Concorde made its inaugural flight from Paris to Rio de Janeiro in 1976.

should be a co-operative activity, and the function of D.R.U. is to focus on every project it undertakes the combined knowledge and experience of several creative minds since it believes that only by pooling the talents of a team of designers is it possible to offer a service capable of meeting every demand from the wide and varied field of present-day industry.'

Amongst the many projects undertaken by the D.R.U. the mention of just a few key works provides ample evidence of the industrial design team's versatility and potential. D.R.U., in association with Sir Hugh Casson and architect Michael Rosenauer, worked on the prestigious Time & Life building, opened in 1952. In 1959 the Unit designed the public areas of the P & O ship *Oriana*; in 1956 D.R.U. undertook one of its most complex programmes, the complete renewal of British Rail's corporate identity.

## Aircraft Design

More dramatic than any developments in ground transport has been the refinement of aircraft design in recent decades and, of course, the evolution of space vehicles of a functional but potently symbolic beauty. A significant step forward was made with the advent in 1955 of the Boeing 707, designed by the Boeing team in collaboration with Walter Dorwin Teague Associates. This plane heralded the arrival of regular international jet travel. A 707 with sleek body painting by Raymond Loewy became a stylish U.S. Air Force 1, the Presidential plane. Loewy played an important role as design consultant to N.A.S.A. His team was invited in 1967 to propose interior schemes 'to help insure the psycho-physiological safety and comfort of the astronauts.'

Anglo-French co-operation led to the exploration of a new phase in international air travel, the supersonic era, with the successful development of the 'Concorde', an airplane of considerable beauty,

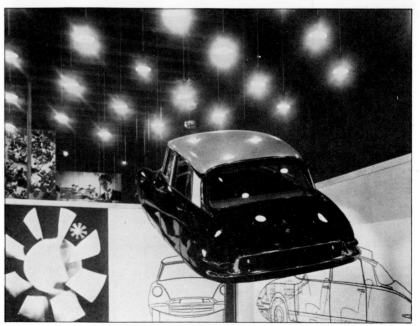

*Right: The Citroën 'D.S.19' on show at the 1957 Milan Triennale. The car soon acquired the nickname 'Déesse', French for 'goddess'.*

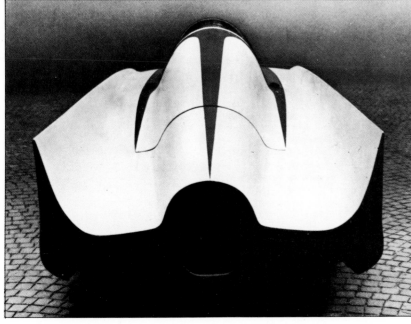

with its long, tapering nose, sleek body and swept-back wings expressing in every line its speed and power – industrial design at its most sophisticated and the fruit of government sponsorship of design research.

## Automobile Design

Germany has had an especially influential motor-car designer in the person of Ferdinand Porsche. His early triumph was the classic Volkswagen of 1936, the sound design of which has assured its lasting popularity with only minor modifications through the post-war decades. The aerodynamic silhouette of the V.W. was adapted by Porsche in the luxury high performance cars which bear his name and which developed from the Model 356 launched in 1952 with the sleek bodywork designed by Erwin Kommenda. The pared-down refinement of the Porsche and the honest good-sense of the V.W. have demonstrated the ability of rationalized, functionalist designs to transcend fashions in styling.

The French motor-car manufacturing company Citroën has developed a reputation for good design, combining practicality and performance with a distinctive but unfussy approach to body styling. The company's classic designs are the 2CV, designed in 1939 and launched in 1946, and comparable in many respects with the V.W. and, most notably, the D.S.19, which has been described as '. . . one of the celebrated pieces of modern industrial design, a masterly combination of visual flair and mechanical ingenuity.' Designed in 1955, the D.S. went into production in 1957 in which year it was presented at the Milan Triennale, without wheels, suspended in mid-air so as to effectively emphasize its aerodynamic beauty.

While American motor cars, with their exaggerated chrome trims, elaborate fins and fenders, were the most eye-catching cars in the post-war years, symbols of the

*Above:The 'E-type' Jaguar. Launched in 1961, this car was destined to become a symbol of the sixties, with its long thrusting curves expressing the energy of that era.*
*Left: 'Nibbio 2' racing car designed by Karmen Ghia of Turin. Silver and red. Illustrated in the survey of 1957 'Forme Nuove in Italia'.*

*Right: The 'Sovereign' pocket calculator designed for the British firm Sinclair Radionics Ltd by a team led by John Pemberton. The casing shown is of satin finish stainless steel.*

consumerism in the United States, European designers evolved body styles based on more practical criteria and created more lasting standards. The Italians, with such talented designers as Pinin Farina and Karmen Ghia, have brought a distinctive blend of sophistication and sound design sense to the creation of motor-car bodies. Perhaps the most influential British figure in contemporary motor-car design has been Sir Alex Issigonis, if only for his revolutionary 'Mini' of 1959. The most richly symbolic British car of the post-war years, however, is surely the 'E-type' Jaguar, its swollen, forward-surging curves expressing the vitality of the sixties dream.

## Corporations and Design

The diversity of the industrial designer's task in our present highly-industrialized world is truly phenomenal and, perhaps more than any other designer, he has the power to influence greatly the quality of life. Numerous corporations have realized their responsibility in this direction and their design programmes are far more than a sales-catching gimmick. In fact, many of the finest examples of industrial design survive beyond the whims of fashion and are outmoded more by technological than stylistic evolution.

An exemplary case is that of the Italian company Olivetti which has branched out from its original exclusive manufacture of typewriters into a wide area of electronic equipment, showing always a concern for the work situation both of its own staff and for those who use its products. A major retrospective exhibition 'Design Process – Olivetti 1908-1978', held in 1979 at the Frederick S. Wright Art Gallery, University of California, gave opportunity to survey the achievements of the firm. The drive towards Olivetti's strong image in the contemporary period came from Adriano Olivetti who had become executive director in 1933. Under his leadership Olivetti's design image has involved not only a meticulous concern for product design but has extended from architecture and graphics to every area of design on which a major industrial concern depends.

The list of designers who have worked for Olivetti is a roll-call of merit and includes some of Italy's foremost industrial designers, notably Mario Bellini, Ettore Sotsass and Marco Zanuso. Marcello Nizzoli was employed in 1936 to co-ordinate the development of new products and was responsible for several award-winning designs, including his Lexicon 80

Left: A pioneering exercise in typewriter casing design, the 'Lexicon 80' designed by Marcello Nizzoli for Olivetti in 1948.
Above: The '82 M' memory typewriter manufactured by IBM.

Top: The 'Lexicon 83 DL' typewriter designed for Olivetti by a team led by Mario Bellini, 1976. The design was amongst twenty-five selected in 1977 by Fortune magazine as the best examples of industrial design on the U.S. market.

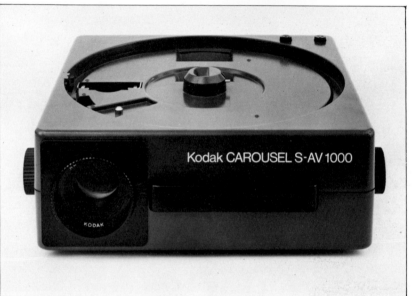

of 1948, a breakthrough in typewriter casing design, Lettera 22 of 1950, and Divissuma of 1956. The Los Angeles exhibition catalogue closed with a sleek design by Mario Bellini, an electronic typewriter designed in 1978 for the eighties.

The strong contemporary image of the American I.B.M. corporation was inspired by the desire to emulate and rival Olivetti, whose strong marketing was making incursions on home ground. Eliot Noyes was employed as design consultant and he succeeded in giving a recognizable and stylish look to the wide range of products manufactured by I.B.M. The example of one Italian firm, Pirelli, the rubber goods manufacturers, has clearly demonstrated that a forceful concern for image can make a household word of a company name whose products are surely less well-known than their advertising.

A hard drive combined with a high technical competence has given many Japanese industrial products a large slice of the international markets. In recent years, the Japanese have consolidated a reputation for competitively-priced, well-designed, quality goods and have made a speciality of miniaturization. Japanese motor cars, cameras and sound equipment have found an international market and the brand names of Toyota, Datsun, Pentax, Nikon, Minolta or Sony are as familiar in the West today as the names of our own products.

Miniaturization has been a notable trend through the seventies and research has evolved a new micro-technology which in turn has allowed new design possibilities. Electronic 'pocket' size calculators have become commonplace within the last decade, with designs

*Top left: The Polaroid 'SX-70' camera, launched in 1972.*
*Top right: The Pentax 'Spotmatic' SLR camera.*
*Above: The Kodak Caroussel projector, designed in 1964 by Reinhold Hacker and Hans Gugelot.*

shrinking down to the size of a credit card. Perhaps the most sophisticated pocket-calculator design and in itself a symbol of the micro-technology, was the 'Sovereign', by Sinclair Radionics Ltd. The soft-contoured satinized metal casing, rationalized key system and red display-panel combine to make this a classic of modern industrial design. Sinclair, winner in 1975 of the Queen's Award to Industry, has featured prominently in the British contribution to micro-technological research and has combined scientific progress with a concern for aesthetics.

## Photographic and Audio-Visual Design

One popular area of industrial design in which the major manufacturers have ben-

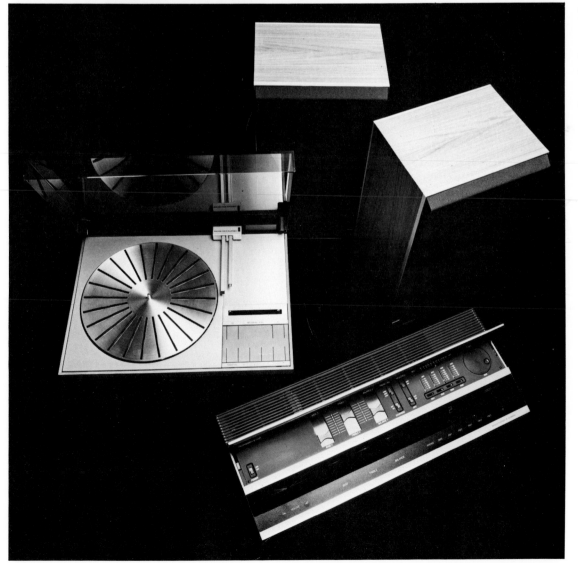

*Above: The 'C7' video unit launched by Sony in 1980. The style is one of aggressive, no-nonsense efficiency.*
*Left: Elegantly designed stereo equipment from the Danish firm Bang & Olufsen.*

*A 1954 Studebaker Commander.*
*The pursuit of style inspired the exaggerated, streamlined trim of American cars of the post-war years with functionalism becoming a justification rather than a genuine explanation. The prime function was to please the eye.*

efited from a trend towards miniaturization has been in the design of photographic equipment, especially in the amateur market. The Minox designed in 1937 by Walter Zapp was the precursor of today's pocket cameras, though it was the Kodak Instamatic 100 which, launched in 1963, heralded a new phase of popular photography. It is perhaps to be regretted that Eastman-Kodak, despite the easy recognizability of its logo and a pre-eminence ensured by the firm's historical priority in the market, has failed to create a distinctive house style for its equipment. The Polaroid corporation has dominated exclusively until recently this specialized area of the market and, with the launch in 1972 by Dr Land of his S X-70 camera, created an instant classic of design, compact, chic and distinctive in satin-finish steel and leather.

Televisions have become increasingly sophisticated and today's sleekest models bear little resemblance to the cumbersome cabinet designs of the fifties. Sound equipment has become equally sophisticated and designers have explored countless ways of packaging what are essentially the same technical components. International leader is the Danish firm Bang & Olufsen who have stated succinctly in their advertising that 'there are few secrets in today's technological world. The same components and materials are available to hi-fi designers throughout the industry. Yet

some products succeed while others fail. Perhaps it's a case of fulfilling promises on our part and accepting compromises on theirs.'

**Contemporary Taste and Design**

Well-designed manufactured goods often have a quality of rightness which somehow transcends fashion and it is certainly true that numerous designs have sold in virtually unchanged form through several decades. It would be wrong to assume, however, that there is an absolute rightness of design, and changing tastes can alter basic precepts.

In the post-war years, industrial design was dominated by glamourous American ideas of styling, a sleek, but essentially decorative look which paid lip-service to functionalism but was still seduced by the extremes of 'streamlining' which had developed in the thirties. The leading American industrial designers, Raymond Loewy, Walter Dorwin Teague and Henry Dreyfuss had built their reputations in the pre-war period and evolved their ideas to a style of which Loewy was perhaps the most gifted exponent and which came to symbolize a romantic image of American consumer culture.

These essentially ornamental concerns, American in origin and with chrome trims and curving contours as key features, were outmoded in the sixties by a new design ethos, epitomized in the minimal but

*Changing tastes inspire different approaches to similar problems. R.D. Russell's forties television cabinet, coyly disguised as a piece of furniture, contrasts with Zarach's television of c. 1970 in a transparent plastic bubble or the late seventies British clock.*

impeccably integrated designs of Braun.

A second key thread which has assumed an increasing importance has been wilful exposure of mechanism. After a period of elaborate cosmetic concealment, many designers came to appreciate the aesthetic possibilities of frank exposure of constituent elements. The 'Toio' lamp designed by the Castiglioni brothers in 1962 is a classic early example of this reversal. The Centre Pompidou is its architectural equivalent. Tastes in the look of those consumer goods which have become indispensable to our way of life are just as fickle, just as liable to stylistic evolution as in any area of art, craft or design. The Contemporary period has, through its diversity in industrial design, dispelled the myth that a functional product is a beautiful product per se and has presented an invigorating challenge to those designers whose influence in shaping our aesthetic has become so pervasive.

# GRAPHIC DESIGN

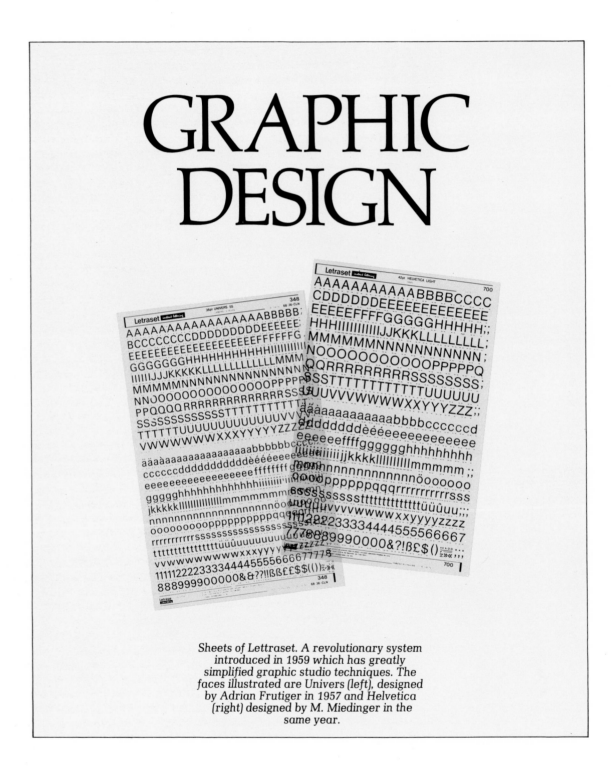

*Sheets of Lettraset. A revolutionary system introduced in 1959 which has greatly simplified graphic studio techniques. The faces illustrated are Univers (left), designed by Adrian Frutiger in 1957 and Helvetica (right) designed by M. Miedinger in the same year.*

────────── 1940 – Present ──────────

## Designers, Design and New Affluence

GRAPHIC DESIGN BOMBARDS US DAILY in a multitude of guises ranging in scale from advertising hoarding to record sleeve. We are surrounded by the largely ephemeral creations of the graphic artist whose work, two dimensional and usually for print, is geared principally to the processes of commerce, with sales figures as the guiding light. Indeed, the commercial nature of the work, serving to heighten the competitiveness of the field, has in the contemporary period encouraged a variety of distinguished talents. At the basis of so much graphic design is the need to catch the eye, to make a vivid impression and convey information succinctly by force of graphic impact. It is, therefore, an area of design very much subject to changes of fashion, its strength residing in the potential for constant innovation and novelty.

Graphic design has flourished as a major by-product of consumerism and especially as a result of the considerable post-war boom in the scope of advertising business. Today graphic design is a full-time study course on art college curricula and the graphic designer a professional with a sophisticated visual and marketing education.

There are many areas in which he can exercise his talent. He is responsible for the packaging of goods. He plays a key role in the world of advertising, though more in the concept and presentation of ideas than in their illustration, since photography has tended increasingly to replace graphic illustration. Graphic designers also create the type-faces and setting styles as well as lay-outs for books, magazines and other areas of print, which, however subtly, are in a constant process of evolution. Occasionally a timely idea, such as the computer-style type-face, has attracted particular attention.

The illustrator's art has by no means been superseded by photography; indeed, in many cases illustrators have used photography as an element within their work or as a visual starting point. Fashion illustration, an art which reached a peak in the years around the First World War, has certainly suffered since the war from the increasing sophistication of fashion photography, though with one or two notable exceptions. One whole industry, however—pop music—essentially a contemporary phenomenon, has provided opportunities for illustrative work, posters and record covers, of a remarkably high standard.

The commercial art of graphic design has, in the Contemporary period, as in previous periods reflected, often very specifically, dominant trends within the fine arts. When Studio Publications issued their international survey of graphic design, *Modern Publicity 1942-48* in 1948, a number of strong trends were clearly discernible as having been directly influenced by the fine arts.

The motifs of Surrealism featured prominently and, together with themes and motifs inspired by the neo-Romantic school of painting, were to form the basis of a repertoire for graphic artists in the immediate post-war years. English artist John Barker was responsible for a number of graphic designs which are highly evocative of their era. One, a poster for I.C.I., is an almost caricatural exercise in the Surrealist style in which life-like gloves create a Daliesque vision. French neo-Romantic painter and theatre designer Christian 'Bébé' Bérard was also an illustrator of rare talent who had evolved a charming, sad, whimsical style before the war and continued in this vein, with a fondness for neo-Victorian detail.

The new post-war schools of painting which were to influence graphic design were strongly linear and often abstract. Abstract Expressionism was coming into vogue and the linear splashes of Hans Hartung, of Franz Klein and, of course,

Jackson Pollock were to influence the graphic arts away from the figurative tendencies of the immediate post-war years. Bernard Buffet's work became very much in vogue and his thin lines were much imitated by graphic designers and illustrators.

The birth of Pop Art in the fifties and its wide-ranging development in the sixties was to provide graphic design with a fund of imagery, colours and viewpoints the influence of which is still very much alive. This situation was especially ironical since Pop had started as an attempt, in Mario Amaya's words (*Pop as Art*) to exploit 'the psychological, sociological, mythological (as well as purely visual) elements in ... images' drawn from the 'widely-accepted trivia of the commonplace world, as seen and understood through movies, television, comic strips, newspapers, girlie magazines, "glossies", high fashion, "High Camp", car styling, billboards and other advertising.' Commercial art inspired a 'fine' art school which in turn has shaped the attitudes of graphic and other commercial designers.

Perhaps the most influential style of

painting on graphic design in the seventies has been the Hyper-realist mode. Hyper-realism has engendered a tremendous concern for finish with a number of graphic artists who have in several cases mastered the air-brush as the ideal tool to achieve the flawless heightened effects which are their ideal. Others have used photo-montage and other skills to create complex, unreal images all the more disturbing for being photographic and therefore notionally 'real'. One of the most influential painters through the seventies has been David Hockney whose appealing, flat, graphic style has provided a tempting source of inspiration to graphic artists.

*Above: Neo-Baroque and Surreal combine in the graphics of Italian designer Fornassetti, c. 1950.*
*Right: Surrealism in a 1948 advertisement by John Barker for ICI.*
*Opposite top left: 1949 Paris Vogue cover by Ph. Jullian.*

## 1940 – 1950
### The New Romanticism

Any appraisal of the graphic design of the war and immediate post-war years would demonstrate clearly that the illustrator was the central figure and figurative motifs his stock in trade. The euphoric post-austerity spirit expressed itself in symbols of romance and optimism amongst which featured prominently heraldic motifs of every kind; joyous motifs of harvest and country life. The opulence of Victorian decorative styles was a revelation after the barren war years and was revived in graphic form with considerable popularity on magazine covers, book jackets and posters.

Amongst the many talented graphic artists in this romantic vein was French illustrator Jean Picart-Le-Doux, whose work is full of charm. His clients included Lucien Lelong and the French government for whom he created tourist publicity. English artist Eric Ravilious created graphic illustrations in a distinctive personal version of the Romantic style which were adapted for various media including ceramics. Italian artist Piero Fornasetti created Surrealist graphic decorations, also for various media. Typical of his style were his unnerving fractured faces printed on ceramic plates.

Perhaps the most talented illustrator of the post-war years, and still active through the seventies, is French artist René Gruau who came to prominence in the forties with an elegant, seemingly spontaneous and effortless style, a timeless style which has gracefully outlived the fashions which he illustrates. Gruau has worked regularly for Vogue and has enjoyed a long and fruitful relationship with the house of Dior for whom he still creates advertising illustrations. His house symbol for Dickins and Jones' store in London is a characteristic example of his graphic style.

The scratchy linear style of the fifties found able exponents in the graphic arts, among them Peynet, Rowland Emmett and American cartoonist – caricaturist Saul Steinberg. Peynet's sweet, sentimental lovers, conducting their courtship to the background of spindly images of Paris, became the subject of book illustrations and advertizing for such products as Vins Nicolas. Rowland Emmett, drawing exclusively for Punch in 1950, was invited to contribute to the Festival of Britain and

*Left: 'Panache'. Page of sketches by Christian 'Bébé' Bérard, 1947.*
*Above: Ashley Havinden advertisement for Simpson's.*
*Above right: Peynet sketch in a 1954 Schiaparelli advertisement.*

*René Gruau emerged as perhaps the most talented fashion illustrator of the post-war years. His seemingly effortless drawings were deceptively simple yet highly sophisticated.*
*Opposite: A 1951 design by Gruau.*
*Left: A 1953 design by Gruau.*

translated into three-dimensional realities the skinny eccentric inventions which he had been concocting in two dimensions.

## Into the 1960s
### Wit and Simplicity in Design

A new professionalism was emerging, meanwhile, in the world of graphic design, taking its lead from the world of advertising. A pioneer of the direct and simple graphic style which was to assert itself so positively by the early sixties was designer Ashley Havinden. As early as 1948, within the survey *Modern Publicity* already quoted, his work showed clear signs of the direction which graphic design was to take. His unfussy lay-outs, in which the typography constituted the main element of the design, were ahead of their time. Working for the London agency of W.S. Crawford Ltd, Havinden led the field with such projects as his publicity for S. Simpson Ltd.

In certain features, notably in its pursuit of graphic strength through simplicity and directness, this emergent style suggested echoes of Modernist ideology. It distinguished itself, however, from the strict pre-war graphic styles by its combination of professionalism and wit. Here was a seemingly terse and dry style in which, however, and by no means in conflict with their professionalism, designers were playing subtle games and having fun. Alan Fletcher, Colin Forbes and Bob Gill hint at this attitude in their introduction to their 1963 survey *Graphic Design: Visual Comparisons*. 'There are,' they write, 'some designers and even clients who insist that the public deserve and will

**92** graphic art; advertising art; applied art
freie graphik; gebrauchsgraphik; angewandte kunst
arts graphiques; arts appliqués; publicité

respond to much higher standards in graphics. They are convinced, as Charlie Chaplin was convinced, that the best way to entertain the public is first to entertain oneself.' Their aim was to show 'a ... number of solutions to advertising and communication problems that are efficient and imaginative.'

Among the many clever typographical ideas which they illustrate are two characteristic, witty examples for Pirelli, an enlightened company in the use of good graphics. This direct style dominated advertising and graphic design through the sixties and, indeed, still enjoys considerable favour. It went hand in hand with a dynamic new approach to magazine lay-out with art directors Harry Peccinotti for *Nova* and Willy Fleckhaus for *Twen* setting a standard which has proved hard to follow. It is hardly suprising that major international firms which have won high reputations for their standards of product design should set equally high standards in the graphic design aspects of their advertising and packaging. Volkswagen is a credit-worthy example, and has favoured the direct and simple approach which came to the fore in the early sixties.

--- The 1960s ---

### The Push Pin Style

Graphic design in the sixties was fascinating, above all, however, for explosions of talent of a quite different character. The self-conscious minimalism of art directors and advertising agencies with which the decade opened was overshadowed by the sheer vitality and colourful exuberance of other, more overtly decorative graphic styles, in many instances taking their cue from Pop culture or, often, more specifically, from popular music.

The most prominent graphic design studio of the sixties, a studio so exceptionally inventive that in 1970 its brief sixteen years of existence were celebrated by a major retrospective at the Musée des Arts

*Top: Cover design for* Graphis *magazine by Alan Fletcher, one of a generation of graphic designers who evolved a distinctive new style in the sixties.*
*Above: The sixties saw the advent of a bold, new style in magazine layout. A spread from Nova, March 1967.*

*Top and above: Witty ideas for neat, and in one case, symbolic, motifs to incorporate the company names of the two influential Italian firms, Olivetti and Pirelli.*

Décoratifs, was the American Push Pin Studio, founded by Milton Glaser and Seymour Chwast; they and their talented team created many of the decorative graphic styles of the sixties. Both Glaser and Chwast, born in 1930 and 1931 respectively, studied at the Cooper Union Art School and the two came together as fertile minds with an ambition to break new ground in graphics and illustration.

Their sources are numerous, but their style, the way in which they brought elements together, was quite novel. Bold use of colour in the Pop manner, collage, montage, a pseudo-naive graphic style with nostalgic references, ideas lifted from comic strips, visual puns and optical illusions, all were potential ingredients of a lively new approach to graphic design.

Among the Studio's most publicized works was the poster for Bob Dylan, his hair a stylized maze of coloured stripes above a black silhouette profile, drawn by Glaser for Columbia Records, and Glaser's poster for the American Hospital Association, 'There's a Future for You in a Health Career.' Barry Zaid was just one amongst a distinguished band of collaborators to flourish in the creative atmosphere of the Push Pin Studio.

## Pop Art Graphics

The Push Pin style, or rather styles, for the Studio was capable of a considerable diversity, became the most fashionable of the sixties. This exuberant Pop approach found several talented individual exponents, among them the British artist Peter Blake and the American Peter Max. Blake, primarily a painter and a major figure in the early formulation of British Pop Art, had studied at the Royal College of Art and graduated in 1956 with a first-class diploma. In the sixties he achieved renown with his style which mixed painterly textures with bright, hard colours and nostalgic details, often for recent heroes, Elvis *et al.* Blake designed magazine covers and pages for *Nova* and the Sunday newspaper supplements. In 1968 he published, through Dodo Designs, his celebrated *Babe Rainbow*, a definitive expression of his Pop graphic style. Another worthy claim to fame was his design for the sleeve for the Beatles' *Sergeant Pepper* album.

British Pop painters Richard Hamilton and Allen Jones each contributed themes and motifs to the graphic design repertoire but were themselves more involved with the resolution of painterly problems.

Peter Max combined a fertile imagination with a seemingly boundless ambition to fill the world with the decorative products of his graphic art. He was one of a number of graphic artists to encourage a revival of the purely decorative poster, a

There's a
Future for You in a
Health Career

Top left and left: Two late
sixties posters from the
influential Push Pin
Studio by Milton Glaser,
founder, with Seymour
Chwast.
Above: Poster for the
Island record company by
Hapshash and the
Coloured Coat, foremost
British exponents of the
psychedelic style, 1967.

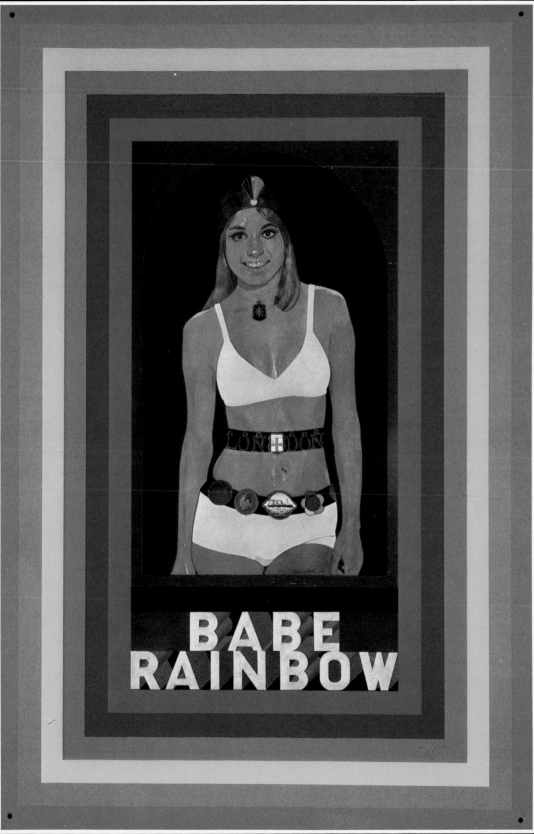

*Above: Poster for the New York shop, The Different Drummer, by Peter Max, 1968.*
*Left: 'Babe Rainbow', silkscreen print on tin by Peter Blake, published in 1968 by Dodo Designs, London.*

trend which has developed in the seventies to become a major international industry, largely through the sale of blow-up photographic portraits of cult figures. Max's name should survive if only on the strength of a spectacular decorative poster of 1967 depicting the legendary characters of the current Pop scene in brilliant Day-Glo colours. In the same year, and in similar psychedelic colour schemes, Richard Avedon published his manipulated photographic portraits of the four Beatles.

British and American artists dominated the story of the pictorial revitalization of graphic art in the mid- and late-sixties. Andy Warhol, father-figure of American Pop, has been described as the godfather of modern graphic design and appropriately enough started his career as an illustrator before finding success as an artist, cinéaste and controversialist.

British illustrator Alan Aldridge achieved notoriety as a daring graphic innovator who upset the conservative traditions of Penguin Books where he was employed as art director. Aldridge, nicknamed the 'Wild Man of Penguin', unleashed a torrent of often startling ideas in a firm known for the straight-laced appearance of its paperbacks. The uneasy collaboration lasted two years and ended acrimoniously. Aldridge's major contribution to British graphic design was his editorship of *The Beatles Illustrated Lyrics* published in 1969, containing examples of his own work and bringing together the work of the most prominent international graphic talents. Here was yet another instance of popular music as a starting point for graphic creativity.

## Pop Music and Graphics

One of the most exciting events of the sixties in graphic design was the presentation of the animated film *Yellow Submarine* (1968), written around the Beatles' *Sergeant Pepper* album. A rich and

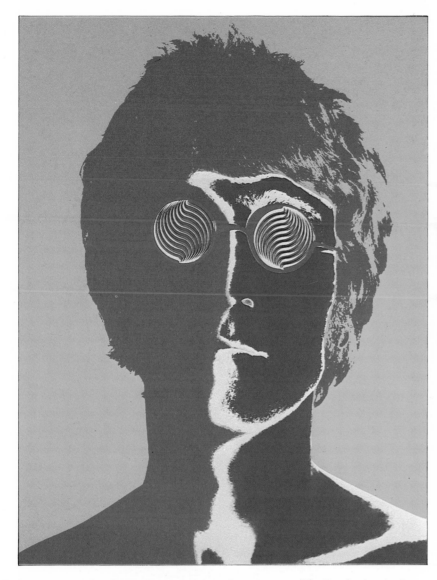

The Beatles inspired a rich variety of graphics during the late sixties.
*Opposite top: In 1967 Peter Blake collaborated with his wife Jan Haworth and photographer Michael Cooper to create this sleeve for their 'Sergeant Pepper' album.*
*Above: Psychedelic portrait of John Lennon by Richard Avedon issued as a poster by the Daily Express, 1967.*
*Opposite below and above right: Stills from the film 'Yellow Submarine' of 1968.*
*Left: 1969. 'The Beatles' Illustrated Song Book'.*

remarkable pot-pourri of graphic styles and imagery, the film encapsulated the decorative trends of the decade – Op, Kinetic, Pop and psychedelic themes melted together in a dazzling expression of youthful culture.

Pop music was the primary inspiration for an extraordinary spate of creativity in poster design in the late sixties, centred in England and in the States on the West Coast. The so-called psychedelic poster was part of a sub-culture which influenced graphics, dress and life-style and had music and drugs as its central themes. The style has been well if cynically described by George Melly as 'a rubbery synthesis of early Disney and Mabel Lucy Attwell carried to the edge of illegibility ... almost a collage of other men's hard-won visions: Mucha, Ernst, Magritte, Bosch, William Blake, comic books, engravings of Red Indians, Disney, Dulac, ancient illustrations of treatises on alchemy: everything is boiled down to make a visionary and hallucinatory *bouillabaisse.*'

The lasting image is of confused, seductive lines, but above all of sharp, almost fluorescent acid colours. The most exciting American posters of the genre were designed for the Avalon Ballroom and Fillmore Auditorium in San Francisco,

203

*Cover designed by illustrator/photographer Antonio Lopez for the April 1975 issue of Andy Warhol's newspaper Interview.*

where artist Wes Wilson was claimed in 1967 as the originator of the style. In England the foremost exponents were artists Michael English and Nigel Weymouth who joined forces in 1967 and worked together under the name 'Hapshash and the Coloured Coat.'

It was in the mid-sixties that album sleeves were first regarded as worthy of serious artistic concern, a potential soon realized by such fruitful collaborations as those between Peter Blake and the Beatles and between Andy Warhol and the Velvet Underground. The seventies have witnessed an explosion of highly sophisticated talent in this area of graphic design, notably from the British team of Hipgnosis started in 1968 by the highly imaginative

Storm Thorgerson and Aubrey Powell.

In an anthology of album covers published in 1977 and edited by Hipgnosis and Roger Dean, the favourite themes are detailed – 'Sleeves have their own visual vocabulary – a counterpart to the obsessive themes of rock music. Narcissism, make-up, "style", and instant gratifications for the body and mind are reflected in "mood" portraits, images of fast cars, fast food, comic strips and violent or fetichistic sexuality . . . Recently, nostalgia has added a new dimension to the source material of designers; old photography and re-worked '40's and '50's graphics have been featuring prominently on covers. The diversity unleashed by the '60's has made possible unexpected superimpositions – the ima-

*Philip Castle airbrush painting used for a poster for his 1978 exhibition at the Thumb Gallery, London.*

gery associated with the American Dream mingles with that of surrealism, fantasy and sci-fi.' The abstract graphics of George Hardie mark a contrast with the heightened graphic or photographic surrealism of the work of other members of the Hipgnosis team.

### 1970 – 1980
### Eclecticism

The sixties contribution to graphic design was a difficult act to follow, so fertile and diversified were the products of this decade. The seventies have, nonetheless, seen the flowering of a variety of talents. Andy Warhol, however intangible his peculiar talent, has continued to play an influential role. The throwaway graphic chic of his monthly newspaper *Interview* has proved a success which has inspired numerous rivals of which only the British *Ritz*, jointly published by David Bailey and David Litchfield, seems to have established itself. *Interview* has published exciting *mondain* photography and has attracted contributors such as the talented New York-based Antonio Lopez, probably the most interesting fashion illustrator of today, who has moved away from the purely graphic style which he had favoured since the late sixties and who now combines graphics with the instamatic sequence portraits which have become his obsession.

The concern for finish of the American Hyper-realists, and indeed their iconog-

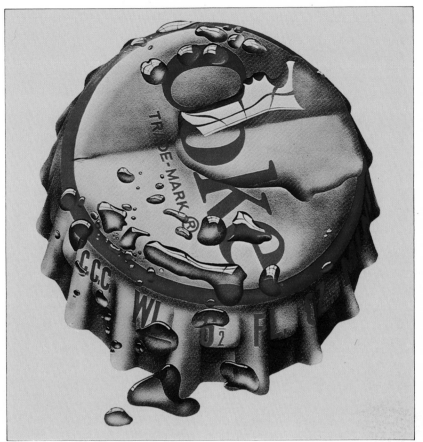

*'Coke'. Airbrush drawing by Michael English from a series on the theme 'Rubbish', 1970. Published as a large-format print.*

raphy, has found its equivalent in the purely commercial sector. Cottingham, Bechtle, Eddy, Estes, Goings and Salt have opened up a new repertoire of images and techniques. An internationally acknowledged maestro of the air-brush whose work owes much to the language of Hyper-realism is British graphic artist Philip Castle who has worked hard since the sixties to perfect his talent and whose work has taken on a new vitality in the seventies. Michael English, abandoning his psychedelic phase, used the air-brush first in a series of stylized representations of 'Rubbish' and 'Erotic Food Subjects', and more recently on meticulously realistic close-ups of mechanical details.

With the close of the seventies graphic design would seem to have reached a turning point. The negative contributions of New Wave culture would tend to confirm that the ideas of the sixties and early seventies have been explored to the full. The time is ripe for a new lead, a fresh phase for the eighties which has yet to be defined.

Record album cover by the Hipgnosis team for the rock group 10cc's 'Deceptive Bends', 1977. The cover image is a composite of several transparencies by Hipgnosis and retouched by Richard Manning with graphics by Colin Elgie. Below: New Wave record sleeves of the late seventies, including the cover for the Sex Pistols' single 'Anarchy in the U.K.'. These deliberately eschew sophistication, as a reaction against the pervasive slickness of consumer-oriented graphics.

# PHOTOGRAPHY & FILM

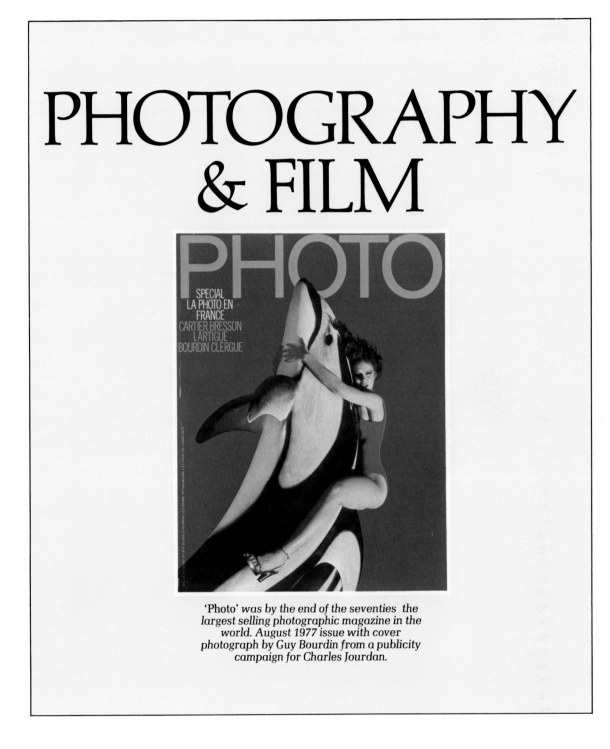

'Photo' was by the end of the seventies the
largest selling photographic magazine in the
world. August 1977 issue with cover
photograph by Guy Bourdin from a publicity
campaign for Charles Jourdan.

──────── 1945 – Present ────────
## The New Image

'SO SUCCESSFUL has been the camera's role in beautifying the world that photographs rather than the world have become the standard of the beautiful.' Susan Sontag's words in *On Photography* (1977) pin-point a pervasive aspect of Western life in post-war years – the insidious and highly potent persuasiveness of photography in shaping the ideals and directing the desires of a consumer society.

The post-war era has become increasingly dominated by the obsessive cult of the photographic image and by the proliferation and quality of such imagery. The force of the image has been strengthened by the considerable strides made since the war both in quality and versatility of colour film stocks and in the techniques of colour separation and printing processes. Commercial photography and especially colour, can today be of a remarkably high standard, its professional slickness adding to the impact of the imagery.

Alexander Liberman, art director of Condé Nast Publications, wrote in his foreword to *The Art and Technique of Color Photography* (1951), 'The public demanded pictures, and bought magazines that gave them what they wanted. The magazines in turn gave means to create and send talented men all over the world in search of visual nourishment ... colour photographers have brought us report and stimulation as no other art form has been able to do.' A distinction between commercial photography and other art forms, however, has made both the weakness and the fascination of such photographic images. For they are images of the all-important 'now', destined rapidly and inevitably to be superseded to keep the attentions of a neophiliac public.

The cult of the photographic image has been reflected in the cult of the commercial photographer as popular hero. The young Richard Avedon provided the model for the hero of *Funny Face*, the skittish 1957 film on the world of image-making. More significant, however, was Antonioni's *Blow Up* of 1967, for beneath the superficial glamour of the hero, the film exposed, through every layer of the plot, the essential and frustrating intangibility of the photographic image.

One might justly restyle a Wildean aphorism and propose that Life now imitates Photography, and Art has undeniably already done so. Art has paid homage to commercial photography in the 'Hyperrealist' or 'Photo-realist' movement of the early seventies.

The seventies have witnessed the official coming of age, the consecration of the photographic medium, as subject for commentary and analysis, as a new facet of the art market and as the subject of a spate of books and exhibitions.

Photography has eased itself into the official pantheon under the cloak of its fine art aspirations and pretensions. This museum- and market-inspired 'Photography-for-Art's-sake' viewpoint has encouraged a disproportionate emphasis on the literary 'Fine Art' genre, photography's equivalent of Tom Wolfe's *Painted Word*. Commerce on the other hand has spawned some of the most vital images of our immediate past, and photography has provided a memory bank of stylistic clues to the aspirations of successive generations.

Photography has become a major tool of the commercial sales process. It is everywhere in the form of advertising, on every scale from magazine advertisements to hoardings, through poster, point-of-sale and publicity materials of every kind. No business has benefitted more than the fashion and cosmetics industry from the promotion of sales through creative photography, nor has any industry provided greater inspiration to commercial photographers.

Just as photography's frozen images

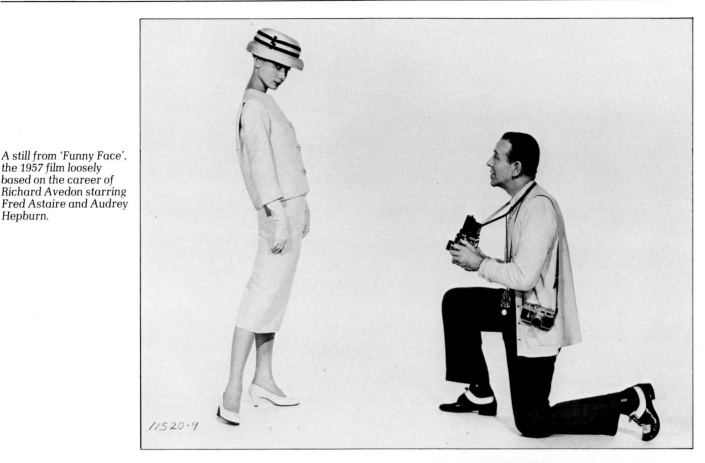

*A still from 'Funny Face', the 1957 film loosely based on the career of Richard Avedon starring Fred Astaire and Audrey Hepburn.*

have pervaded the collective sub-conscious, so, similarly, has the public's potential for fantasy been nourished by the film industry. Key films have created new heroes, and anti-heroes, suggested new life-styles and provided escapist fantasies of which the strongest thread has been the fascination with the imagery of space.

**Colour Photography and the Magazine**
The development and exploitation of colour has been an increasingly dominant feature of commercial photography since the first marketing of Kodachrome still film in September 1936. An improved form of Kodachrome became available also in sheet film in 1938, though war-time restrictions slowed the development of its commercial applications. *The Art and Technique of Color Photography*, published in 1951, stands therefore as an early résumé of the first successes of the Condé Nast stable of photographers. These included Serge Balkin, Cecil Beaton, Erwin Blumenfeld, Anthony Denney,

Horst P. Horst, Frances McLaughlin, Norman Parkinson and Irving Penn, leaders in their fields of still life, fashion, glamour, beauty and interior photography.

The tendency of those early colourists was to compose within a limited colour range, to cautiously exploit a dominant hue, favouring low-key and washed-out effects, using vivid details or contrasts with a painterly discipline and restraint. The high-key, pin-sharp colour image is the exception. A gracious diffusion of colour and line characterizes the majority of the published colour work of the late forties and fifties.

Erwin Blumenfeld is among the most interesting of this post-war generation of colourists. Having explored aspects of creative photography in pre-war Paris, where he was closely involved with avant-garde artistic circles, Blumenfeld came to New York in 1940 to adopt the cloak of commerce and ran a highly successful studio, turning out work mainly for *Vogue*, for which he did countless covers. A typical master of the restrained palette, Blumenfeld would exploit the brilliance of red lips, nails or ribbon to electrify an otherwise virtually colourless image. At the same time he explored the potential of colour in images which survive as uncanny precursors of the so-called 'psychedelic' colour distortions of the late sixties.

The sixties will be remembered as the decade of colour, the brash colours of Pop Art, the Hard-Edge primaries of a new generation of American Abstractionist painters. In commercial photography the closing of the decade saw the crystallization of an emphatic primary, high-saturation approach to colour, made possible perhaps as much by the improved quality of Kodachrome II as by the influence of schools of painting.

Perhaps the greatest promoter of the saturated, high-key colour image has been the Paris-based Filipacchi publishing organization whose star photographer, Francis Giacobetti, has proved his mastery of the genre. In their magazine *Photo*, launched in September 1967, Filipacchi has consistently and successfully promoted the commercial side-by-side with the purely creative aspects of contemporary photography. *Photo* is today internationally the biggest selling magazine on photography.

Amongst the most influential picture magazines of the post-war decades have been *Vogue* and *Harper's Bazaar*, each in a variety of editions and formats and each depending on the perception of an inspired art director. The Condé Nast organization, publisher of *Vogue*, has had the benefit of Alexander Liberman's guidance, his shrewd prescience of his public's needs and his ability to discover and develop nascent talent. American *Vogue* enjoyed a period of particular brilliance under the editorship of the impulsive, wonderfully unrealistic Diana Vreeland. Today French *Vogue* leads the field with the quality of its photography, both advertising and editorial, and its printing.

American *Harper's* flourished under the art directorship of Alexey Brodovitch, enlisted before the war by editor Carmel Snow. Brodovitch's catalystic influence in the sphere of commercial photography has been likened to that of Stieglitz in formal photography. Richard Avedon was his greatest protégé.

Numerous other magazines have enjoyed a passing success. In the sixties two notable newcomers were the German magazine *Twen*, art directed by Willy Fleckhaus and the English *Nova* launched in 1965, for which fashion editor Caroline Baker commissioned some of the most exciting photography of the day. Amongst the best-produced magazines on the luxury aspects of living are the art and interior design reviews *Connaissance des Arts* and *Architectural Digest*, both of which rely on a high standard of photographic presentation. All such magazines, however, depend upon the advertising revenue for their continued existence and the advertising content, which often outweighs the editorial content, can be just as visually stimulating.

## Masters of Commercial Photography

From the mass of work published in the world of commercial photography, so much of it weakly derivative and tasteless,

*Verushka and David Hemmings as model/photographer in Antonioni's 1967 film 'Blow-Up'. The two make a strong contrast in style with Astaire and Hepburn in 'Funny Face'.*

METRO-GOLDWYN-MAYER presents VANESSA REDGRAVE · DAVID HEMMINGS · SARAH MILES in **BLOW-UP** (x) in COLOUR

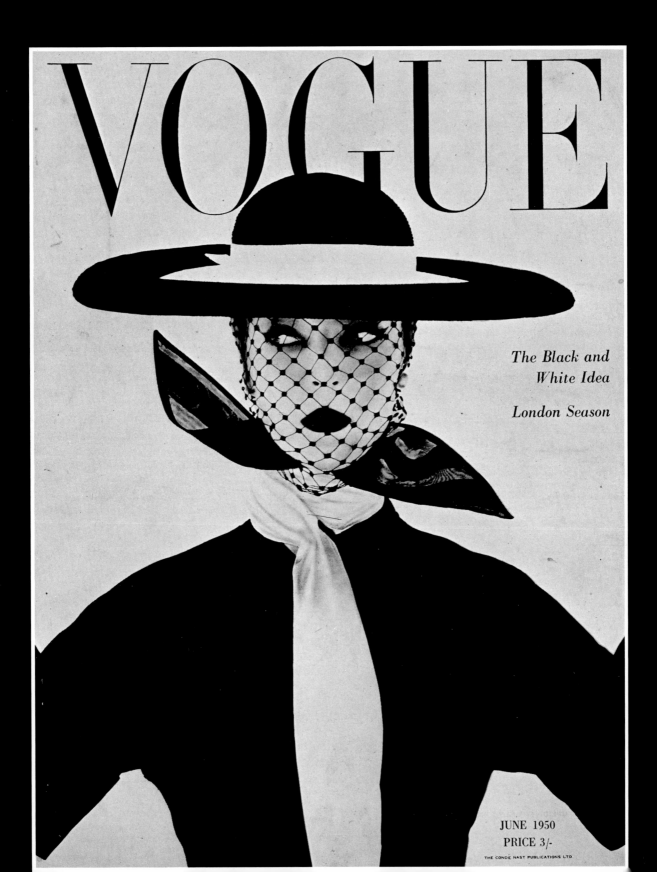

VOGUE

The Black and
White Idea

London Season

JUNE 1950
PRICE 3/-

THE CONDE NAST PUBLICATIONS LTD.

the real talent emerges and shows lasting qualities.

The most masterful commercial photographer of the post-war era is surely the American Irving Penn, an unnervingly intense, totally committed talent who has given a new grandeur to still-life and fashion photography, as well as taking some of the finest classic yet most severely penetrating portraits of recent decades. Penn has been called the 'spiritual child' of art director Alexander Liberman who early recognized his talent and brought him to Vogue in 1943. Beaton has written of Penn's meditative, analytical style that his 'are the virtues that abide after (the) febrile electric shocks of sensation-seekers have long since been forgotten'. The appearance in 1960 of Penn's *Moments Preserved* was a milestone in photographic publishing and confirmed his mastery and versatility. Capable of such precious, fine-detailed observations as his composition 'Theater Accident', Penn was equally at ease in a grainy, soft, Impressionistic style which he can justly claim to have invented. Sarah Moon and David Hamilton have re-explored this genre in the last decade.

Penn can create sublime compositions from simple elements. Through his lens a flower or a shoe, a plate of food, half empty liqueur glasses or butter sizzling in a skillet take on a symbolic presence. In his fashion work from the late forties and early fifties, his best period, Penn is without peer. Grandeur and simplicity are combined in his inimitable studies of the fabulous creations of Balenciaga, Dior, Fath, Rochas and their contemporaries. Under his minute scrutiny fashion loses its frivolity and Penn makes an art of treating it as an art.

The excitement of post-war Paris fashion inspired a number of new talents and heralded a new chapter in the history of fashion photography, that most fascinating aspect of commercial photography. The two giants of the period were Penn and Avedon, the latter taking his models out of the studios and into the streets, photographing them in restaurants, cafés, or night clubs, capturing the vitality of a re-awakened Paris in lively anecdotal photographs. There is a thread of excitement running through Avedon's earlier work which has gradually evolved towards his present masterful, but more impersonal studio objectivity.

The pages of post-war Vogue and Har-

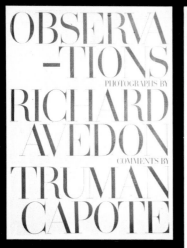

OBSERVA
-TIONS
PHOTOGRAPHS BY
RICHARD
AVEDON
COMMENTS BY
TRUMAN
CAPOTE

*Above: 'Observations'.
A compilation of Richard
Avedon's work published
in 1959 with a series of
essays by Truman
Capote.
Right: Irving Penn's 1960
anthology 'Moments
Preserved', perhaps the
most influential
photographic book of the
post-war era.*

# MOMENTS
# PRESERVED

BY
IRVING PENN

$17.50

*Elegant layouts and photography were combined in the German magazine Twen. Opening spread of a fashion feature photographed by Hans Feurer, published in February 1971.*

per's became a showcase also for the work of many other talented photographers, including John Rawlings, Louise Dahl-Wolfe, Arik Nepo, Norman Parkinson, still active and particularly good at colour fashion/travel assignments, the ever-versatile and inspired Cecil Beaton and Erwin Blumenfeld. For a period of about ten years, through the late fifties until 1965, William Klein injected a distinctive blend of chic and parody into fashion work for *Vogue*. He was one of the first to use extremely wide-angle lenses and his pictures often convey at once the absurd facade, as well as the glamour of fashion.

English photographer John French set a new standard for fashion photography in newsprint with his work through the fifties for the *Daily Express*. French ran a large and successful studio and several of his assistants were to achieve fame independently during the sixties, most notably David Bailey, *enfant terrible* of fashion photography in the 'swinging sixties'. Bailey found initial success with his aggressive black/white images but has based his lasting success on a capacity for hard work rather than any distinctive, dateable style. His name is often associated with those of Terence Donovan and Brian Duffy, two other self-consciously working-class photographers who shared the limelight with him during the sixties and have consolidated their reputations more quietly during the seventies.

The sixties was the great decade of exotic fashion/travel stories, often photographed in far-flung corners of the world. Henry Clarke photographed several such extravaganzas with the model Verushka, before she worked in the late sixties with Italian photographer Franco Rubartelli, who brought out her full potential in photo-essays for French *Vogue* and the *Telegraph Colour Magazine*.

The former Swiss-born art director, Hans Feurer was one of the brighter talents of the late sixties and early seventies with a strong-coloured, hard, polished style, a style which was to dominate the seventies and which found its greatest exponents in Helmut Newton and Guy Bourdin. After recovering from a heart attack suffered in New York in 1971, Helmut Newton's work seemed to find a new edge and vitality. The brittle sophistication and aggressive mood of Newton's images has probably been the strongest

215

Three memorable
publicity campaigns using
photography.
Right: Surreal imagery by
Duffy for Smirnoff.
Below: Advertisement for
Gordon's Gin by the
London agency,
Foote, Cone & Belding.
Below right: Pirelli 1970
calender. Photography by
Francis Giacobetti.

single influence of the decade in fashion, erotic and advertising photography and his imitators are legion. Chris Von Wangenheim, German-born like Newton but based in New York, is foremost among them. Bourdin, the withdrawn painter-turned-photographer, loves hard colours and harsh lighting and manipulates his painted models in symbolic and highly-charged scenarios.

The greatest creativity and expenditure in advertising is often in the area of luxury, largely unnecessary goods, for which the impulse to purchase must of necessity be artificially stimulated. Advertising must help create a brand image on the strength of visual associations. The finest campaigns have consistently been associated with the perfume industry, and with cigarette and drink advertising.

The sixties and seventies, especially, saw the injection of an increased sophistication into the concept and preparation of photographic advertising images. Perhaps the single most distinguished campaign of recent years has been the series of photographic essays prepared for Charles Jourdan, the shoe manufacturer, by the French painter-turned-photographer Guy Bourdin. His strongly composed and brilliantly coloured images have a distinctive *piquant*.

The American Revlon company has set the pace in cosmetic advertising since shortly after the war, using such top photographers as Richard Avedon and top models, among them Suzy Parker, Dorian Leigh and more recently Lauren Hutton, in consistently stylish images. Nina Ricci has created a romantic image for the perfume 'L'Air du Temps' through the photographs of David Hamilton. Surreal images by Michael Joseph, Brian Duffy and John Thornton have respectively made strong campaign themes for White Horse whisky and for Smirnoff Vodka. A sophisticated, minimal approach to 'pack-shot' photography has given Gordon's Gin

Advertisement for Nina Ricci's 'L'Air du Temps'. Photography by David Hamilton who has made a speciality of soft, grainy images.

a special place on the hoardings.

Japanese photographer Hiro has been responsible for memorable product images. Coming to New York in 1954 he worked briefly for Avedon and became a protégé of Brodovitch, working freelance for *Harper's*. Among his most interesting images is his 1969 study of Piaget gold and lapis watches, set monumentally in a psychedelically coloured 'lunar' landscape.

Calendars have become a flourishing by-product of photographic advertising since the Italian company Pirelli, in the late sixties, saw the wisdom of employing top photographers and transformed the annual launch of their calendar into an event eagerly awaited by art directors. Pirelli employed Giacobetti on more than one occasion, most memorably in 1970, Sarah Moon in 1972, Hans Feurer in 1974,

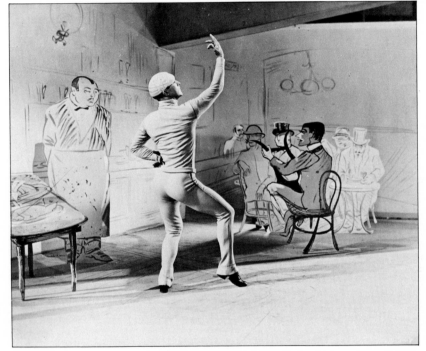

*Gene Kelly mimics a figure from a drawing by Toulouse Lautrec. From 'An American in Paris', 1951.*

of 1951 capture the sparkle of post-war Paris, once again the centre of the fashionable world, while the ballet finale to George Gershwin's score remains a masterpiece of creative cinematic fantasy.

A distinctive thread in the mid–fifties was the emphasis on the developing teenage market and a whole spate of films appeared which helped give an identity to this commercially significant age group. Teenagers were becoming consumers, savouring the first tastes of post-war prosperity and in search of heroes. They found them in Marlon Brando, the moody bikeboy of *The Wild Ones* of 1955 and James Dean, whose sulky looks shot him to fame in *Rebel Without a Cause* in the same year. Federico Fellini had analyzed this restless generation in *I Vitelloni* of 1954.

The young discovered their own style of music, rock'n'roll, when Bill Hayley and his Comets made a brief but memorable appearance in *Blackboard Jungle* in 1955 and capitalized on their success with *Rock Around the Clock* the following year. The transformation of young hero into instant legend is perfectly demonstrated in the meteoric rise to stardom of British homegrown rock idol Tommy Steele.

Discovered in a suitably Italianate coffee-bar to a background of futuristic hissing Gaggia equipment, Steele's success was recorded in the film *The Tommy Steele Story* of 1957. Here was the blueprint for the working class youth success stories of the sixties. Colin McInnes observed shrewdly that same year in an article in *Encounter*, 'This picture, which I believe to be enormously revealing of contemporary English folk ways, was, as far as I could check, entirely ignored by serious film critics.' The working-class vitality of Steele, the poses of Brando and Dean, the iconography of motorbikes and the rhythms of rock and roll were the significant ingredients of a new identity for a forceful young generation.

Since the fifties there has been a con-

and combined photography and graphic techniques in 1973 in a series of images by English artist Allen Jones. Few other companies have showed such initiative, though the Japanese photographic Pentax company have commissioned Helmut Newton (1976), Hans Feurer (1978) and most recently Guy Bourdin (1980) to great effect.

### The Contemporary Film Image

The study of the commercial applications of still photography within a history of Style inevitably involves the exclusion of so much worthwhile photography in other areas. Similarly, in such a history, only a small number of films can be deemed relevant, and these not always by virtue of their intrinsic quality, but simply because they provide the necessary clues to the shapes of prevalent fantasies and aspirations in life-styles. How perfectly, for instance, does *An American in Paris*

stant emphasis on youth-oriented films. Antonioni's *Blow-Up* consecrated the hollow myth of the young photographer hero, an archetype of his decade. *Blow-Up* is littered with throw-away clues to the mood of the sixties. The hero's home/studio is the ideal 'pad', with *objets trouvés*, chairs from Anderson Manson and Pop objects; the set-piece fashion session is a wittily observed parody. Here also are the significant threads of anarchic violence and the drug sub-culture that was to dominate the 'psychedelic' late sixties.

The sixties saw a number of films from four new young heroes from Liverpool, the Beatles. Their first film in 1964 was Dick Lester's *A Hard Day's Night*, emphatically shot in the hard black-and-white style which enjoyed a vogue in the mid-sixties, along with the fad for Op Art in fashion and interiors. The classic Beatles film, however, was George Dunning's

brilliant animation, *Yellow Submarine* of 1968, perhaps best discussed in the context of graphics, so strongly did it reflect and influence the arts of illustration and graphic design.

Youth, and again the symbolic motorbike, led the way into the seventies with Peter Fonda in *Easy Rider*. The irreverence of the sixties was to harden into an anarchic vein during the seventies, an anarchy which adopted stylistic symbols in the Punk movement. Film critic Alexander Walker of the London *Evening Standard* has dubbed Stanley Kubrick's violent fantasy of 1972, *A Clockwork Orange*, 'film of the decade'. Both the empty, vicious mood of Punk and the extraordinary styles associated with it were brilliantly distilled in Derek Jarman's *Jubilee* of 1978.

If the new, young markets have dictated the mood and style of so many films since the mid-fifties, two distinct genres have

*The two greatest idols to emerge in the mid-fifties: Left: James Dean in 'Rebel Without a Cause', 1955, the second of two films made before his tragic death. Right: The sulky good looks and tough image of Marlon Brando in the classic movie 'The Wild Ones', 1955.*

developed with a far wider appeal to collective fantasies: the secret agent film and the space film. When Sean Connery first hit the screen in the 1962 film version of Ian Fleming's *Dr. No*, James Bond immediately captured the public imagination. *Dr. No* and the James Bond films which followed, including, notably, *Goldfinger* of 1964, created a violent consumer-fantasy world of expensive gadgetry, the jet-age world of push-button living, a dream world in which villain masterminds plot against society from their futuristic lairs. *Dr. No's* underground kingdom created by set designer Ken Adams, in which space-age elements vie with natural rock walls, is like a parody of Frank Lloyd Wright's Taliesin home. The most recent Bond movie, *Moonraker* (1979), has taken

the fantasy element to its logical destination, outer space.

Space, in the decade which saw man on the moon and through the seventies, has provided the inspiration for a succession of visually stunning films. The classic, Stanley Kubrick's *2001* (1968), is doubly fascinating for having already become so dated in many visual details, despite its futuristic subject matter. The manipulated

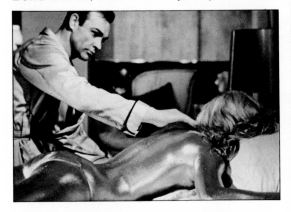

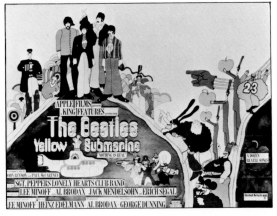

Top left: Sean Connery discovering the gilded corpse of his adversary's victim in 'Goldfinger', 1964.
Above: Poster for 'Yellow Submarine', 1968.
Right: Poster for the science fiction spoof 'Barbarella', 1968.

*Left and below: Two stills from Stanley Kubrick's '2001 — a Space Odyssey'. The space landscape (below) adopts the fashionable colours of psychedelic graphics.*

colour of the space landscapes owe a great deal to the 'psychedelic' age and the Hilton Space Station decor seems equally outmoded. The film is a haunting master-piece, however, by any standards. The same could hardly be said of Roger Vadim's sex-space fantasy *Barbarella* of 1968. Jane Fonda brought the strip-cartoon heroine to celluloid life, travelling in a fur-lined space ship to galaxies 38,000 years hence clad in erotic costumes designed by Jacques Fonteray, with more than a glance at the futuristic creations of Paco Rabanne.

The genre was explored with ever-greater extravagance in the record-break-ing *Star Wars* of 1977, memorable for the spectacular, sinister space-station. The success of *Star Wars* spawned a revival of the space fantasy with such films as *Close Encounters of a Third Kind* (1977) and *Alien* (1979).

Aside from the broader trends and amid the predominant contemporary genres, numerous films have made their indivi-dual mark in the story of the decorative arts. It is difficult to overlook the impact of Cecil Beaton's designs for *My Fair Lady* of 1964 in encouraging the Art Nouveau revival in interior design. Ten years later, in 1974, the post-war period was already turning full circle and the nostalgic, touch-ing film *American Graffiti* highlighted rev-erentially the iconography of American Youth in the fifties: the language, the music, the clothes, cars, drive-ins and movies. American photographer William Klein made two notable films during the sixties, first his *Qui Etes-vous Polly Magoo?* of 1967, a cruel and brilliantly observed satire on the world of fashion, and *Mr Freedom* (1968), a satirical obser-vation of Pop fantasy and consumerism.

# INDEX

Page numbers in italics
refer to illustrations

Aalto, Alvar 62, *63*
Aarbuim Eeri 62m *71, 72*
Abstract expressionism 9,
33, 193
Adams, Ken 220
Adler, Ruth 138, *139*
Adnet, Jacques 59, *59*
Aircraft *183,* 184-5
Aldridge, Alan 202
Amies, Hardy 151
Andersen, David 93
Andreason, Jeus *91*
Andrew, Gordon 46
Arabia (Finland) 101, 107,
*133*
Arbeid, Dan 100
Archizoom Studio 69
Arflex (Milan) *59,* 60, 78
Arneson, Robert 105
Arnstöm, Folke 92
Arredamenti, Chiesa 60
Art & Industry, Committee
on 182;
    Council for, 177, 182
Artek 62, *63*
Arteluce 95, 96
Artemide 96
Art nouveau 40, 132, 141
Arts & Crafts & Industrial
Design, Society of 180
Asko 62
Asprey 91
Asquith, Brian 88
Aubert, Jungmann & Stinco
67
Auld, Ian 100, *101*
Aulenti, Gae 96
Automobiles *178, 184,*
185-6, *185, 190;*
    Custom cars 17
Avedon, Richard 145, 202,
*203, 209, 210, 211, 213, 214,*
217

Bailey, David *11, 11,* 20, *21,*
205, 215
Balenciaga, Cristobal 145,
148, 149-51, *150*
Balkin, Serge 210
Balmain, Pierre 145, *146,*
148, 151, *155*
Bang & Olufsen *189,* 190
Barker, John 193, *194*
Barnes, Karen 100
Barovier, Ercole 123, *124,*
*124*
Bartoli, Carlo 78
Barton, Glenys 106
Bauer, Wolf *140,* 142
Beardsley, Aubrey 41
Beatles, The 20, *21,* 41, 202,
*203,* 219
Beaton, Cecil *35,* 145, *146,*
*150, 154,* 210, 215
Beene, Geoffrey 175
Behrens, Steven *113*
Bellini, Mario 72, *75,* 76, 77,
*77, 96, 176, 186, 187,* 188
Beltzig, Gunter &
Wuppertal *50*
Benney, Gerald 87, *87,* 88
Bérard, Christian ('Bébé')
193, *195*
Bergström, Hans 95, *95*
Bertoia, Harry 33, 51, 53,
*54*
Bestegui, Carlos de 7, *8,* 81
Bianconi, Falvio 124
Biba 41, *161, 163*
Birolli, Renato 138
Birtwell, Celia 164
Black, Misha 182

Blake, Peter 13, *13,* 37, 199,
*201, 203*
Blass, Bill 175
Bliny, Jacques 95
Blumenfeld, Erwin 210-11,
*213, 215*
Boda Nova 92
Boggeri, Antonio *140,* 142
Bojesen, Kaj 90
Borsani, Osvaldo 60, *61*
Boucheron 109, *110*
Bourdin, Guy *208,* 215, *217,*
218
Bowie, David *11,* 13
Braun A.G. 180-2, *180, 181*
Britain Can Make It (1946)
16, 45, 56
British Silverware Group
88
Brodovitch, Alexey 211
Broadhead, C. 120
Brown, Dorothy 130
Brumwell, Marcus 182
Brussels World Fair (1958)
45, 49, *49*
Buffet, Bernard 9, 33, 194
Bülow-Hübe, Torun 114
Burton, Jocelyn 88
Buzelli, J. Anthony 94

Calculators *186,* 188-9
California modern 51
Cameras, *see* Photographic
equipment
Canovas del Castillo,
Antonio 148
Cardew, Michael 99, *100*
Cardin, Pierre 118, 155,
158-9, *158*
Carlson, Tom 104
Carpets *140,* 142
Cartier 109, *111,* 121, *121*
Cassina, Figli di Amadeo
60, *74, 75,* 76, *77,* 78
Casson, Sir Hugh 182
Castiglioni, Achille & Pier
Giacomo 95, *96, 97,* 191
Castle, Philip *205,* 206
Castle, Wendell 24, *79, 79*
Catroux, François 81
Cavanagh, John 153
César 73, *82,* 118, *132,*
Chairs 25, 30, 33, 55-57, *59,*
*61,* 62, 65, 67, *71,* 73-75, *77*
Chanel, Coco 155
Charles de Gaulle Airport
*27, 28,* 43
Cheti, Fede 138
Chow, Michael 13, *13*
Christofle 88, *91*
Cinema 202-3, 218-21
Citroën *184, 185*
Clark, Ossie *161, 163*
Clarke, Dillon 135
Clarke, Henry 215
Clarke, Lord Kenneth 21
Clendinning, Max 72
Clen-Murphy, Desmond 88
Coatstands *31, 41*
Coffey, Michael *78,* 79
Coleman, John *78*
Collingwood, Peter 141, *141*
Colombo, Joe *68,* 69, *69,* 72;
    Studio *179*
Conran, Terence 23, *23,* 69;
    Associates *26,* 69
Consumerism 15, 23, 177
Contemporary style 21-2,
140
Coper, Hans 35, *102, 103*
Copier, Andries 129
Corbusier, Le 49
Courrèges, André 41, *41,*
146, 147, 156-7, *156*
Coventry Cathedral *33,* 35

Crafts *24, 45, 78;*
    Council 25
'Crayonne' *26*
Crippa, Roberto 138, *139*
Cristofanetti, Elena 138
Cruikshank, Robin 69
Cullen, Rea Spencer *172,*
173

Dahlquist, Enga-Britt 114-5
Dahl-Wolf, Louise 215
Dalquist, Ibe 114
Dalton, Sir Hugh 24
Danko, Peter 79
Daum, Michel 130;
    Studio *128, 131,* 132
Day, Lucienne *136, 137, 139*
Day, Robin 55, *56,* 57, 64,
68, 95
Dean, James *20, 219*
De Beers 111, *113*
De Carli, Carlo 60
Deganello, Paolo 78
De Large, Edward *116,* 120
Del Pezzo *131,* 132
Denney, Anthony 210
De Poli, Paulo 93
Design Centre 24, 25, 182
Design Research Unit 177,
182-4, *182*
Designers & Art Directors
Association 24
Dessès, Jean 151
Devlin, Stuart 85, *86,* 87, *88*
Dior, Christian 15, 145, *146,*
148, *148,* 149, *167*
Disderot, Pierre 95
Ditzel, Nanna 114
Donald, John 112
Donovan, Terence 215
Dreiser, Peter 130
Drerup, Karl 94
Dreyfuss, Henry 190
Duckworth, Ruth 100, *101*
Duffy, Brian *11,* 215, *216,*
217
Dumond, Jacques 59
Durbin, Leslie 86, 88, *89*

Eames, Charles 25, 29, 30,
*30,* 51, *52, 53, 55,* 65, 66
Eckhof, Tias 90, 107
Eddy, Don *43*
Edinburgh weavers 137,
*138*
Eichler, Dr Fritz 180
Emmett, Roeland 32, *33,*
195
Enamel 92-4, *92, 94*
English, Michael *39,* 204,
206, *206*
Epp, Paul 79
Ercolani, Lucien 56
Erikson, Sigurd Alf 93
Estes, Richard 42
Ethnic style 41-2, *75, 164,*
167
Expo '67 (Montreal) 45, 49

Famery, Jacques 67
Farina, Pinin 186
Farulli, Nando *106*
Fath, Jacques 145, 148,
151, *152*
Fausing, Age 114
Ferrieri, Anna Castelli 69,
72
Festival of Britain (1951)
45-6, *48;*
    Style 55, *136*
Festival Pattern Group 31,
46, 137
Feuer, Hans 215, *215, 217,*
218
Films, *see* Cinema

Filopacchi 211
Fiorucci, Elio *143, 163,* 164
Fischer, Bernard 94
Flavin, Dan 37
Fleckhaus, Willy 211
Fletcher, Alan *198*
Flockinger, Gertrude 112
Floris 50
Fogh, Federico 65
Fontana Arte *30,* 31, 60, *61,*
95
Fiorucci, Elio *143, 163,* 164
Fontana, Lucio 46, *48,* 104
Fool 42
Formes Utiles 26, *27,* 59, 85
Fornasetti, Piero 194, 195
Forquet, Federico 160
Foster, Norman 43, *44*
Franck, Kaj 101, 107, *128*
Fraser, Robert 10
Frattini, Gianfranco 60
French, John *213,* 215
Freedom, Mr *38, 71, 75,*
143, *163, 164*
Friberg, Berndt 101
Frink, Elizabeth 35
Fritsch, Elizabeth 104
Fry, David 17
Fuller, Buckminster *49*

G.A.B. (Sweden) 88
Gadoin, Jacques 59
Gambone, Guido 93, *94,* 106
Garrard 88, *92*
Gate, Simon 126
Gecchelin, Bruno 96
Geldzahler, Henry 10
Genisset, Jean-Pierre 59
Gense 88, 92
Gernreich, Rudi *164, 165*
Getty, Talitha 41
Ghia, Karmen *185,* 186
Giacobetti, Francis 211,
*216, 217*
Gillgren, Sven 85
Gismondi, Ernesto 72, *95,*
96
Givenchy, Hubert de 148
Glaser, Milton 199, *200*
Glasshouse, The 134, *135*
Goldsmiths, Worshipful
Company of 85, 86, 88
Godden, Robert Y 86, *89*
Gordon, Harold 130
Gorham (USA) 88
Grasten, Viola 141
Gray, Milner 182
Grierson, Martin 79
Grima, Andrew 111, *112,*
121, *121*
Groag, Jacqueline 137
Gruau, René 195, *197*
Gugelot, Hans 182, *188*
Guggenheim Museum *28,* 30
Gustavsberg (Sweden) 101,
107

Habitat style 23, *23,* 69
Hacker, Reinhold *188*
Haile, Sam 99
Hald, Dagny 106
Hald, Edward 126
Halston *174,* 175
Hamada, Shoji 99, *100*
Hamilton, David 213, 217,
*217*
Hamilton, Richard 10, *10,*
*36,* 37, 177, 199
Hammond, Henry F 99
Hanninen, Olavi *22*
Hansen, Carl Gustav 91
Hansen, Fritz 85
Hansen, Hans 90, 114, *115*

Hansen, Johannes *62*
Hard-Edge 40, 118
Hardie, George 205
*Harper's Bazaar* 211
Harris, Stephen 79
Hartnell, Norman 151, *153*
Hartung, Hans 33, 193
Havinden, Ashley *195, 197*
Heal's fabrics *136,* 137
Heesen, Willem 130
Henningsen, Poul 95
Herbst, René 56
Heritage, Robert 69
Herman, Sam *131,* 132, 134
Hermès 121
Heron, Susanna 120
Hicks, David 81, 142
High-Tech style 43, 80, *82*
Hille 68
Hipgnosis 204-5, *207*
Hippies 15, 41
Hiro 217
Hockney, David 13, 16, *18,*
194
Hogbin, Stephen 79
Holdaway, Bernard 67
Horst, Horst P 210
Houghton, Arthur 130
Hovisaari, Annikki 101
Hughes, Graham 134
Hughes, Patrick *192*
Hulanicki, Barbara *161,*
163
Hultberg, Paul 94
Hutton, John *33, 129,* 130
Hvidt, Peter *25*
Hyper-realism 42, 194, 209

International Business
Machines (IBM) *187,* 188
Industrial Design, Council
of 24, 49, 182
Industrial Design
Partnership 182
International modernism
35, 51, 64
*Interview* 204, 205
Issigonis, Sir Alex 186

Jacobsen, Arne *62,* 64, 71
Jaguar *185,* 186
James, Charles 153, *154*
Jarman, Derek 21
Jensen, Georg 31, 85, 90, *90,*
114, *114, 115*
Jensen, Soren Georg 90, 114
Jewellery 38, 108-21
Johns, Jasper 37
Johnson, Philip 35
Jones, Allan *36,* 37, *73, 74,*
199, 218
Joseph, Michael 217
Juke boxes 17, *19*
Jullian, Ph 194
kagan, Vladimir 54
Kalckreuth, Jo v. *30*
Kamali, Norma *174,* 175
Karlby, Bent 141
Karp, Ivan 10, *10*
Kartell (Milan) 69, *69,* 72
Keith, Howard 56
Kelly, Ellsworth 40
Kentish, Simon *39*
Kepax, Mary *103*
Kinsman, Rodney *82*
Kirk (USA) 88
Kjaerholm, Poul 64, 71
Klein, Calvin *175, 175*
Klein, Franz 193
Klein, William 37, 40, *40,*
215, 219
Klepper, Irina 54
Klingenberg, Inge 65
Klint, Kaare 61, *62*
Knapp, Sonja 158

Knoll, Florence 51, 53
Knoll International 35, 53, 54, 66, *140*, 142
Kodak *188*, 190
Kommenda, Erwin 185
Koppel, Henning 90, *90*, 114, *114*
Kosta 126, *126*, 127, 135
Kukkapuro, Yrjo 71

Labino, Dominick 123, 130
La Falaise, Lou-Lou de 13
Laffon, Dupré 59
Lagerfeld, karl *12, 13*, 170
Lalanne, Claude 118
Lalanne François *72, 74*
Landberg, Nils 126
Landin, Ingeborg 126
Lane, Ken *111*, 112
Lapidus, Morris 81
Las Vegas *14*, 35-7, *35*
Laszlo, Paul 31, 53, 95
Latimer, Clive 55, *56*
La Trobe-Bateman, Richard 79
Lauren, Ralph 175
Leach, Bernard *98*, 99, *100*
Leleu, Jules 59
Levine, Marilyn 106
Levi-Strauss *147, 147*
Lewis, Robert 51
Liberman, Alexander 211, 213
Libhart, Miles 94
Lichtenstein, Roy 10, 37, *39*, 73, 118
Liertz, Hildegard 95
Lighting 94-6, *95, 96, 97*, 191
Lindberg, Stig 93-4, *94*, 107, 137, 141
Lindh, Francesca 101
Lindstrand, Vicke *126*, 127
Lipofsky, Marvin 132, *132*
Litchfield, David 205
Little, Anthony 41
Littleton, Harvey *122*, 130
Loewy, Raymond 178, *178*, 182, 190
Lopez, Antonio *204*, 205
Louis, Morris 40
Low-Cost Furniture competition (1948) 24, 51, 55, *56*
Lundin, Ingeborg 126
Lunds, Alice *139*
Lunning, Frederik 24, 26, 90

McDermott, Mo 75
MacDonald, Grant 88
McHale, John 16-17
McLaughlin, Frances 210
Magistretti, Vico *72, 74*, 76-7, 96
Mahler, Marion 137, *138*
Majella, June 130
Makepeace, John 79, *79*
Malmsten, Carl 64
Manheim, Julia 120
Mannheim, Celia *119*
Martens, Dino 124
Martini, Piero de 78
Mathesson, Bruno 64
Max, Peter 199-202, *201*
Mazza, Sergio 72
Meaker, Charlie 134
Meech, Annette 135, *135*
Mellor, David 88, 92, *93*
Maydam, Floris 129-3ʊ
Mies van der Rohe, Ludwig 35, 51, 66;
    Mies chair 69

Milan Triennale 45, 88, 123;
    (1951) 46, *48;*
    (1957) *22, 49*, 185
Miller, Herman 31, 32, 53, *55, 56*, 66, 67, 72
Mills, Edward 46
Mlinaric, David 81
Molgaard-Nielsen, Orla 25
Mollino, Carlo *30*, 31, 60, *61*
Monpoix, André 59
Montana, Claude *170*, 173
Moon, Sarah 213, 217
Morris, Roger *108*, *117*, 119
Morton Sundour Co Inc 137, *138*
Motte, J 59, *59*
*Mourgue, Olivier 71*
*Mucha, Alphonse 41*
*Mugler, Thierry 173*
*Mujake, Issey 175*
*Murano glass 123, 124*
Murray, William Staite 99
Museum of Contemporary Crafts (NY) 85, 91
Museum of Modern Art (NY) 24, *25*, 51

Natzler, Otto & Gertrud 100
Nayler Bros 88
Nelson, George 32, 66
Nepo, Arik 215
Nesbitt, Eileen *103*
Neutra, Richard J 52
New realism, *see* Hyper-realism
Newton, Helmut *12*, 43, *45*, 215, 218
Niau, Costan 137
Nizzoli, Marcello 186, *187*
Noguchi, Isamu 31, 53, *56*
Noland, Kenneth 40
*Nova 198*, 211
Noyes, Eliot 188
Nurmesniemi, Antti 71
Nyman, Gunnel 128

Odawara, Yuki 141, *142*
Ohrstrom, Edvin 126
Oldenburg, Claes 37
Olivetti *176*, 186, *187*, 199
Omega 121, *121*
OMK 69, *82*
Oneida 88
Op-Art 40, *40*, 72, 147
Organic Design in Home Furnishing (1940-1) 24, 51, 52
Organic modernism 29-30, 54
Ornamo 180
Orrefors 126, *126*
Orup, Bengt 128
Osman, Louis 88
Otis Art Institute 104

Pallenberg, Anita 42
Palmquist, Sven 126-7
Panton, Verner 51,72
Paolozzi, Eduardo 107
Parisi, Ico 60
Parkinson, Norman 210, 215
Parzinger, Tommi 54
Paulin, Pierre *67*, 71
Pedersen, Bent Gabriel 91, *114*, *115*
Pemberton, John 186
Penn, Irving 145, 210, *212*, 213, *214*
Pentax *188*, 218
Peretti, Elsa 111
Permanente, Den 26, 62
Perriand, Charlotte 57
Persson, Sigurd *84*, 91

Pevsner, Sir Nikolaus 177
Peynet 32, 195, *195*
*Photo 208*, 211
Photographic equipment *188*, 190
Photo-realism, *see* Hyper-realism
Piaget 121
Piaggi, Anna 13
Piano, Renzo 16, *17*, 43
Picart-Le-Doux, Jean 195
Picasso, Paloma *12, 13*
Pick, Frank 182
Piper, John 35
Pirelli 188, 198, *199, 216*, 217
Piretti, Gian Carlo *76*, 78
Plenderleith, John 119
Pleydell-Bouverie, Katherine 99, *100*
Polaroid Corporation 190
Poli, Flavio 123, 124-6, *125*
Pollock, jackson 9, 33, *35*, 194
Pomodora, Joe 118
Pompidou Centre (Paris) 16, *17*, 28, 43, 191
Poncelet, Jacqueline 104
Ponti, Gio 46, 60, 124
Poole Pottery *105*, 107
Pop-art 10, *36*, 37-40, 72-5, 105, 118, 143, 147, 164, 194
Pop music *11*, 13, *17*, 202-5
Porsche, Ferdinand 185
Posters *20*, 199-202, *200, 201*, 203
Post-modernism 43
Pothier, P 59
Pott (Germany) 88, 92
Powell, Aubrey 204
Prampolini, Enrico *33*
Prestini, James 51
Price, Anthony *169*, 173
Prouvé, Jean 57
Psychedelic style 41, *41*, *200*, 203
Pucci, Emilio 160
Punk 13, 21, *21*, 44, 46, 148, 173-4, *173*, 219
Push Pin Company 199, *200*

Quant, Mary 146, *160*, 163
Queen's Award to Industry *178*, 182

Rabanne, Paco 117, 146, 147, 159, *159*
Race, Ernest *33, 33*, 46, 55, *56*, 69
Ramos 59
Rams, Dieter 182
Ramshaw, Wendy 119
Rancillac 67
Rava, Carlo Enrico 60
Ravilious, Eric 195
Rawlings, John 215
Read, Herbert 182
Record sleeves *11, 41, 42*, 199, 204-5, *207*
Reich, Tibor 141
Reid, John & Sylvia 69
Renon, André 59
Rhead, A B *105*, 107
Rhodes, Zandra 167, 173, *173, 174*
Ricci, Nina 148, *155*, 217, *217*
Rickard, Stephen *129*, 130
Rie, Lucie 103
Riley, Bridget 40, 142
Roberts, Martin *26*
Roberts, Tommy 164
Robinson, Janet E *119*
Robsjohn-Gibbings, T H 54
Rochas, marcel 151

Roche-Bobois 81
Rogalski, Walter 94
Rogers, Mike *163*
Rogers, Richard 16, *17*, 43
Rolex 121
Rosenauer, Michael 182
Rosenquist, James 37
Rosenthal 106, 107, *107*
Rowenta *188*
Royère, Jean 59, *59*
Rubartelli, Franco 215
Russell, Gordon 54
Russell, RD 69, *191*
Rya rugs 141

Saarinen, Eero 29, *29*, 30, 51, *52*, 53-4, *54*
Sachs, Gunter 73
Sainsbury Centre for the Visual Arts (Norwich) 43, 44
Saint-Laurent, Yves 13, *81*, 82, *83*, 118, 149, *165*, 167-70, *169*
Salon des Artistes Décorateurs 59
Salto, Axel 101
Sapper, Richard 95, *96*
Sarpaneva, Timo 107, *127*, 129, 132, *132*
Sartre, Jean-Paul 7, *10*
Sassoon, Vidal 160
Scandinavian modern style 61
Scarpa, Carlo 124
Scarpa, Tobia 76, *77, 77*
Schlumberger, Jean 111
Schön, Mila 160
Schummi, Heinz 173, *173*
Schwast, Seymour 199, *200*
Screens 51
Seagram Building (NY) 35
Seguso, Archimede 124
Sempre, Astrid 141
Shrimpton, Jean *11*, 13
Sinclair Radionics 186, *189*
Silton, E H *91*
Site Inc 43
Socota (Milan) 138
Sognot, Louis 57
Solven, Pauline 134
Sony *189*
Sottsass, Ettore *38, 143*, 186
Space age 15, *16*, 41, *142*, 143, 146, 156, *156, 158, 159*
Spence, Basil 35, 56
Squires, Eddie 143
Stainless steel 85, 91-2
Stalhane, Carl harry 101
Stapley, Jack 86, *88*
Steinberg, Saul 195
Stella, Frank 40
Stephen, John 163
Stephensen, Magnus 90
Steuben glass 130
Stiebel, Victor 153, *153*
Stilnovo 95
Storage units 55, *56*, 69
Styles, Alex 87, 88, *92*
Superior, Roy 79
Surrealism 30-1, *193, 194*
Sutherland, Graham 35
Svenska Slöjdföreningen 26, 64, 180
Synthetics *26*, 28

Tables 53, 54, *56, 61, 67, 73, 77, 82*
Takada, Kenzo 173
Tallon, Roger 65, 71
Tamesa Fabrics 141, *142*
Tapiovaara, Iimari 62
Teague, Walter Dorwin, Assoc. 182, 190
Teddy boys 18

Televisions 190, *191*
Teller, Bonwit 31
Thatcher, Sue *142*, 143
Thorgerson, Storm 204
Thornton, John 217
Thurston, Gerald 95
Tiffany & Co 109-111
Tilson, Joe 37
Toikka, Oiva 132, *133*, 135
Trattoria style *22, 23*
Turner, Helen Munro 134
*Twen 211, 215*
Tynell, Paavo 95
Tyssen, Keith 87, 88, *89*
Typewriters 187

Ungaro, Emmanuel 117-8, 157-8, *157*
Union des Artistes Modernes 26, *27*, 57
Untracht, Oppi 94, *94*
Utility furniture 54

Valentino 160
Vallien, Bertil 135
Vasarély, Victor 40, 107, 142
Vavadi, Susan 120
Venini, Paolo 123, *124, 131*
Vianello, Vinicio 124
Viners 85, 87, 92
Vivier, Roger *80*
Volkswagen 185, 198
Von Wangenheim, Chris 217
Voulkos, Peter 104
Voysey, Charles Annesley 41, 141
Vreeland, Diana 211
Vuitton, Louis 121

Walker & Hall 92
Wallpapers 41
Warff, Goran & Ann 135
Warhol, Andy 6, 10, *10*, 37, 44, 73, *83*, 202, 205
Warner's Textiles *142*, 143
Watches 120-1, *121*
Watkins, David 119
Waugh, Sidney 130
Weallans, Jane 143
Weallans, Jon *38*, *71*, 75
Webb, David 112
Webster, Jane 130
Weckström, Bjorn 114, 115
Wegner, Hans 26, 62, *62,* 64
Weinrib, David 100
Welch, Robert 88, 92
Wesselman, Tom 37, 74
Weymouth, Nigel 204
Whiles, Gerald 88
Whistler, Lawrence 130
Whitechapel Art Gallery 37
Whitehead, David 137, *138*
Wiggin, J & J 91
Williamson, Rupert 79
Wilson, Wes 204
Wines, James 43
Winston, Harry 111
Wirkkala, Tapio 25, 26, 46, 49, 62, 91, 106, *127*, 128
Wlodarczyk, W D 31
W.M.F. (Germany) 88
Wolfe, Tom 16, 17, *36*, 165
Wright, Frank Lloyd *28*, 30

Young, Dennis 55, *56*
Yuki *169*, 174

Zaid, Barry 199
Zani 92
Zanuso, Marco 186
Zapp, Walter 190
Zarach 81, *191*
Zavanella, Renzo 46, 60, *60*

# BIBLIOGRAPHY

**Books** Aldridge, Alan, *The Beatles Illustrated Lyrics*, London, 1967. Amaya, Mario, *Pop as Art*, London, 1965. Anscombe, Isabelle, *Not Another Punk Book*, London, 1978. Antonioni, Michelangelo, *Blow-Up*, Turin, 1968. Art and Industry, Council for, *Design and the Designer in Industry*, London, 1937. Avedon, Richard, *Avedon Photographs 1947-1977*, New York, 1978. Capote, Truman, *Observations*, London, 1959. Baldwin, James, *Nothing Personal*, London, 1964. Bailey, David, *David Bailey's Box of Pin-Ups*, London, 1965. *Good-By Baby and Amen*, London, 1969. Ballard, Bettina, *In My Fashion*, London, 1960. Balmain, Pierre, *Balmain*, London, 1964. Banham, Mary, et alii. *A Tonic to the Nation*. London, 1976. Banham, Reyner, *Theory and Design in the First Machine Age*, London, 1960. Beard, Geoffrey, *International Modern Glass*, London, 1976. Beaton, Cecil, *The Best of Beaton*, London, 1969. *Cecil Beaton's Fair Lady*, London, 1964. *The Glass of Fashion*, London, 1954. Buckland, Gail, *The Magic Image*, London, 1975. Beer, Eileen Harrison, *Scandinavian Design — Objects of a Life Style*, New York, 1975. Bettarini, Enrico, et alii, *Forme Nuove in Italia*, Milan, 1957. Birks, Tony, *Art of the Modern Potter*, London, 1976. Blake, Avril; John, *The Practical Idealists*, London, 1969. Blumenfeld, Erwin, *Jadis et Daguerre*, Paris, 1975. Booker, Christopher, *The Neophiliacs*, London, 1969. Caplan, Ralph, *The Design of Herman Miller*, New York, 1976. Carter, Ernestine, *The Changing World of Fashion*, London, 1977. Charles-Roux, Edmonde, *Chanel*, New York, 1975. Chase, Edna Woolman; Ilka, *Always in Vogue*, London 1954. Chase, Linda, *Les Hyperréalistes Americains*, Paris, 1973. Clark, Garth; Hughto, Margie, *A Century of Ceramics in the United States 1878-1978*, New York, 1979. Clark, Sir Kenneth, *What is Good Taste?* London, 1958. Clemmer, Jean; Rabanne, Paco, *Nues*, Paris, 1969. Dean, Roger; Hipgnosis, *'Album Cover Album'*, Limpsfield, 1977. Design Council, The, *The Design History: Past, Process, Product*, London, 1979. Devlin, Polly, *Vogue Book of Fashion Photography*, London, 1979. Digby, Wingfield, *The Work of the Modern Potter*, London, 1952. Dior, Christian, *Dior by Dior*, London, 1957. Dorner, Jane, *Fashion in the Forties and Fifties*, London, 1975. Esslin, Martin, *The Theatre of the Absurd*, London, 1968. Fiorucci, *Fiorucci Image*, Milan, 1978. Fletcher, Alan; Forbes, Colin; Gill, Bob, *Graphic Design: Visual Comparisons*, London, 1963. Garland, Madge, *The Changing Face of Beauty*, London, 1957. *The Changing Form of Fashion*, London, 1970. *Fashion*, London, 1962. Hall-Duncan, Nancy, *The History of Fashion Photography*, New York, 1979. Hennessy, Val, *In the Gutter*, London, 1978. Herbst, René, *25 Années UAM*, Paris, 1956. Herdeg, Walter, *International Window Display*, London, 1951. Hockney, David, *David Hockney by David Hockney*, London, 1976. Hodin, J P, *Bernard Leach — A Potter's Work*, London, 1967. Hughes, George Ravensworth, *The Worshipful Company of Goldsmiths as Patrons of their Craft 1919-1953*, London, 1965. Hughes, Graham, *Modern Silver*, London, 1967. Hutchinson, Harold, *The Poster*, London, 1968. ICI, *Landmarks of the Plastics Industry*, Birmingham, 1962. Inchbald, Jacqueline., ed., *Interior Design and Decoration*, London, 1965. Jenks, Charles, *The Language of Post-Modern Architecture*, London, 1978. Joel, David, *Furniture Design Set Free*, London, 1969. Johnson, Philip, *Mies Van der Rohe*, New York, 1978. Jones, Allen, *Allen Jones — Figures*, Milan, 1969. *Allen Jones — Projects*, London, 1971. Keenan, Brigid, *The Women We Wanted to Look Like*, London, 1977. Krivine, John, *Juke Box Saturday Night*, London, 1977. Kron, Joan; Slesin, Suzanne. *High-Tech*, New York, 1978. *Décor et aménagement de la maison*, Paris, 1952. Kultermann, Udo, *New Realism*, New York, 1972. Lambert, Frederick, *Graphic Design — Britain*, London, 1967. Leach, Bernard, *Michael Cardew, A Collection of Essays*, London, 1976. Levin, Bernard, *The Pendulum Years*, London, 1970. Liberman, Alexander, *The Art and Technique of Color Photography*, New York, 1951. Loewy, Raymond, *Industrial Design*, London, 1979. Lynam, Ruth., ed., *Paris Fashion*, London, 1972. MacCarthy, Fiona, *All Things Bright and Beautiful*, London, 1972. MacInnes, Colin, *England, Half English*, London, 1961. *Absolute Beginners*, London, 1959. May, Chris, *Rock 'N' Roll*, London, n.d. Meadmore, Clement, *The Modern Chair*, London, 1974. Mercer, Frand; Rosner, Charles, *Modern Publicity 1942-1948*, London/New York 1948. Miyake, Issey, *East Meet West*, Tokyo, 1978.

Newton, Helmut, *Sleepless Nights*, New York, 1978. *White Women*, New York, 1976. Penn, Irving, *Moments Preserved*, New York, 1960. Pentagram, *Living by Design*, London, 1978. Pinter, Harold, *The Caretaker*, London, 1960. Polak, Ada, *Modern Glass*, London, 1962. Polhemus, Ted; Procter, Lynn, *Fashion and Anti-Fashion*, London, 1978. Scarfe, Gerald, *Gerald Scarfe's People*, London, 1966. Sontag, Susan, *On Photography*, New York, 1977. Stennett-Wilson, R., *Modern Glass*, London, 1975. *The Beauty of Modern Glass*, London, 1958. Stewart, Richard, *Modern Design in Metal*, London, 1979. Untracht, Oppi, *Enamelling on Metal*, New York, 1957. Venturi, Robert, et alii., *Learning from Las Vegas*, London, 1977. Warhol, Andy, *The Philosophy of Andy Warhol*, New York, 1975. Weidert, Werner, *Private Houses — An International Survey*, London, 1967. Welch, Robert, *Design in a Cotswold Workshop*, London, 1973. Wolfe, Tom, *The Kandy-Kolored Tangerine-Flake Streamline Baby*, London, 1965. *The Painted Word*, New York, 1975. Young, Dennis; Barbara, *Furniture in Britain Today*, Milan/London 1964.

**Exhibition Catalogues** City Art Gallery, *Peter Blake*, Bristol, 1969. Corning Museum, *New Glass*, Corning, 1979. Crafts Advisory Committee, *Ceramic Forms*, London, 1974. *Glenys Barton at Wedgewood*, London, 1977. Crafts Council Gallery, *The Work of Alison Britton*, London, 1979/80. Jacques Damase Gallery, *Bijoux d'Artistes Contemporains*, Paris, n.d. East Midlands Arts, *Synthetic Jewellery*, 1978. The Fine Art Society, *Sam Herman*, London, 1951. Garrard & Co. Ltd., *Garrard — The Crown Jewellers*, London, 1977. The Goldsmith's Hall, *Explosion — Talent Today*, London, 1977. *Loot*, London, 1975 and subsequent. *Seven Golden Years*, London, 1974. The Guggenheim Museum, *Roy Lichtenstein*, New York, 1969. Holbourne of Menstrie Museum, *Twentieth Century Craftsmanship*, Bath, 1972. Leeds Art Galleries, et alii., *Elizabeth Fritz — Pots About Music*, Leeds, n.d. London County Council, *Festival of Britain Guide*, London, 1951. Musée des Arts Décoratifs, *L'Art du Verre*, Paris, 1951. *The Push Pin Style*, Paris, 1970. Musée des Beaux Arts de Nancy, *Daum — Cent Ans de Création*, Nancy, 1979. Museum of Modern Art, *Charles Eames — Furniture from the Design Collection*, New York, 1973. *Italy — The New Domestic Landscape*, New York, 1972. Neue Galerie der Stadt, *Kunst Um 1970*, Aachen, 1972. Scottish Arts Council, The, *Jewellery in Europe*, 1975/76. Serpentine Gallery, *Photo-Realism, Paintings, Sculpture, and Prints from the Ludwig Collection and others*, London, 1973. The Tate Gallery, *Warhol*, London, 1971. Trienale di Milano, *Trienale di Milano*, Milan, var. Dates. Ulster Museum, *New Ceramics*, Belfast, 1974. Union des Artistes Modernes, *'Formes Utiles'*, Paris, var. dates. U.S. Travelling Exhibition, *The Sterling Craft*, 1966/67. Victoria and Albert Museum, *Fashion — An Anthology by Cecil Beaton*, London, 1971. *International Ceramics 1972*, London, 1972. Whitechapel Art Gallery, *Modern Chairs*, London, 1970. Worshipful Company of Goldsmiths, *Modern British Silver*, London, 1963. *Modern Silver*, London, 1954. (G.R. Hughes, ed.), *Worshipful Company of Goldsmiths as Patrons of their Craft 1919-53*, London, 1965. Wright, Frederick, S. Gallery, *Design Process — Olivetti 1908-1978*, California, 1979.

**Magazines and Periodicals** Ambassador; Association of Illustrators First Annual, The; Architectural Digest; Art Director's Index to Photographers; Commercial Photo Series (No. 26, 1974; No. 27, 1975); Connaissance Des Arts; Daily Mail *Ideal Home Book*; Decorative Art and Modern Interiors; Design; Design and Art Direction; Designers in Britain; Domus Editoriale; Harpers Bazaar; Harpers & Queen; House & Garden; Image: Interview; Lui; Mobilia (special issue Georg Jensen 1866-1966, June-July 1960); Nova; Photo Technique; Playboy; Queen; Ritz; Realites; Stern; Studio Yearbook of Decorative Art; Twen; Vogue; Zoom.

**Trade Catalogues** Anonima Castelli; Aram Design; Artemide; Artek; Cassina; De Sede; Flos; Form International; Garrard, The Crown Jewellers, 1977; Habitat; Herman Miller; OMK; *Sculptures en Pate de Verre*, Cristallerie Daum.